FUTURE

FUTURE

A RECENT HISTORY

LAWRENCE R.
SAMUEL

University of Texas Press   Austin

Requests for permission to reproduce material from this work should be sent to:
    Permissions
    ˙University of Texas Press
    P.O. Box 7819
    Austin, TX 78713-7819
    www.utexas.edu/utpress/about/bpermission.html

♾ The paper used in this book meets the minimum requirements of ANSI/NISO
Z39.48-1992 (R1997) (Permanence of Paper).

LIBRARY OF CONGRESS CATALOGING-IN-PUBLICATION DATA

Samuel, Lawrence R.
    Future : a recent history / Lawrence R. Samuel. — 1st ed.
        p.   cm.
    Includes bibliographical references and index.
    ISBN 978-0-292-71914-9 (cloth : alk. paper)
    1. United States—Civilization—20th century—Forecasting.   2. Twentieth
century—Forecasting.   I. Title.
    E169.1.S2415   2009
    973.91—dc22
                                                    2008042035

TO BAYLOR,
WHO KEPT
MY EYES ON
THE FUTURE

"Would you tell me, please, which way I ought to go from here?"

"That depends a good deal on where you want to get to."

—Alice and the Cheshire Cat, in
Lewis Carroll's *Alice's Adventures in Wonderland*

CONTENTS

ᗩCKNOWLEDGMENTᔑ

M ANY THANKS TO ALL THE FINE FOLKS AT THE UNIVERSITY OF TEXAS Press and to the anonymous readers whose comments and suggestions made the manuscript that much better. Much gratitude to the staffs at the New York Public Library, Miami-Dade Public Library, University of Miami Richter Library, and Wolfsonian Library. Above all, deep appreciation to the hundreds of futurists who dared to offer their vision of tomorrow and without whom this book would not be possible.

FUTURE

ꟿNTRODUCTION

Every present is great with the future.

—Gottfried Leibniz, 1703

BUCKLE YOUR BUCK ROGERS SEAT BELT TO TAKE A JOURNEY THROUGH
time. Although any time is a good time to look back on the future, the
first decade of a new century and millennium is an especially apt moment
to reflect on how visionaries of the last 100 years or so saw tomorrow playing out. The history of the future is as important and revealing as our "standard" history—the history of the past—but is undervalued and relatively little known, the reason why this book was written and why it might be worth
spending a bit of your own future with. "In the recorded history of man,"
wrote Anne Fremantle in 1955, "it may well be that the visions of the future,
of other worlds, of the shape of things to come, have played as great a part
as the remembrance of things past," the remembrance of things future being
the story of this book.[1]

Besides the obvious but largely overlooked need for a full telling of how
visionaries imagined the recent history of the future, particularly that of
America, there is considerable need for additional context by which to locate
today's vision of tomorrow with those of yesterday. A look back on how people looked forward reveals that while it possesses certain common themes—
technological progress, scientific breakthroughs, and a utopian (or dystopian) perspective, among them—the future is not a fixed idea but a highly
variable one that reflects the values of those who are imagining it. There is, I
argue, not one narrative of the future in America since the end of World War
I but rather six, each one strongly tied to the cultural dynamics of its time. It
also becomes clear how the idea of the future, largely limited to "experts" in
the early decades of the twentieth century, grew in both volume and importance as it rode the technological wave into the new millennium. For better
or worse, we're all futurists now, the need for each of us to anticipate tomorrow part and parcel of everyday life.

It should hardly come as news that the future, that is, that which is yet to be, has always been viewed as a highly charged cultural site loaded with significance and meaning. The future, David Remnick explained in 1997, consists of "stories we tell to amaze ourselves, to give hope to the desperate, to jolt the complacent," implying that thinking about tomorrow really serves the needs of today. The future is indeed "always about the present," Remnick continued, a catharsis for "what confuses us, what we desire, what we fear."[2] Likewise, "prophecies and predictions tell us little or nothing about what will happen," David A. Wilson argued in his *History of the Future*, but rather "tell us a great deal about the fears, hopes, desires, and circumstances of the people who peer into their own future and imagine what it will be like."[3]

More than this, however, futurism (the practice dedicated to anticipating the future) is often propagandist, a cause attached to whatever, whenever, and however is being predicted. Just as history is "written by the winners," as the popular phrase goes, official versions of the future also carry an agenda and, at times, serve as a kind of political act. With many (actually an infinite number of) futures to choose from, prediction is thus typically not a random exercise but more often an attempt to turn a particular scenario into reality. And while symbiotically connected and codependent, the future and futurism can of course be going separate directions, the two concepts in fact often sharing an inverse relationship. Positive views of the future do not imply a positive state of futurism, in other words, the latter enjoying some of its best days during the darkest days of the former. Concern and fears about the future not surprisingly spark a greater demand for futurism, thus accounting for the field's popularity during the economically depressed 1930s, the paranoid 1950s, and the self-loathing 1970s.

It is the pure unknowability of the future, however, that has made it such a powerful force in our imaginations and daily lives. "The future: have any two words excited more hope, prompted more dreams and visions?" asked William A. Henry III in 1992, the limitless possibilities of tomorrow at the core of the visceral response those two words elicit.[4] Our pervasive interest in the future—whether it's reading one's horoscope, watching the weather forecast, betting on a ballgame, subscribing to Bloomberg to get the inside scoop on what the stock market might or might not do, or feeling the world might end in 2012—reflects our common desire to know the unknowable in order to anticipate it or, even better, control it. "The itch to know what's going to happen next seems engrained in modern man," Thomas Griffith observed in 1979, all of us competing with one another in what could be viewed as a marketplace of potential futures.[5] The survival of any species is in fact a kind of leap of faith in tomorrow, the idea of the future firmly entrenched in the act of creation. "Every garden and child is an expressed belief in the future," Stefan Kanfer wrote in 1976, the origins of life itself grounded in a commitment to the yet-to-be.[6]

While "to be human is to ponder the future," as David Rejeski and Robert L. Olson succinctly put it in 2006, actually knowing what's to come is of course impossible.[7] Like Philadelphia for W. C. Fields, there's no "there" there when it comes to the future, a new horizon always appearing as soon as you reach the last one. It is, though, this inherent elusive and ephemeral quality of futurism that makes it so compelling, not unlike the thought of peering into Pandora's box to see what forbidden goodies might be inside. "It [the future] is more creative, more beautiful and strange than can be imagined by the past," Lewis Lapham mused in 1979, seconded by James Poniewozik's view almost a quarter-century later that "nothing is more shimmeringly beautiful than the next big thing in our imagination."[8] That major world events have been considerably shaped by factors impossible to predict—insanity, genius, randomness—as Nassim Nicholas Taleb convincingly argued in his 2007 *The Black Swan: The Impact of the Highly Improbable*, attempting to know the future is only that much more desirable, one of our most powerful fantasies.[9] And, as David Orrell pointed out in his 2006 *The Future of Everything: The Science of Prediction*, recent scientific thinking such as chaos theory and the butterfly effect have made the forecasting method du jour—mathematical modeling—fundamentally unreliable, thus making it impossible to know if the stock market will go up or down or if one should take an umbrella to work.[10]

Besides being an inherently losing proposition, it hasn't helped that more than one charlatan has hung out a futurist shingle, interested only in telling people what they want (or don't want) to hear in order to make a buck. Whether populated by those with alleged special powers—soothsayers, oracles, crystal ball gazers, clairvoyants, palm readers, dream interpreters, stargazers, and the occasional witch—or professional futurists with reams of "data" up their sleeves, the field has always been viewed as a bit shady, some considering the whole enterprise to be plain quackery. "To talk about history, you have to have your facts in order, but, to talk about the future, all you have to do is say you work in research," complained George F. Mechlin in 1983, a typical sentiment among the more skeptical.[11] A dozen years later, David Bouchier griped that "financial advisers, think tanks, opinion polls, market researchers, the Federal Reserve and the CIA all specialize in getting the future completely wrong at enormous cost," while he himself believes that "only mothers really know the future." "But the world pays no attention to mothers," Bouchier grumbled, "the world wants to hear the bad news from a genuine prophet with a long white beard."[12]

Even some genuine prophets, long white beards notwithstanding, regretted their career choice and felt they might be better off with a "real" job. "How did I ever get into the predicting business?" asked one of the best, Isaac Asimov, at the top of his game in the mid-1960s, convinced that "predicting the future is a hopeless, thankless task, with ridicule to begin with and, all too often, scorn to end with."[13] While he had a legitimate point, Asimov was actually overestimating how much the public (especially Americans) have looked back to see if prognosticators were right or wrong. And although futurists have indeed often been treated as Rodney Dangerfields by critics, they have on occasion received the credit they richly deserve. "We desperately need prophets, even false ones, to help us narrow the infinity of plausible futures down to one or at least to a manageable handful," thought Lev Grossman in 2004, a refreshing take on those treading in tomorrow's waters. "They are our advance scouts, infiltrating the undiscovered country, stealing over the border to bring back priceless reconnaissance maps of the world to come," he continued, an all-too-rare expression of appreciation for futurists.[14]

The ambivalence surrounding futurists and the field itself reflects the fact that its history has been a polarized one, the world of tomorrow often imagined in utopian or dystopian language and imagery. If not a Rousseau-like peaceful kingdom where we all will one day live happily ever after, the future is frequently a place of impending catastrophe or, just as often, one in which the individual will be crushed under the foot of a totalitarian regime. The future has served as an opportunity to both vent our worst fears and air our greatest hopes, the most profound of the latter that we'll live on after our bodies die. The notion of an afterlife—the core of many religions—is futurism in its purest form, tomorrow conceived not as a place made much better by the next great invention or much worse by an alien invasion but as an alternative universe with its own rules. Futurism has always carried with it a sense of mystery, the ability to know the unknown deemed limited to those with special and, sometimes, evil powers. Prophets were, centuries ago, considered divinely anointed in some way, the strange art common to members of certain families who possessed a genetic predisposition for it.[15]

This off-the-beaten-track aspect of futurism can be most readily seen within science fiction, the primary launching pad of twisted tomorrows over the past century. The standard tools of the sci-fi trade have served as some of the most familiar tropes of futurism, these not just an entertaining diversion but a way to safely contain the darkest side of our imagination. Mad scientists, master races, mutation, barbarism, and disembodied heads are just a few scenarios of future-gone-bad, most of these kinds of narratives not much more meaningful than those found in your typical horror movie of the week. The granddaddy of dystopia, however, is the creation of machines more intelligent or powerful than ourselves, this one reflecting our real-life (and, according to some current futurists, justifiable) fear of technology run amok. Not surprisingly, then, the robot or automatic man has been a ubiquitous figure in the recent history of the future, both appealing to our quest for perfection and acknowledging the threat that we may lose the essence of what makes us human.

Likewise, the idea of perfect, mistake-free, and emotionless machinelike beings, often blended with human (and therefore flawed) traits, as in the case of *2001*'s HAL or *Star Trek*'s Mr. Spock, has been a recurring theme within both fictional and nonfictional views of tomorrow, this perhaps best illustrating the love-hate relationship we share with technology. The loss of individuality due to rampant mechanization and conformist mass society has frequently served as cause for alarm for the future, the thought of people being turned into automatons the stuff of cold sweats in the middle of the night. Real-life events in Europe in the 1930s and 1940s served only to fuel fears of a universal state akin to Huxley's disturbing and prescient *Brave New World* (1932) and Orwell's equally prophetic *Nineteen Eighty-Four* (1948), prime evidence that futurism thrives best in periods of instability and insecurity. In her 2007 *A Brief History of the Future*, Oona Strathern considered Orwell, Huxley, and H. G. Wells nothing less than the "three witches of futurism," their vision of the twentieth century a long nightmare that one couldn't wake up from.[16]

The elephant in the futuristic room, however, has undoubtedly been our on-again, off-again relationship with science and technology, this queer romance at the very heart of tomorrowism for at least the past 500 years. Since the Renaissance, in fact, science and technology have dominated our visions of tomorrow, our common dream to, as one mid-twentieth-century futurist put it, go where no man has gone before. Flying machines have been, of course, a staple of futurism, this despite the sensible argument within much of the day's scientific community that they would never get off the ground (the internal combustion engine was never really anticipated, even by the genius of the millennium, Leonardo da Vinci). Time machines also have been commonplace in narratives of the future, these too believed by most to defy the laws of the physical universe (until relatively recently, when travel through time, at least backward, is considered possible, according to some string theorists).[17]

Overall, however, the actual pace of technology has almost always surpassed that expected by those peering into the future, the quantum leaps made possible by a new discovery impossible to anticipate. In his 1898 *The Sleeper Awakes*, for example, H. G. Wells nailed a number of technologies that were to be—radio, movies, air-conditioning—but underestimated how quickly they would appear—about forty years instead of his projected 200.[18] Wells, whom British "alternate history" novelist Harry Harrison credits with having created almost all themes of science fiction in his own "scientific romances," was off by almost a century when it came to man's landing on the moon, analogous perhaps to how futurists of the twentieth century missed the rapid evolution of information technology by a country mile.[19] Even more than overshooting technological achievements, however, it has been futurists' failure to anticipate major social change, most egregiously the women's and civil rights movements of the twentieth century, that has most seriously and justifiably damaged the reputation of the field. The bias toward predicting technological versus social progress has been and continues to be the Achilles' heel of futurism, the next wave of gadgets and gizmos easier to see coming than a cultural tsunami. It is, as Arnold Toynbee has pointed out, ideas, not technology, that have stirred the biggest changes in history, something that more futurists could and should have taken to heart.

Future focuses on the United States from 1920 to today, a way to contain a vast subject that is inherently global (cosmic, actually) and spans millennia. Another reason why this book is so American-centric is that the idea of the future is so American-centric. Since the nation's founding, the notion that tomorrow will be better than today has been a principal strand in America's DNA, our "future-mindedness" rooted in our enduring faith in progress, self-improvement, and limitlessness. The social critic David Brooks considered future-mindedness "a distinctly American trait," an essential and unique part of our national character. Future-mindedness is, Brooks wrote in 2002, "the ability to see the present from the vantage point of the future," as well as "the freedom to feel unencumbered by the past and more emotionally attached to things to come," each of these things making us fundamentally different than every other civilization that has existed on earth.[20]

Brooks was of course hardly the first to notice this streak of tomorrow-ism that ran through the United States and its people. In fact, futurism was embedded within the nation's very birth, the founding fathers eager to toss out the historical baggage of the Old World like it was a rotten tomato. "I like the dreams of the future better than the history of the past," Thomas Jefferson wrote as the American experiment unfolded, the New World a tabula rasa on which to write something original and, in short, better. Other great minds of the last couple of centuries noticed that America and the future were kissing cousins. "America is . . . the land of the future," wrote Hegel two centuries ago, the German philosopher thinking that "the American lives even more for his goals, for the future, than the European." Albert Einstein (who happened to be fascinated by psychics) also saw Americans as somehow different than other people around the world. "Life for him is always becoming, never being," the genius wrote, detecting the classic American faith in the limitless possibilities of the future.[21]

Americans' preference for the future over the past remained strong throughout the twentieth century and still shows no signs of easing up. Hugh Stevenson Tigner felt in 1942, for example, that "It has been a notable characteristic of American life during the last fifty years that the definition of an inconvenience has called forth an invention—another gadget, a new medicine, an improved model, an extra cushion, a change in the rules, a new bridge, one more personal service on trains and ships."[22] Kanfer felt similarly, suggesting a few decades later that "The profound belief in posterity seems uniquely American," the primary reason for this being that the United States had "no yesterday of its own."[23] Even in this postmodern, post-9/11, seemingly post-everything day, social critics remain moved by Americans' optimism rooted in the nation's utopian principles. "If there's a common faith in America, it's our faith in the future," the editors of *Wilson's Quarterly* observed in 2006, convinced that "we can't shake a deep-seated conviction that we'll be able to deal with any problem."[24]

While no other society has embraced futurism as the United States has, prognostication can be traced back thousands of years. The text of the *I Ching*, the ancient Chinese book of prophecy, is essentially a master collection of predictions, employing a set of symbols to create order out of chance events. In ancient Greece, the Delphic oracle provided guidance and was consulted before all major undertakings, and in Greek mythology, Cassandra was granted the gift of prophecy by Apollo (all for naught when she did not return his love). Ancient Romans preferred watching the flight of birds before making major decisions like whom to conquer next, while the early Egyptians preferred stargazing for such matters. Astrology, the system of celestial omens, goes back as far as ancient Babylonia (as does weather forecasting, a favorite hobby of Aristotle's as well), the heavens believed to wield control over man's destinies. It being common knowledge that one's fate was determined by the relative position of heavenly bodies at the precise moment of birth, having an astrologer as a key adviser was de rigueur for kings, emperors, and even popes for thousands of years, and these seers were consulted on everything from military matters to whether the coming years would be ones of plenty or lean.

For Jews and Christians alike over the centuries, futurism arrived in literally biblical proportions. Prophets, of course, notably Jeremiah, Isaiah, and Daniel, made the futuristic rounds in the Old Testament, knowing what was to come because they heard it firsthand from God. Both the Old and the New Testament make a number of references to the need to anticipate the future ("Without vision, the people perish," says Proverbs 29:18), with the Gospels, we all know, promising a place for the saved in a New Jerusalem. Many Europeans believed the Day of Judgment promised in the Book of Revelation would occur in the year 1000, the Second Coming probably both the most anticipated and the most feared prediction in Western civilization. As the millennium approached, any notable event in the natural world— shooting stars, failed crops, deformed livestock—was viewed as an ominous warning that one had better repent pronto if one was planning on salvation. "In 999, Europe was awash with mystic pilgrims preparing for the end and collapsing in despair at every thunderclap," noted Peter Andrews, something that would happen much the same way in a thousand years, when Armageddon would arrive in digital form when our computers failed.[25] Such was the concept of the future in agriculture-based, preindustrial times, general scholarship agrees, with tomorrow rooted in spirituality and folklore and marked by intuition and faith.

Things began to change in a big way midway between the first and second millennia. Although Mother Shipton, a sixteenth-century English soothsayer (who some experts now believe was a purely fictional character), gained considerable fame making a number of predictions that supposedly turned out to be accurate (all of them seemingly tragic, such as London's Great Plague and Great Fire), it was the infusion of science that redefined futurism. Borrowing from Plato and others and newly equipped with the printing press, English writers such as Thomas More shifted the concept of utopia ("nowhere" in Greek) from a mythical place to a future time, a key turning point within the realm of the imagination. Beginning with the best-known, most over-interpreted, and probably most overrated futurist in history, Nostradamus, the art of prediction increasingly strove to become more of a science. (Because his writings were, more than anything else, cryptic,

David A. Wilson considered the sixteenth-century physician and astrologer "the perfect prophet.")[26] Physicists imbued tomorrow with their quest for reliability and validity—literal "predictability"—the scientific method and new obsession with "proof" significantly weakening folklorist methods of futurism. Copernicus's discovery in the 1500s that Earth revolved around the sun, rather than vice versa, also pushed futurism decidedly toward left-brain thinking (and, as a sidebar, made many astrologers rather suddenly decide to call themselves astronomers). With futurism elevated to the realm of science, the predictive arts of the past—reading palms, tarot cards, or tea leaves—lost much of their credibility, and were left for those on the cultural fringe to claim as their own.

Equally important, the ideals of the Enlightenment—logic, reason, order—were applied to the future of Man, the dream that one day people might be as perfect as the increasing number of instruments and machines being invented. "With the coming of the machine, which enabled man to telescope time in unimagined ways, the tempo of change rose in a wholly unprecedented and explosive manner," wrote Roderick Seidenberg in 1955. Seidenberg believed that with mechanization, Europeans in the seventeenth century started to change their orientation to the past toward one looking to the future, this decisive shift "symboliz[ing] a new relationship in respect to nature, to himself, and to his destiny."[27] With the rise of science and technology, the idea that it was humans, not God, who determined the future gained traction, a giant leap in cosmology and its relationship to tomorrowism. Society would ultimately benefit from industrialization, the scientific revolution, and the rise of financial capitalism, visionaries of the period believed, a natural result of the accumulated knowledge of civilization. "By the eighteenth century the future was increasingly seen in terms of progress," David A. Wilson wrote, "the triumph of technology and reason over nature and passion."[28] The establishment of "universal" time and the mapping of the world too helped create organization out of chaos, each a major achievement that would lead humanity to its ultimate destiny of pure rationalism. The Age of Discovery thus also recast mythologies of space to those of time, changing the very dimensions and parameters of the imagination and leaving the future as the only true realm of the unknown.

Technological developments of the eighteenth and nineteenth centuries—the steam engine, the factory system, the exploitation of coal and oil, and the phenomenon that was the locomotive, to name just a few—served only to accelerate both the tempo and the possibilities of tomorrow. It was such progress that led to the realization then that "the future would be fundamentally different than the past," as Merrill Sheils put it, the second wave of the Industrial Revolution causing a radical shift in the temporal plates.[29] Major technological change could, for the first time in history, be measured in a single lifetime, this development also recalibrating the workings of futurism. Propelled by nineteenth-century technology, "time itself appeared to be accelerating, and futures—big and small alike—seemed to be coming and going with breathtaking speed," wrote Daniel Rosenberg and Susan Harding in the introduction to their 2005 collection of essays, *Histories of the Future*, the result an upheaval in the very concept of tomorrow.[30] As well, there was now the possibility, even probability, that machines and processes not yet imagined could, in a half-century or much less, be creating new things not yet imagined, a rather frightening revelation for those used to change occurring at glacial speed. "Nineteenth-century fears and hopes for the technological future crystallise[d] in turn-of-the-century fantasies about the fully mechanized state," wrote editors Alan Sandison and Robert Dingley in the preface to their 2000 *Histories of the Future: Studies in Fact, Fantasy, and Science Fiction*, some of those fantasies coming close to realities within mid-twentieth-century fascist and totalitarian regimes.[31]

Technology wasn't the only thing rocking the boat of tomorrow in the eighteenth and nineteenth centuries, however, as intellectuals appropriated the future as a device to speak their minds. Philosophical approaches to futurism emerged as powerful ideological tools (Hegel and Marx come to mind first), and novelists such as Bacon and Swift located their stories in a time yet to be, as a means to satire the political climates of their day. A new form of utopian science fiction also was born in the Victorian era, as Edward Bellamy, H. G. Wells, and Jules Verne brought the future to the masses through their wildly popular novels. Bellamy's *Looking Backward from 2000 to 1887* (which, interestingly, presented Boston circa 2000 as a locus of democratic ideals) was less a prediction than a political treatise using the safe device of fiction, a formula other socialists used to criticize capitalism (and, ironically, sell more books). While Bellamy was disturbed by the unrest within American industry in the 1870s and the out-of-control power of the trusts of the 1880s, Verne and Wells zeroed in on the late-nineteenth-century British class system, the latter's 1895 *The Time Machine* (which jumped forward all the way to the year 802,701) a scathing critique of its vast inequities (and an homage of sorts to Plato's *Republic*, in which biologically superior "guardians" rule over the peasants). Verne too actually didn't try to predict the future, his intent simply (or not so simply) to create imaginative stories based on conditions that then did not exist (a method that would a century or so later become all the rage in the field when rebranded as "scenario planning.")[32] Those practicing this allegorical style of futurism were sometimes referred to as "mythologists," their stories of tomorrow political wolves in sheep's clothing.

By 1900, it was clear that the future had become part of the public's consciousness but, in many respects, this was only the beginning. As modernity beckoned in the early years of the twentieth century, the concept of the future now had the ideal cultural climate in which to flourish. Henry Adams's turn-of-the-century proposition to create a legitimate science out of the future was a bold one, but it would be the Jules Verne–inspired "Amazing Stories" in popular magazines of the 1920s and 1930s that propelled futurism as a form of entertainment.[33] Equally influential was H. G. Wells, whose stories would serve as the bridge between the romantic sensibilities of Victorian futurism and the colder, crueler versions forged in the Machine Age. Wells's most significant contribution to the field was the realization that the tools of Man had changed but Man had not, posing major trouble ahead in his future as new, much more lethal tools were discovered. With the social consequences of technological change now part of the conversation, dystopian themes now entered the discourse of futurism, with science not only our best ally of tomorrow but also our worst enemy, that is, the ways and means of mass destruction. In his 1933 *The Shape of Things to Come*, for example, Wells located utopia a couple of generations away, after the fall of capitalism, a double whammy in which things would get a lot better only after they got a lot worse. Universalism would ultimately triumph over nationalism and ideology, Wells envisioned, a world state the only political system that could lead to peace and abundance for all. Interestingly, Wells saw intellectual revolutionaries using violence to create this world of peace and love in the 1960s and 1970s, a very rare instance of a futurist accurately predicting major social change or, at least, the idea of it.[34]

It was after the "war to end all wars" when the field took its biggest leap to date, as a distinctively rational brand of futurism continued to blossom. "We emerged from the First World War with a wholly new concept of our possibilities," remembered Charles M. A. Stine in 1942, fully aware that the world and America had irrevocably changed over those few years. "We learned that it was possible not only to emulate nature but even to excel her in certain fields of creation," he continued, acknowledging the dramatic leaps in science made during the war.[35] Importantly, the future could never again be "perfect," the horrors of this war forever making the idea of a coming utopia seem, if not messianic, insincere or naïve. Postwar jitters about a looming economic depression and/or social revolution also helped propel futurism to a new plane, with quantitative forecasting techniques used for the first time to calm nervous businessmen. The explosion in transportation and communications that followed in the 1920s—the commercialization of the automobile, aviation, radio, telephone, and movies—as well as major advances in both agriculture and industry were a direct result of the new possibilities that the war had seeded. It is right after World War I, then, that our story begins, when it can be said that futurism, as we know it today, was officially born.

Indeed, the twentieth century proved to be a golden era of futurism as economists, sociologists, and political scientists entered the burgeoning field, applying their particular tricks of the trade to advance the rational brand of prediction originally conceived during the Enlightenment. The milestones reached during these hundred years, especially the flying machine and eventual landing on the moon, the development and use of atomic and nuclear weapons, the women's and civil rights movements, the commercialization of the birth control pill, and the advent of biological and genetic engineering, fueled the possibilities of tomorrow in the public's imagination, and helped make the twentieth century the first one to be significantly more about the future than the past. The rise (and temporary collapse) of Wall Street in the 1920s contributed heavily to the popularity of futurism, with the winners and losers separated only by their relative skill in predicting what would go up, what would come down and, most important, when. With the present a difficult one for many, the Depression years also were ripe for thinking about the future, this decade the first in which a concerted effort was made not just to foresee tomorrow but to enable or engineer it (Keynesian economic policies being just one example).

After World War II, a new breed of futurists arrived on the scene, all of them committed to the seemingly noble cause of "planning." Demographers, academics, and other assorted experts and pundits from foundations, government agencies, and think tanks (the Rand Corporation, especially) dwelled in futurisms in order to shape public policy, provide advice to industry, and serve on advisory boards (all of these men in gray flannel suits completely missing the yet-to-be alliance between the USSR and Cuba, not so incidentally). While the between-the-wars era of futurism was grounded firmly in the cultural dynamics of the machine and wartime, tomorrowism looked to the domestic paradise that lay ahead; the future of the postwar years was more fragmented, a function of the new world order. "Faith in a meaningful collective narrative of the future [became] progressively eroded" beginning in the postwar years, Sandison and Dingley argued, with rapidly expanding globalization and new technologies in particular discouraging a narrow vision of tomorrow.[36]

As with the first world war (wars are essentially battles over opposing visions of the future), however, World War II undoubtedly shifted the foundation of the field, the use of atomic weapons changing the rules of the game of the future. In a nuclear world, thought Kanfer, "the very idea of a future was arguable," as "anti-utopias grew like botulisms in a sealed jar."[37] Indeed, for many thinking outside the box after the war, existential despair was the lingua franca, with Kafkaesque and Orwellian nightmares now part of the vocabulary of tomorrow. Angst would become virtual panic in Alvin Toffler's 1970 *Future Shock*, the bestseller singlehandedly making futurism cool despite the bummer of a message. Change itself now was the problem, Toffler insisted, the pace of society simply too fast for humans to process.

Beginning in earnest in the 1980s, however, the wonkish and depressing future of postwar intellectualism took a sharp (right) turn toward the corporate world, with technology now prime cultural currency. The province of the radical fringe in the late nineteenth century, futurism had become, a century later, a tool of consumer capitalism, as American as mom, apple pie, and Chevrolet. Strategic planners, trend spotters, marketing consultants, and other gurus from disparate backgrounds and with varied experience (myself included) took to the now-lucrative field of advising companies what to do next. Whether methodologies were based on historical inquiry (W. Warren Wagar), studying long-term cycles (Arthur Schlesinger, William Strauss, and Neil Howe), scenario planning (Herman Kahn, Peter Schwartz), computer modeling and simulation (Department of Defense), opinion polling (Elmo Roper, George Gallup), chaos theory (James Gleick), or pure crystal balling (Faith Popcorn, "the Nostradamus of marketing," according to *Fortune*), the essential, decidedly ambitious goal remained the same—to know the unknowable. At the beginning of a new century and millennium, the future of the future is undoubtedly a promising one as it gets increasingly compressed and driven forward by exponential change. "If anything has a future, it's futurism," concluded Stefan Kanfer; tomorrow is as certain as death or taxes as long as we're around to imagine one.[38]

While a number of themes emerged out of my research for this book, especially that of the love-hate relationship between Man and machine, it became clear that the evolution of the idea of the future over the past century or so was the real and biggest story. A chronological approach was thus chosen over a thematic one, as the former provides a stronger narrative and, in short, a better story. *Future* covers a wide swath, each chapter viewing the idea of the future as it relates to (1) the public or civic arena, i.e., issues relating to government, politics, religion, education, law, geography, nationalism, war, race, ethnicity, class, age, and gender; (2) popular and consumer culture, i.e., the arts, media, communications, lifestyle, recreation/leisure, sports, entertainment, fashion, food, and the home; (3) the economic arena, i.e., business, jobs, and money; (4) travel and transportation, including space; (5) architecture and cities, especially New York; and (6) science and technology, including energy (especially atomic), medicine, weather, the environment, and weapons. Through both a vertical (chronological) and horizontal (thematic) lens, I offer a 360-degree perspective of a recent history of the future; this dualistic approach, I believe, is the best way to take on such a complex subject.

The outline of *Future* follows my argument that there have been six narratives of the future in America since the end of World War I. The first chapter, "The Shape of Things to Come, 1920–1939," explores how America's tomorrow was imagined between the world wars, when leading visionaries foresaw a new age steeped in the rationalism of modernity and, more specifically, the unprecedented power of the machine. The new sights and sounds to be seen and heard in the movies and on the radio were harbingers of, as H. G. Wells famously put it, "the shape of things to come," with the possibilities of future mass communication seemingly endless. Chapter 2, "Great Day Coming, 1940–1945," examines how the future was envisioned during World War II, when America's present was "out of stock," as a popular phrase went, and the future was fully expected to overflow with the bounty of postwar abundance. "Tomorrow" was in fact one of the seminal words and ideas during the war, as Americans sacrificed for, as *Time* expressed it in June 1942, the "great day coming." Chapter 3, "The Best Is Yet to Come, 1946–1964," discusses visions of the future during the postwar years. As fears of another depression ebbed and citizens started to enjoy the fruits of their victory, the future of the American way of life appeared brighter than ever, with science and technology being counted on to make life as easy as that of everyone's favorite future family, the Jetsons.

Chapter 4, "Future Shock, 1965–1979," shows that as America's postwar triumph faded in the mid-1960s, so did much of its faith in a future defined by unlimited progress, a leisure-based society, and urban utopias. In its place, a new future emerged in the late 1960s that reflected the social, economic, and political turmoil of the time, with Toffler's book a poster child for this era's dominant narrative of tomorrow. Chapter 5, "The Empire Strikes Back, 1980–1994," considers how the future played out in the 1980s and early

1990s, when America's confidence was restored under President Reagan's red-white-and-blue leadership. As free-market capitalism flourished and the nation flexed its global muscles as a modern-day empire, much of the doom and gloom of the 1970s evaporated, replaced by the traditional American jeremiad proclaiming our special place as a "city on the hill." The final chapter, "The Matrix, 1995–," deals with how we've imagined the future over the past decade, when the crossing over into a new century and new millennium turbocharged our instincts to look forward. The future was irrevocably altered in the mid-1990s, when it became clear that the Internet was going to be a major force in our lives, shifting many visions of tomorrow from the real world to a virtual one popularly perceived as an all-encompassing online grid. In the book's conclusion, I consider the current state of futurism, and suggest where it should go from here in order to chart a course for future historians of the future.

In terms of sources, the spine of the story relies on how leading visionaries imagined the future as reported in newspapers and magazines, both popular and trade. Literature in the field, both books and journal articles, is used to frame the story and provide valuable context. Primary texts—books, movies, television and radio shows, comics, advertising, etc.—too are used to glean images of what's around the corner. I also use high school and college yearbooks as primary texts, believing them to be an underutilized resource offering special insight into how both youth culture and adult authorities envisioned tomorrow. Finally, *Future* is filled with dozens, perhaps hundreds, of predictions from experts of their day in their own words, my feeling that it's best to hear it direct from the horse's mouth, as the saying goes.

Welcome to a recent history of the future.

CHAPTER 1

THE SHAPE OF
THINGS TO COME,
1920—1939

I Have Seen the Future.

—Button at General Motors' Futurama ride
at the 1939–1940 New York World's Fair

IN 1933, JULIAN HUXLEY, NOTABLE BRITISH BIOLOGIST AND BROTHER
of futurist extraordinaire Aldous, was asked to predict what was "in our
stars" by describing what the world might be like in fifty years. Included in
his imaginative forecast was the belief that the "conditioning" of air would be
"well-nigh universal," a common sight in both public buildings and private
homes. Huxley's prediction was not at all unusual; many visionaries of the day
saw some kind of technological manipulation of the air as almost a given, just
one way nature would be improved by Man and his many future machines.
Unlike others, however, who saw the ability to control the temperature and
composition of air as simply an agent of comfort or possibly health, Huxley
saw air-conditioning playing a truly "revolutionary" role in the future. By
1983, this particular technology would, he thought, "make it possible for the
white man to invade the tropics, not merely as an exploiter but with a view to
making of them a permanent home." Given the coming age of scientific and
technological miracles, Huxley's questions—"Will economic facts justify that
invasion? And will it be tolerated by the black and brown peoples who now
inhabit those of our planet?"—were considered not at all unreasonable.[1]

Such was the world of tomorrow as it was imagined between the world wars, when futurism as an authentic field came into its own. After "the war to end all wars," leading visionaries of the 1920s foresaw a new age steeped in the rationalism of modernity and, more specifically, the unprecedented power of the machine. The new sights and sounds to be seen and heard across the cultural landscape were harbingers of, as H. G. Wells famously put it in 1933, "the shape of things to come," with the possibilities of the future seemingly endless. Economic and political chaos throughout the 1930s—what Wells saw as just the beginning of an "Age of Insecurity"—would prove to be an ideal climate to imagine "Amazing Stories," as the popular pulp serial of the day was called. This era of the future fittingly climaxed at the "World of Tomorrow" world's fair in New York in 1939, specifically at General Motors' "Futurama" exhibit, which promised an American paradise even as another world war beckoned. The future had officially begun.

DAZZLING HORIZONS

As World War I brought the nation out of its rather prurient and isolated cocoon, the rise of mass culture and the reshuffling of the international deck sparked a new way of looking at things that was mightily receptive to the idea of tomorrow. Achievements by women in the 1920s—getting the vote, the popularity of larger-than-life personalities such as Dorothy Parker, Coco Chanel, Josephine Baker, and Mae West (not to mention D. H. Lawrence's Lady Chatterley and other women in love) and, of course, the sheer presence of the flapper—alone were cause to think the nation's seismic plates were shifting, if not crumbling into dust. Race too was fundamentally altering the nation's DNA, with African Americans' increasing presence in popular culture reflecting our fascination with black culture. Not coincidentally, sex was also finally coming out of America's Victorian closet, as everything from the first Miss America pageant to Rudolph Valentino's *The Sheik* to Freudian theory raised the country's collective libido. The debut of Trojan condoms and the rubber diaphragm as well as the AMA's endorsement of birth control too were scrambling gender dynamics like one of those new Waring blenders, reflected by the rather startling rise in divorces following World War I.

Popular culture of the 1920s and 1930s, newly fueled by mass production and mass consumption and increasingly informed by European and Asian goings-on, also helped set the stage for a bigger and better American future. Modernist novels by F. Scott Fitzgerald, Sinclair Lewis, Ernest Hemingway, Henry Miller, Virginia Woolf, and James Joyce were changing the rules of literature or perhaps showing that there were no longer any rules. The witty musings of the Algonquin Round Table in the new magazine *The New Yorker* and poetry from Eliot, Pound, Cummings, and Crane also were widening the gap between a more abstract literary future and its flowery past. Meanwhile, in the art world, the wave of Dada and Surrealism crossing the Big Pond had a major effect on American visual culture, climaxing with the opening of MOMA in New York in 1929. Whether through the rarified air of modern art—Duchamp's industrial objects-as-sculpture, Moore's sensuous sculptures, Calder's curious mobiles—or populist architecture of streamlined deco, a new vocabulary of aesthetics was smashing the traditional boundaries of high and low.

The rise of radio broadcasting also signaled that a new age had arrived, and music by modern composers such as Gershwin (especially his 1924 *Rhapsody in Blue*, a self-described "experiment in modern music") suggested that, after a century and a half, a truly original American culture had been born. Movies, arguably the nation's most original art form, somehow looked forward while looking back, reflecting the increasingly tenuous relationship between Man and Nature as the Machine Age ground on. *Frankenstein, Dracula*, and *Tarzan the Ape Man* (all from 1931), *King Kong* (1933), and the era's cinematic coup de grâce, *The Wizard of Oz* (1939), were undoubtedly escapist fantasies from the economic chaos at home and rising totalitarianism and fascism abroad but, as important, spoke to our collective fears about out-of-control science and technology and questioned in their own way the very identity of the human being of the future.

With this kind of fertile ground seeding change of all stripes, most visionaries between the wars believed that the arts and entertainment would be radically transformed by a variety of technological innovations in the works. All of the arts would benefit in the future, a best-of-both-worlds blending of Man and machine, many experts foresaw, as new technologies made the impossible possible. "The Vitaphone is the successful experiment which makes a dream a fact, and its possibilities for the future of music as well as the moving-picture art are extremely important," reported Olin Downes in the *New York Times* in 1926, after seeing one demonstrated.[2] Two years later, Downes saw another technology that he thought would revolutionize music, this one based on "ether waves." "What is before us now is a successful scientific experiment which unfolds new and dazzling horizons for a future that should certainly have much to do with music," he wrote in 1928 after witnessing an exhibition by Professor Theremin of his yet-to-be-named instrument.[3]

Along with major advances in movies and music, an incredible new age of communications beckoned that promised to do nothing less than change the way that people talked to each other. Writing for *Le Figaro* in 1927, Andre Maurois presented what he felt was a realistic scenario for communicating in the near future:

> Within a few years we shall surely be able both to see and hear our interlocutors with the assistance of a wireless contrivance which will perhaps be called the "telephotophone." Pocket models will enable us to continue a conversation with a friend during a journey or walk. Lovers will make dates at twenty minutes and sixteen seconds past four at a wave length of four hundred and fifty-two metres. An ether police force will monopolize certain wave lengths for secret government communications. There will be wave lengths for unmarried ladies, and others for schools . . .[4]

Although it would take much longer for Maurois's kind of communications scenarios to actually happen, he was clever enough to also recognize some of the implications of these new technologies. "Lying will become more difficult," he believed, with "a woman no longer able to say on the telephone that she is out simply by imitating the voice of her maid," apparently a common ploy within some circles in Jazz Age Paris. Maurois would have it backward, of course—cell phones and e-mail make it easier to misrepresent one's geographic whereabouts—but his foresight of tomorrow's communications landscape was undeniably startling.[5]

Another dazzling technology on the horizon, called "radio-television," was cause for major alarm to many in the media business as it became less of a dream and more of a reality. Some recalled how the debut of radio soon after the end of World War I was met with derision by newspapermen who dismissed it as a plaything but soon regretted their misjudgment. Within a decade, radio had proved to be a serious threat to the newspaper business, as advertisers shifted some of their promotion money to be part of this most modern of media. As this new technology came closer to commercialization, more visionary journalists recognized that an even more serious threat to print could very well be waiting in the wings.[6] Writing in 1929, Silas Bent found the idea of "the transmission of colored pictures and talking movies by air" quite a disturbing development, asking readers to

> Fancy what this means. Sitting in your home you may witness distant events, observe the natural colors of the surroundings, and hear simulta-

neously the accompanying sounds. All the imperial pageantry and exotic color of a Sultan's nuptials, dancing-girls and warriors, wild horsemen and chanting priests, might have their being in our very presence, so that we could all but touch them. Even if color-printing be perfected, what can the daily press offer in competition with such a lure, or what pale promise make?[7]

Bent argued that, in order to survive, the newspaper business would have to split into two segments, one devoted to delivering serious information to intellectuals, the other to "the journalism of triviality and entertainment." The latter was in fact already in circulation, with the Hearst-owned "tabloid picture paper" dedicated to "downright fakery, fiction, picture serials, [and] comics and eroticism" the poster child for this kind of journalism. Bent believed it was just the beginning for the tabloids, however, as newspapermen scrambled to compete with the rising threat of radio and the looming threat of "radio-television." "Their photographers will scour the earth to make snap-shots of the bizarre and the shocking and the freakish," he predicted, forecasting the kind of newspaper readily available today at one's favorite supermarket. These papers "will not be much concerned with news," Bent noted, their assigned purpose "to entertain and thrill the mentally deficient," again perhaps not too far off the mark.[8]

On the other hand, the future possibilities of radio and television were thrilling to those in the broadcasting business, both in the United States and across the pond. The Earl of Clarendon, who happened to be chairman of the BBC, recognized the potential of television in 1930, almost a full decade before its official debut at the 1939 New York World's Fair. "It is quite possible a day will come when people will see the world before their eyes as they sit by the fire at home," he said, likening the new medium to how many used their radios as a kind of electronic furniture. The earl also foresaw the populist appeal television would likely have, with viewers "able both to see and hear a play, or an opera, or the Derby, or the world's series, or the heavyweight championship," in essence a multisensory radio.[9]

With the possibilities and uses of television still unknown, however, imaginations about it ran wild. Television was commonly believed to become a two-way medium, to be used for everything from medical diagnoses and military surveillance to even committing crimes.[10] Television would also, some visionaries believed, be used one day in the business world to, naturally, improve efficiency. Dr. Zay Jeffries, a leading metallurgist of the day, told his colleagues at their annual meeting in 1930 that television would allow the businessman of the future to, as the *New York Times* reported, "project himself instantly through space and attend half a dozen board meetings from the Atlantic to the Pacific Coast in one day" (a classic case of futurists' ability to predict the benefits of a new technology that would, ultimately, prove to be those of a subsequent one, i.e., videoconferencing and, later, Internet conferencing). Not only would this new technology save time and effort, Dr. Jeffries added, but it would also "make harmless the odors from foul cigars" that pervaded the typical business meeting of the time—a true leap forward.[11]

As with most revolutionary technologies past and present, television was also assigned a higher, nobler purpose that went far beyond its potential practical applications. Every home equipped with a television "may become an art gallery," Floyd W. Parsons believed in 1931, the new medium capable of uplifting the tastes and intelligence of the masses. Not only would "the treasures of great museums then be able to extend their cultural influence to millions of homes," Parsons wrote in the *Saturday Evening Post*, but "the artist will be brought to the public, the lecturer to his audience and the educator to his student body." As originally intended for the last great medium, radio, television could and would be put into public service, an instrument of high culture versus crass commercialism.[12]

Those in the business, not surprisingly, had other ideas. David Sarnoff, president of RCA in 1936 and already well on his way to becoming a legendary media mogul, was not surprisingly tickled pink as television, by then clearly the medium of tomorrow, loomed on the horizon. Not only would television be used as a communications medium (making the telegraph as passé as the "pony express," Sarnoff predicted), but it would eventually complement radio by offering "new functions, new entertainment and new programs." The "General" remained bearish on radio, however, believing that the new medium would in no way completely replace sound broadcasting. According to Sarnoff, "an unlimited array of mass communication services" lay ahead in the radio universe, in fact, with someday "each one of our millions of citizens hav[ing] his own assigned frequency, wherever he may be" (something that materialized not in radio but via the World Wide Web). With radio a primary source of advertising revenue for RCA, and its competitors and engineers still tinkering with television in their labs, Sarnoff was hardly ready to write it off.[13]

As commercial television started to become a reality in the late 1930s, some imagined other possibilities for the medium beyond entertainment. William Ogburn, a sociologist at the University of Chicago, believed in 1938 that television might very well reshape the way people shop and, in the process, shift America's cultural geography. "Why should Mary visit the grocer if she can see the fresh vegetables by [television]," he asked, presuming that Mary would then get her vegetables delivered. Similarly, why would people "fuss with trolleys or parking for a visit to the department store?" he wondered, if the goods could be seen and ordered via television (apparently channeling the gods of the infomercial). The professor also recognized that this kind of "virtual" shopping might stir people to move from crowded, dirty cities to the bucolic bliss of the wide-open spaces. "Country life may have allure; there may be little reason for living near city stores," he suggested, much like how, some sixty years later, many prophesied that online technology would make hordes of city mice become country mice. Even with his keen foresight, the good professor did get at least one thing wrong. "Fifth Avenue real estate might be a good short sale," he added, underestimating the continual draw of the urban experience despite its major problems and minor annoyances.[14]

OUR ECONOMIC MACHINE

Buoyed by the boom economy of the 1920s, the business world saw dazzling horizons ahead, beyond just those in entertainment and communications. "The business of America is business," famously proclaimed new president Calvin Coolidge in 1923, putting his money where his mouth was by encouraging a laissez-faire economy that would define the decade. John Maynard Keynes's 1926 *The End of Laissez-Faire* made a convincing case for government intervention in the marketplace, however, a policy that would serve the nation well after the crash of 1929. With unemployment at historic highs and coast-to-coast Hoovervilles, free-market capitalism was apparently not as "self-correcting" as once believed. For the first time, more people in the 1930s left the United States than arrived, a clear sign that the American Dream had become just that, an elusive fantasy. The Florida land boom that reigned through much of the 1920s had gone bust, with real estate ventures for most now limited to the new board game, Monopoly. With FDR's election in 1932, however, a new chapter in America's future was about to be written, via the launching of the New Deal, the largest public works program in history. The creation of the TVA in 1933, the FCC and SEC in 1934, and the Social Security Act and WPA the following year were the foundation for a happy (and rare) alliance between the federal government and its citizens, seeding a progressive spirit and belief that a new and improved American Dream loomed in the future.

For business leaders, the logic and efficiency of modern times and the more modern times to come was a natural fit, the ideal climate for organizations to run like well-oiled machines. "Business is passing out of the pioneer stage," observed Edward Filene, the leading Boston merchant, in 1928, locating commerce at the very center of the progressive ideals of the 1920s. "Snap judgments were often necessary in the old days, because quick action was called for and there were few facilities for scientifically determining business facts [but] there is too much at stake in the great business of today to take chances on anything," Filene concluded.[15]

Others in industry were equally sure that objective truth should be the beacon pointing the way to tomorrow. "The world has finally learned its greatest lesson," argued William B. Stout, a top designer for Ford, in 1929, the lesson being that "facts rule, and that any person or institution or entity of any kind that gets in the way of facts to suppress them, hinder them or in any way obstruct them, no matter how powerful it may be today, will eventually be conquered by facts." Stout believed his decidedly fact-obsessed boss Henry Ford was not just a great industrialist but a great preacher delivering a message that was particularly relevant and meaningful for the times. Ford's pursuit of "more jobs for more men at more money" was, in Stout's eyes, not a corporate mission but, rather, "the forerunning gospel of this religion of industrial progress, which is elevating the standard of living and the standard of thinking." In the future, he himself preached, "it is what we do, what we can do, what we shall do with our widening and deepening knowledge of facts that will be the religion," raising the role of commerce to an act of God.[16]

Only three months after Stout's confident words, however, the mother of all facts—the great stock-market crash of 1929—threw a major monkey wrench into the works of consumer capitalism. It was, as many noticed at the time, a kind of futurism itself—the trading of securities on margin—that was to blame for the collapse, as greedy investors bet on a richer tomorrow without having the cash today. Some viewed a somewhat different dimension of futurism, however, the installment buying craze of the 1920s, as the principal cause of the crash. "By 1929 America, with the whole Western world, had in its frenzy of to-morrow chasing so bought and made for its future that, by 1930, it had made more than it could buy and it had bought more than it could pay for," argued Roy Helton in *Harper's* in 1932. Rather than the conventional wisdom, which held that investors had been caught with their hands in the cookie jar, Helton felt it was more consumers' limitless pursuit of luxuries that brought down the economic house of cards. It was, for Helton and others, the relatively new concept of buying on time (an "economic steeplechase so habitual that we accept it as the proper way to live," he called it) that was at fault for the sorry state of affairs. The Depression was vivid evidence illustrating "what tinkering with to-morrow can do," he convincingly believed, holding that "every such attempt to reach forward into time is in some way capitalized out of the pockets of the future which we wish to control."[17]

Still, however, most captains of industry believed the machine remained fundamentally sound and would again be purring like a kitten in the not-so-distant future. "We shall go over our economic machine and redesign it," Ford himself wrote in 1931, "not for the purpose of making something different than what we have but to make the present machine do what we have said it could do." Describing himself simply as an "industrial experimenter," Ford looked out eighty years and saw a future "so full of promise as to make the present seem drab in comparison," not unlike the progress civilization had made in the past eighty years. By 2011, Ford believed, we will have entered "an ante-room of self-searching and through something very like penitence for our past stupidity" become much wiser creatures, joining a chorus of voices predicting an exponential evolution of the species.[18] Five years later, Ford was more convinced than ever that the good life was just around the corner, with the machine paving the way. "The Machine Age has not only come to stay but is only beginning," Ford said in 1936, deeming the worst economic slowdown in the nation's history a mere bump in a very long road.[19]

Ford's brother-in-arms, Alfred P. Sloan, Jr., head of General Motors, also believed that America's economic machine could and would be repaired. "No depression since man began to use machines effectively has lasted long enough to break down the consistent optimism of generation after generation of inventors and industrialists," he wrote in 1934, seeing great times ahead for the nation and for industry. With "new ideas and methods developed by research," Sloan maintained, "we shall be on our way toward a higher standard of living than the world has ever seen." Sloan perceived the bigger threat to America's future to be not a massive economic depression but organized labor, the latter much more capable of gumming up the works of a full recovery. "Looking forward, either for a year or for a century, who can doubt the limitless ability of America to continue its industrial progress, provided men are left free to organize their activities?" he asked, frustrated by the greater friction between management and labor that was a byproduct of shrinking revenues. Still, Sloan looked down the road of tomorrow with clear optimism, convinced a new and better day was coming. "The good life lies ahead somewhere along the road of abundance," he concluded, "and we shall find it by continuing in that direction with stout hearts and open minds."[20]

Although Henry Ford and Alfred P. Sloan were especially, perhaps pathologically, fervent believers in the forward thrust of history, most visionaries of the Depression years maintained if not escalated their own utopian concept of tomorrow. Whether a means to deflect the realities of bad times, put things in long-term perspective, or restore hope and confidence, futurism in the early 1930s was generally designed to, as the song went, keep one's sunny side up. As in other especially tough times, a common device was to look back on the Depression from a future time, a more powerful technique than simply making predictions. In 1931, The *Magazine of Wall Street* published an article called "Looking Backward on the Depression," which did just that from what seemed to be the very far-off year of 1935.[21] In just four years, the magazine believed, there would be

> Nothing on the front page about wage slashes. Nothing about relief plans for the unemployed. No strikes. No prospective increase in taxation. Nothing is said about bank failures. No mention of a Senate investigation of Wall Street. The nation is prosperous and happy again.[22]

Besides having none of the bad news of 1931, this article added, the world of 1935 was going to be an appliance paradise filled with radios, television sets, refrigerators, and "home-cooling units."[23] While consumer culture in the 1920s was more about enjoying the rather suddenly liberated present, consumerism in the 1930s more often traded on the hope and optimism that were embedded in the language of the future. "During the Depression, the future began to secure a permanent place in advertising illustration and copywriting," Corn and Horrigan observed in their amazing book, *Yesterday's Tomorrows*, as a parade of consumer products and industrial materials were somehow plucked from the world of tomorrow to be made available today. "By explicitly linking products with popularly perceived images of the future," they argue, "advertisers encouraged buyers to think of their products as not merely modern, but . . . ahead of the cutting edge." Leapfrogging over the literally depressing present to the much more exciting future was a brilliant strategy among marketers of the 1930s, a way to make the redesigned economic machine a reality.[24]

Some of the most utopian ideas about the future, in fact, originated during the darkest days of the Depression. In a 1931 book, *Tomorrow's Business*, for example, the National Education Association listed a number of "probable achievements" that would be realized by 1950, all things for which businessmen should prepare. In just twenty years, the NEA told either delighted or skeptical men of commerce, most contagious diseases would be wiped out, medical care and insurance would be made available to all, and crime would be virtually abolished, all this somehow with a shorter workweek and workday. How businessmen should prepare for these and many other equally amazing achievements was not made exactly clear, but the book was a good example of how Depression-era futurism was used to ease the sorrows of today and to encourage a certain kind of tomorrow to happen.[25] "Let no one doubt that American business is going to do a lot of traveling in the next ten years," Floyd W. Parsons declared that same year, viewing the nation's economic collapse, like other optimists of the day, more as a period of "adjustment" and "housecleaning" than as a crisis. "Life will be carried rapidly to a new and higher plane," he promised readers, with "a wider diffusion of our high standard of living among the masses" to come. The hard times that Americans were experiencing were just a bump in a very long road, Parsons insisted, with good times waiting just around the corner. "People in 1940 will be following practices, thinking thoughts and dreaming dreams that only a few visionaries now contemplate," he predicted, assuring both businesspeople and consumers that the American way of life would one day be bigger and better than ever.[26]

Norman Bel Geddes, already an industrial designer extraordinaire, also put his futuristic hat in the ring in 1931, offering an equally rosy outlook for businessmen and nonbusinessmen alike. Within the next decade, Bel Geddes told *Ladies' Home Journal*, economic slumps (or booms, for that matter) would be a thing of the past, due to the efforts of a "Commercial League of Nations" that regulated international commerce, a riff on the Geneva-based peacekeeping organization League of Nations founded after World War I. Bel Geddes, who had been a highly successful portrait painter and theater set designer before applying his skills to the business world, believed that future artists would follow his path by using their talents to solve industrial problems of the day. Not quite as good as Bel Geddes's news that all incurable diseases and epidemics would be eliminated, but still pretty exciting, was his prediction that men's clothing in 1941 would be both "rational" and "comfortable," a happy development for wool-heavy captains of industry.[27]

More useful, however, were outlooks that pointed the way to the future dynamics of work and play. "The Industrial Revolution is now approaching its end," proposed Julian Huxley in 1933, convinced that "fifty years hence we shall be well into the Technological Revolution." While Huxley was dead on about that, he missed the boat when it came to how the end of one revolution and the beginning of another would affect our work lives. "Labor-saving machinery will have so effectively saved labor that four-and-a-half hours will be the average working day," Huxley prophesied, believing, like others, that new technologies would naturally result in more leisure time. Also like others, Huxley perceived that, while a godsend, having much more leisure time in the future also presented some serious issues. How would we fill all these hours, many reasonably wondered, as the coming wave of miracles turned our workday into a part-time affair? How would the nation reconcile a leisure-based society with its Puritan past grounded in hard work and delayed gratification? The new American middle class that had emerged in the 1920s was currently enjoying a host of leisure activities for the first time, their attraction to "low culture" already a concern to those of higher socioeconomic stature. The possibility of one day having twice as much leisure time available was to some a truly frightening prospect, raising the distinct possibility of a major spike in at least a few of the seven deadly sins. By 1983, Huxley thought, "it will have been realized that the problem of leisure is not merely one of finding ways in which not to work," but "the problem of finding ways of working which people shall enjoy." Huxley's solution was a Department of Social Welfare, which would work with educational authorities and private organizations to help people discover a personal hobby or some kind of worthwhile enterprise. There would thus be two kinds of occupations, one providing "the basic needs of society" and the other designed "to make life richer and more interesting," not too much unlike that which actually occurred as prosperity spread in the latter part of the century.[28]

Dixon Ryan Fox, a professor at Columbia University, also saw lots more leisure time ahead, especially for highly successful businessmen like bankers. Even if it was the middle of the Depression, Fox believed that businessmen had better get used to the idea of less work and more play, whether they liked it or not. "You will have to accustom yourselves to the regulation of business; you will have to be content with smaller fortunes; you will have to develop yourselves as men as well as bankers by the wise use of a larger leisure," Fox told alumni of the university at their annual meeting in 1934, who were no doubt unhappy to hear this news.[29]

The editors of *Good Housekeeping* couldn't agree more that leisure and more leisure loomed ahead, refusing to be a party pooper when the magazine celebrated its fiftieth anniversary in the less than celebratory year of 1935. "We'd like to be editor of *Good Housekeeping* in 1985," wrote William Frederick Bigelow, because "this is going to be such a magnificent world to live and work in then, and any one would be silly not to want to be doing his part in it." Bigelow had a good point, having heard from "the dreamers" that just ten hours of work a week would allow anyone and everyone to "get along passably." With that and other signs of "the most amazing progress," Bigelow reasonably asked, "Can you blame us for wanting to stick around for *Good Housekeeping*'s Centennial?"[30]

MACHINEJ FOR LIVING

Although *Good Housekeeping* was hardly a neutral observer, who would dare question that housekeeping would not be especially good in the future? Nearly everyone agreed that houses would undergo radical changes as form and function became indelibly linked, the sign of a perfectly designed machine. The "home of tomorrow"—both the concept and the phrase itself—became a staple of futurism between the wars, a "cultural symbol of the American obsession with the single-family house," according to Corn and Horrigan. Whether it was avant-garde (European design) or state-of-the-art (electrical appliances), owning a modern home was envisioned as almost a universal birthright for the future. Inspiration for such "modern thinking" was not in short supply, as architects such as Le Corbusier, Richard Neutra, and Frank Lloyd Wright broke new ground with their approach to design, materials, and construction. Buckminster Fuller's much-celebrated 1928 "Dynamaxion House" took Le Corbusier's idea of the house as a "machine for living" to a whole new level, the home reinvented as a mass-produced, factory-assembled, and technology-equipped industrial unit made of aluminum, glass, and rubber. George Fred Keck's "House of Tomorrow" displayed at the Century of Progress world's fair in Chicago in 1933–1934, along with his Crystal House the following year, also challenged all assumptions about the home, each proposing the rather radical idea that high design and low cost were by no means mutually exclusive.[31]

As Walter Pitkin wrote in 1931, however, the design of the home of the future would be determined not by any "architect's fancy," but rather by what he called "the three laws of social revolution: mass production, mass distribution, mass credit." Just like the defining product of the Machine Age, the automobile, the home too would be turned into something that could be easily standardized and efficiently replicated, many believed. The $5,000 prefabricated house would be the logical solution to one of the nagging problems of the 1920s and 1930s, how to deliver the core of the American Dream—one's own "Home, Sweet Home"—to the Everyman. Henry

29

Ford and Alfred P. Sloan were probably the two people in the world most interested in turning this idea into a reality, seeing the mass-produced house as the obvious way to keep their assembly lines humming for perhaps generations. Another world war would delay the development of cookie-cutter communities filled with cookie-cutter homes, but the vision of what would become the postwar American suburb was crystal clear decades earlier. Buying large tracts of land near major cities on the cheap, using standardized building materials and construction methods, and participating in one-stop-shop financing was the formula for creating the house of the future, Pitkin knew, with "a fifty-billion-dollar order" (10 million families coming up with $5,000 each) just waiting for the savvy businessman who could get there first. Pitkin even recognized that the design of this new kind of house "must harmonize the demands of mechanical efficiency with the taste of the occupant," knowing that residents of the Levittowns of the future would insist on turning their ticky-tacky homes into personalized works of art.[32]

Julian Huxley was of similar mind, believing that "the first specimen of the methods of scientific mass-production applied to housing" on display at the Century of Progress world's fair was the start of something big. "Fifty years hence, most of the new houses being erected will be of this type," he stated, "as different from the constructions of to-day as a modern automobile is from a gasoline buggy of the B.F. (Before Ford) Era." Like Pitkin, Huxley thought individual tastes in and customizing of homes wouldn't go away, "but plain economic necessity and common sense will have driven the majority to plump for the cheapness and scientific planning of mass-production." The parallels between the mass-produced automobile of the present and the mass-produced home of the future would be carried even further, according to Huxley. "People will talk, enviously or proudly, about the make and model of their houses as to-day they talk of the make and model of their cars," he predicted, something that may one day still come to pass.[33] Although mass-produced homes have yet to achieve the popularity that visionaries of the 1920s and 1930s believed they would (the Sears kit home being the most successful example), they definitely helped popularize the idea of the future and probably helped fuel the broad appeal of the forward-looking Art Deco style.[34]

Outside of the mass-produced home, big changes were in store for the design and construction of houses in the future. "Houses ten years hence will have flat roofs that can be utilized for outdoor living rooms or roof gardens," believed Herbert U. Nelson, executive secretary of the National Association of Real Estate Boards in 1930, with the Old World pitched roof no longer necessary because of modern gutters and waterproof materials. Nelson also thought basements "will be eliminated entirely" in just a decade, considering them "costly, inefficient, and serv[ing] few useful purposes to the modern family except as a storage place for the heating system." Recalling Jefferson's vision of the yeoman family farmer, Nelson saw the home of tomorrow as being less reliant on the outside world, a self-sustaining paradise on the new frontier. "The house of the future will have one plant which will heat it, make its ice, and wash and cool its air when necessary," he foresaw (an idea just now becoming realized as some of us find ways to get off the public utility grid).[35]

Zay Jeffries, the metallurgist, also saw a new age for the old-fashioned house as it became liberated from external forces, even those of nature. Like many visionaries before and after him, Jeffries saw windowless buildings on the horizon, artificially ventilated and lit by man-made ultraviolet rays. No longer subject to the vicissitudes of weather, Modern Man had, quite literally, a bright future ahead of him.[36] The wave of electrical appliances coming into the home also of course posed especially big implications for our future. In just ten years, Norman Bel Geddes believed in 1931, "the home will become so mechanized that handwork will be reduced to a minimum," a key contributing factor for the more leisure-based society that loomed and beckoned ahead.[37]

These two decades were also the era in which cerebral figures such as Le Corbusier, Wright, Fuller, Hugh Ferris, and a bevy of industrial designers weighed in on what the city of the future might look and be like. As Fritz Lang's 1926 film *Metropolis* and the "City of Tomorrow" exhibit at the Century of Progress world's fair suggested, urban areas would one day be transformed into perfectly efficient machines, although it was unclear whether this new mechanical beast would be more like heaven or hell. A firm believer in the latter, Wright proposed Americans retreat from the modern (and doomed) metropolis for a new kind of rural community, his (never built) Broadacre City of the mid-1930s another twentieth-century version of Jefferson's self-sustaining family farm. The New Deal–backed Greenbelt movement of the 1930s was yet one more attempt to create a progressive and planned community of tomorrow as an alternative to the disordered and dysfunctional city of yesterday. Three Greenbelt communities were actually built but, by the end of the decade, such social programs had taken a backseat to much more threatening forces at work abroad.[38]

With the rapid growth of many cities in the 1920s, compounded of course by the rise of the automobile, it was not surprising for many to call for nothing short of a wholesale reengineering of the urban landscape. Triumphs such as the first cloverleaf highway intersection (1928), the Boulder Dam (begun in 1930), the George Washington Bridge (1931), and the Golden Gate Bridge (1937) proved a key axiom of futurism: Man will not let Nature stand in his way when "progress" is at stake. Architectural miracles such as the 1930 Chrysler Building and the 1931 Empire State Building offered a corollary to that axiom, that state-of-the-art technology and beauty were not mutually exclusive when done right. Until Lewis Mumford's 1938 book *The Culture of Cities*—the first shot in what would be a volley of warnings about massive, badly designed, and less than people-friendly public works that threatened to take the soul out of urban life—it was considered vital that the city of the past be rebuilt for the future.

With Robert Moses becoming state parks commissioner of New York in 1924—the beginning of an almost half-century career during which the "master builder" would remake much of Gotham and its surrounding area— the quintessential American city had a firm (arguably too firm) model for its future. That city's future had actually begun two years earlier, however, with the formation of the Committee on a Regional Plan of New York and its Environs (an organization that basically still exists today, as the Regional Plan Association). In order to plan for future growth, a handpicked group of experts asked themselves what the city should look like in 1965 ("the year selected as having the most interest for contemporary New Yorkers," they explained). Continued growth was a certainty, everyone agreed, although two Harvard professors on the committee believed 14.5 million people would live in New York in the mid-1960s, while the team from Johns Hopkins expected a whopping 21 million residents (each a hefty overestimate). Most importantly, the committee felt the development of New York should not be "the result of a blind rush" but rather a product of "laws of psychology and physics which can be studied and upon which predictions can safely be made." The city's current and much greater future congestion could be fixed, just as a machine operating at less than maximum efficiency could be tuned up. "The evils of the present situation are not due to overgrowth but to bad housekeeping," a reporter for the *New York Times* described the commit- tee's findings in 1928, with getting rid of obsolete structures and expanding into underutilized areas just a couple of ways the city could achieve its full potential. "In short," the reporter summed up the committee's plan, "what the New York region needs is not depopulation—though that would be an effective remedy for some evils—but reorganization."[39]

A big part of the "reorganization" that New York and other cities needed had much to do with issues of race, ethnicity, and class. The immigration boom and "Great Migration" from the south through the 1920s and 1930s flooded northern cities with new residents, stirring up the American melting pot along racial, ethnic, and class lines. "Even now congestion is so frightful in areas like the Semitic and Italian sections of New York and the Negro districts in that city and Chicago, as well as in all business sections, that we would now have buildings two and three hundred stories high if the elevator companies could build machines safe enough and fast enough to care for traffic," wrote William B. Stout in 1929 for *Collier's*.[40] With major cities chaotic, messy, and inefficient, due to occupation by actual people, it was broadly accepted that a different kind of metropolis was needed for the future, one that embodied the rationalism and order of the Machine Age.

To the rescue came the Swiss architect Le Corbusier, along with members of the Bauhaus school such as Walter Gropius and Ludwig Mies van der Rohe, each showing how the skyscraper could mesh with modern systems of transportation to form the core of the city of the future. Neutra also advanced this concept of urbanism that clearly prioritized buildings and vehicles over people, efficiency over livability. With their aerial gardens and sky golf courses, Ferris's 1925 "The Titan City" exhibit at Wanamaker's department store and 1929 book *The Metropolis of Tomorrow* brought more humanity into the urban landscape of the future, but the imagined city of tomorrow was unquestionably more machine than man.[41] Ironically, visions of a more mechanical city were often the product of concerns over machines themselves. The idea of mechanically organized underground cities became a popular one between the wars, for example, partly because of the real rise of urban problems but also because of an imagined threat of a much more dangerous airplane (or even flying tank) in a future war.[42]

Although undeniably highbrow, the fantastic landscapes of the city of tomorrow proposed by the leading visionaries of the day trickled into the popular discourse of futurism, heavily influencing mainstream thought of things to come. As so many interpretations of the urban tomorrow portrayed, often in elaborate detail, cities would take to the skies as space ran out on the ground. "We are headed for multideck cities with various kinds of traffic stories above the ground levels," wrote Floyd W. Parsons, clearly inspired by Lang's *Metropolis* (which in turn was inspired by an actual trip to New York). Unlike Lang's dystopian city of the future, however, in which citizens were dominated and enslaved by machines, Parson's vertical metropolis would encourage "new industries, the expansion of social activities, community betterments, engineering projects, town planning and the rehabilitation of blighted urban areas." Life down on the ground also would be a whole lot better as a new kind of cooperative apartment building replaced the bane of city life, the tenement. "Judging by what is taking place in New York City, darkness, dirt and squalor will be eliminated," according to Parsons, rectified by "built-in bathtubs, gas or electric refrigerators, self-operating elevators, incinerators, good air, sunlight and inner courts with shrubbery, flowers and fountains, all for a cost of $12.50 a room a month." Old World grit and grime would be cleaned up by New World planning and efficiency, this expression of the future proposed, anticipating the scorch-the-earth brand of urban renewal that would reign in the postwar years.[43]

THE RHYTHM OF LIFE

To better serve the most mechanistic machine of the Machine Age, the automobile, the grit and grime of the nation's roads too would be a thing of the past, many hoped. With the Federal Highway Act of 1921 standardizing the building of roads, the first step toward the endless highway system that would help define America in a few decades was formally put in place. The ubiquity of Ford's Model T (over half the cars in the world in the mid-1920s were Tin Lizzies) and the founding of Greyhound in 1926 suggested that the future of transportation would be on wheels, furthered by the introduction of the mobile home that same year (and the drive-in movie theater in 1933).

Even greater possibilities could be found above, in the wide blue yonder, however, as the miracle of flight presented the idea that even the sky was no longer the limit. The use of the airplane in the Great War proved that the invention was by no means a frivolous plaything and, once its kinks could be worked out, it would play a major role in the world of tomorrow. "If the methods of transport employed before the advent of aerial navigation have modified the rhythm of life to a great extent," said Henry Farman, a French airplane pioneer, in 1921, "aviation promises, little by little, to transform it entirely." Farman saw air travel as not just reshaping how we got around but affecting our entire lives. "Its practical development will determine the evolution—the transformation, I may say—of all our habits and our manner of living," he declared, seeing in the future flat roofs of homes as personal landing strips and the redesign of entire cities to accommodate short hops around town. Although by the early 1920s relatively few Americans or Europeans had yet to have any personal experience with an airplane, as it was still mainly the domain of adventurers and daredevils, Farman clearly recognized the commercial potential of the machine. "It must cease to be an 'exploit' in order to become a reality and . . . a suitable means of establishing more speedy communication between nations," he argued, for it to realize its full potential. The airplane would one day be "the essential factor of economic pre-eminence or of military strength, the propagator—or the destroyer—of civilization," Farman concluded, knowing that victory in both war and peace would be won in the air versus on the ground.[44]

Well before Leonardo's aeronautic doodles, flight had been a staple of futurism, of course, the ability to soar in the clouds one of civilization's most profound dreams. With Lindbergh's nonstop solo crossing of the Atlantic in 1927, however, few possibilities in the air now seemed too implausible. Air travel (like that on the ground, via superfast, ultraluxurious autos and trains) would be both faster and safer, more comfortable yet more convenient, with no compromises necessary. Until the *Hindenburg* disaster in 1937 emphatically ended the era of airships, some felt that the zeppelin would play a big role in our future travel plans. Many in fact believed that giant airships, not puny airplanes, would emerge as the future of flight, with these ocean liners of the sky taking us overseas in high style.[45] Hugo Eckener, head of the zeppelin works in Germany in 1928 (and ex–right-hand man to Count Zeppelin himself), was not surprisingly gung-ho on the airship as long as funding could be found to realize his dream. Regular transatlantic service and even the ultimate trip—a nonstop, round-the-world flight—were close to becoming reality, he believed, now that an alternative fuel to the not-very-efficient and highly combustible hydrogen gas was near development.[46]

By the late 1920s, Lindbergh mania and the slow commercialization of the airplane had turned the flying machine into an icon of popular and consumer culture and a seminal symbol of the future. Farman's words were already being realized, as the airplane infiltrated our "manner of living," including fashion. This was readily apparent when Arnold Constable & Company, a New York department store, celebrated its 101st birthday in business in 1928 by holding a "future fashion show," a subtle way to let shoppers know they intended to be around for another century. (The company made it almost another half-century, with the last of its luxury department stores closing in 1975.) After showing past and present-day fashions, the New York store showed an audience of some 1,500 people what women's clothes in the coming decades might look like. While projected into another time, all the fashions reflected the between-the-wars obsession with the machine, especially the airplane. With aviation so safe by 1950 that it would be a "woman's preferred method of transportation," the store's fashion experts believed, suits of chiffon and sheer velvet along with soft kid leggings and a leather windbreaker would be all the rage. Women ten years later would be fond of wearing "flying costumes of a feathery composition of materials and electrical attachments," Arnold Constable prophesied (not all that inaccurately, apparently channeling designer-to-be Bob Mackie). Women at the close of the twentieth century would have moved on to "gowns of metal and synthetic velvet fashioned in tubular effects," the store informed the no-doubt-fascinated crowd, a preview of what one might have actually seen on a runway in the late 1990s. That the airplane would become not just a means of transportation but the inspiration for style and design illustrates the profound power it held over the imagination some eighty years ago.[47]

Although journalist Josephine Daskam Bacon agreed with Arnold Constable that the airplane would become the transportation of choice among women, she disagreed that it would shape the kind of clothes they would wear. "That she will fly to her job in a plane [in 1979] we cannot well doubt," Bacon declared in 1929, although she didn't think her method of commute would have too much effect on fashion. "We shall be foolish if we think she shall therefore wear an aviator's costume," Bacon thought, recalling how women's accessories of the early days of the automobile—goggles, veils, and big coats—turned out to be just a fad. Despite the popularity of this advanced form of transportation, Bacon also had doubts that the airplane would alleviate the growing congestion of city streets and lessen the increasing number of collisions, each a worsening problem as the automobile became a ubiquitous presence in urban life. "The most airplanes can do is ease the traffic a little, and spread the accidents over a wider surface," she reasoned.[48]

Fashion sense aside, Bacon was keenly aware that women, having by the late 1920s realized a degree of intellectual, economic, and political freedom that their mothers could only dream of, had an even more promising future. "I wish I could see the faces of the women in 1979," she exclaimed in *Century*, adding that "they will have forgotten long ago that there was even a day when women hadn't independence!" With access to university educations, job opportunities beyond just that of schoolteacher, and the right to vote, what were the next frontiers for women to cross? Bacon knew it would involve the intersection and conflict between family and career. "I feel safe in forecasting, before the next fifty years, an adjustment between the woman, her man, her child and her job," she presciently sensed, also knowing that different women would juggle these balls in different ways. Interestingly, Bacon believed that women of the future would not be content simply spinning the wheels of capitalism after having earned full independence, with the possibility that they could even avoid some of the limitations of the male-dominated Machine Age. "Surely our grandchildren . . . will refuse to keep working so that more and more people may jump prosperously from a bath-tub to an automobile—and then jump back again!" she argued, believing a higher purpose was in store for the woman of 1979. "They will have more powerful tools than we did," Bacon confidently and correctly stated, adding, "I firmly believe that they will carve out a greater America!"[49]

Until such noble aims could be pursued by women or men, however, it seemed enough to try to figure out ways to make machines better and, in the case of the flying machine, safer. The safety issues surrounding air travel were at the time "not so much mechanical as meteorological," as one reporter put it, but these also would be solved if we put our modern minds to it. "By the year 1950," wrote Waldemar Kaempffert in 1928 for the *New York Times*, "the weather forecasting services of the civilized world will be coordinated to make transatlantic flying safe," an accurate prediction. Like the postal ser-vice, neither rain nor sleet nor dark of night would prevent flying machines from making their appointed rounds as weather-forecasting technologies like the box kite, balloons, and a new idea called radar were put into use.[50]

As the airplane solidified its role as a primary icon of the future and sym-bol of progress in the Machine Age, more visionaries looked to the skies to ply their trade, including some who had focused on other arenas shaping things to come. Norman Bel Geddes's design for a giant (528-foot wing-span) Transoceanic Passenger Plane of 1929 made an impressive case for what intercontinental travel might be like in 1940, but it was probably for the best that the proto–Spruce Goose never left the ground or was even built.[51] The following year, Thomas Edison (who had actually patented a kind of flying machine twenty years earlier) began to get more interested in flight, inviting a local pilot and airplane designer, Assen Jordanoff, to his Menlo Park research lab. Upon hearing that flying through fog remained a particular problem for pilots, Edison latched on to Jordanoff's dream of a "fog-penetrating artificial eye," seeing the possibilities for its realization. "This far we have converted sound into light and light into sound," Edison proclaimed, so "there is no reason for not being able to solve the artificial eye."[52] With the ability to fly safely through fog realized relatively soon through radar, the doors to future aviation miracles were swung wide open. G. T. R. Hill, an engineering pro-fessor at London University and an airplane designer, believed in 1935 that we would soon be cruising at 40,000 feet at 300 miles an hour, impressive figures indeed but a long way from the 2,000-miles-per-hour speed others were predicting.[53]

It was, however, less such speedy or massive flying machines than the personal, mass-produced airplane that dominated our vision of the future of flight between the wars. The freedom of the road that became a permanent and essential part of the American experience would simply and literally be elevated to the sky, each of us taking off to places near and far at a moment's notice. By the late 1930s, aeronautics experts envisioned a new, urban air age made possible by the biggest development in the field since the Wright Brothers first flew at Kitty Hawk, the helicopter. One expert in 1938 envisioned aerial commuter service between the suburbs and the centers of large cities by helicopter within ten years, just one of many predictions that anticipated Jetsons-style travel by a full generation. In New York, for example, passengers would take off from Westchester and then get off at their particular stop in the city, whether it be in midtown, Wall Street, or the Battery. "The machine probably will be much like a bus," predicted Haviland H. Platt, a top engineer. Whatever the aircraft, the ability to fly around the block or into deep space at one's convenience was in Man's destiny as we harnessed the full power of the machine through our unfailing faith in science and technology.[54]

ƒCHEMEƒ OF COƒMIC MAGNITUDE

Science and technology would not only make flying to points near and far as easy as catching a bus, some futurists in the 1920s and 1930s believed, but actually solve the mysteries of life. Amazing progress had been made since the turn of the century, both experts and laypeople agreed, but these paled in comparison to what lay ahead. One of the core predictions of futurism—that cures would be found for all major diseases (as well as for the common cold)—had its basis in a host of medical breakthroughs in the 1920s and 1930s, including a vaccine for TB (1921 in Europe, almost two decades later in the US), the use of insulin for diabetics and discovery of vitamin D (1922), the iron lung (1927), penicillin (1928 in the UK), the first sulfa drugs (1935), and antihistamines (1937). Scientific innovations such as Heisenberg's theory of quantum mechanics (1925), Edwin Hubble's theory of an expanding universe (1929), the atom-smashing Cyclotron (1930), the electron microscope (1931), radar (late 1930s in Europe), atomic fission (1938), and DDT (1939) were each considered major advancements, finding application both in peace and war.

Scientific and technological innovations of the 1920s and 1930s also found their way to the marketplace as consumerism emerged as a principal strand of the American Way of Life. Band-Aids, GM's Frigidaire, the self-winding wristwatch, Schick's electric razor, the Laundromat, GE's fluorescent light, the photocopier, and the ballpoint pen (not to mention Spam) were just a few things that pointed the way to a more comfortable and more convenient future. It would be, however, MIT professor Vannevar Bush's apartment-sized electromechanical computer—the first such modern analog device—followed by Alan Turing's theory for the digital computer (as well as Hewlett and Packard setting up shop in a garage) that would set the stage for the future of a half-century later, the seeds of the Information Revolution planted, rather ironically, in the Depression.

As new medical technologies allowed scientists of the 1920s to gain much more understanding of the workings of the human body at a micro level, the doors to the future were swung wide open. Within the field of biology, for example, "the solution of the problem of rejuvenation, the prolongation of life and the blessing of children in homes previously childless" were just a few of the possibilities floating around in 1924, believed Russell Porter, writing in the *New York Times*. Even the kind of genetic research being pursued today was anticipated as new methods made virtually anything possible. "Current experiments . . . may even lead to the ability to control the transmission of hereditary characteristics to the children of men," Porter wrote, "and may enable the man of the future to reverse his mental and physical characteristics at will."[55] Through science, nothing short of the secrets of the universe would be revealed, he believed:

> Is science to go still further in its progress toward the ultimate truth, toward the hoped-for solution of the riddle of the universe, toward an explanation of the origin of man and the world we live in, toward all the perplexing mysteries of the unknown? . . . If the discoveries of the nineteenth century revolutionized life, those of the twentieth century will produce changes that defy classification. If there is anything more revolutionary than revolutionary, that shall be the word to describe the life that modern science is preparing for the coming generation.[56]

Besides being the Machine Age, the 1920s and 1930s were not coincidentally the heyday, if you can call it that, of the science of eugenics. The Nazis' goal to create a master race and eliminate "rejects" via an assembly-line-like process was just the most egregious example of what was in fact a field of study widely accepted in mainstream academic circles. Pioneered in futurism by H. G. Wells, eugenics-related ideas not surprisingly spread throughout the field, sometimes with serious moral and ethical consequences, sometimes without. Andres Maurois, the Frenchman who envisioned the "telephoto-phone," also foresaw some of the implications that current breakthroughs in biology might one day present.[57] Foreshadowing Philip K. Dick's still-cutting-edge brand of futurism of a full generation later, Maurois claimed that because biologists "now believe that they can explain our emotional and sentimental life by the abundance or lack of secretions from certain endo-crine glands," it would be possible to

> Make people violent or timid, sensual or the opposite, as you please, by simple injections of the products of these glands. . . . It is easy to foresee the time when clever combinations of glandular secretions will permit us to obtain more subtle shades of sentiment . . .[58]

The Earl of Birkenhead, a British politician and diplomat by trade but a very respectable amateur futurist, also believed that decoding the secrets of human biology would shape the world of tomorrow. The earl went even further than Maurois, anticipating today's genetic revolution with uncanny accuracy. "Biologists by 2029 will have learned the secrets of the living chem-istry of the human body," the earl prophesied, with "rejuvenation an ordi-nary and well-recognized matter of a few injections at appropriate inter-vals."[59] Not only age reversal but genetic profiling for all kinds of purposes would be commonplace in the coming age of scientific miracles, according to the earl:

> Most probably by 2029 a clever young man will consider his fiancée's hereditary complexion before proposing marriage; and the young woman of that day will refuse him because he has inherited a gene from his father which will predispose their children to quarrelsomeness. By intelligent combinations of suitable genes, it will be possible to predict with reason-able certainty that truly brilliant children shall be born of a marriage.[60]

In addition to delivering a rash of truly brilliant children, the full tri-umph of the Machine Age would ultimately result in a much more leisurely society, the earl and many others believed. In another century, "men will work as machine minders for one or two hours a day and be free to devote the rest of their energies to whatever form of activity they enjoy," the earl professed, making a case for what would be a long-running theme of tomor-row.[61] Consistently, some experts were concerned that life in modern times had already become too regulated and standardized, producing a "passive type" of citizen or "automaton." "Previously New York produced active citizens, men and women of bodily vigor," argued Harry L. Hollingsworth, a professor of psychology at Columbia, that same year, "but the economic organization of the city has slowly changed and with it the type of citizen." People themselves might be becoming too "mechanical" as the Machine Age reshaped everything in its path, the professor lamented on the eve of the Depression, predicting that "It is the stock of which the citizen of tomorrow will be bred."[62]

Set in London in the twenty-sixth century, Aldous Huxley's 1932 novel *Brave New World* was clearly the most compelling interpretation of the mechanized citizen of tomorrow. Besides anticipating many of the biological and technological advancements made in the twentieth century (including the popularity of depression-fighting drugs, laboratory-created babies, and multisensory forms of entertainment), Huxley captured the prevailing sentiment that more mechanical times may be creating a more mechanical Man. While Huxley's future included many of the utopian themes that other futurists were predicting—healthier people, broad prosperity, more leisure time, sophisticated gadgets, racial equality, and no violence, war, or poverty—he, unlike most others, saw that all this would come at a great cost. The price of "Community, Identity, Stability," the motto of Huxley's world state, was the elimination of those things that most defined what it was to be human, that is, family, diversity, art, literature, religion, and philosophy. The brave new world of the twenty-sixth century was of course simply an extreme, exaggerated version of the increasingly sterile, less individualistic state of affairs that Huxley and many others believed was taking hold in the early 1930s. Writers like Irwin Edman also believed that a more mechanical person could very well be roaming the earth in fifty years. "The days of rugged individualism are numbered, if indeed they are not already over," claimed Edman in 1932, adding the bad news that "Thoreau and Emerson will seem even more remote and irrelevant than they do today."[63]

As cognitive skills usurped both rugged individualism and physical abilities over the course of thousands of years, many experts of the Machine Age believed, the human body itself would gradually be transformed into something quite different. Evolutionary forecasts throughout the 1920s and 1930s thus reflected the transition of Western culture from a labor-intensive society to one in which the middle class was rapidly moving into managerial occupations that demanded more brain than brawn. In 10,000 years, a contributor to the *American Weekly* suggested in 1929, for example, "the average American business man" would not only be taller and thinner but have a much bigger brain. With this larger "master organ of the body," this writer thought, there "will be an increase in organization and activity, the brain-cells being coupled to each other more accurately and complexly, so that thinking abilities now possess [sic] only by the rare genius will be the common possession of normal men and women." Alex Hrdlicka, a noted medical doctor of the day, agreed with this assessment, telling his colleagues at a Philadelphia meeting of the American Philosophical Society that because "the brain is becoming ever more important in human evolution," an ever-expanding skull was destined to be in our evolutionary future. This "increased demand of the brain for blood" would have the unfortunate side effect of pervasive baldness, Hrdlicka explained, although "the future of the beard is uncertain."[64]

Just as biology would reshape the human body in the future, advancements being made in the new field of atomic energy were indeed the stuff that would shape things to come. As early as 1927, Arthur W. Goodspeed, a professor of physics at the University of Pennsylvania, believed humankind was on the brink of "a wonderful age" as the secrets of the atom were revealed, telling graduating students at a commencement address that "the greatest achievements of modern science have to do with the smallest things in nature." Exponential leaps would be made in both speed and power, Goodspeed thought, correctly predicting the rise of atomic energy over the next couple of decades.[65]

Along with the Earl of Birkenhead, another British wonk, one Winston Churchill, too offered his ideas on how science and technology, specifically atomic energy, were going to change the very laws of nature. Between jobs in 1932, the former British Chancellor of the Exchequer was confident that "the scientific achievements of the next fifty years will be far greater, more rapid, and more surprising than those we have already experienced," a prediction that made one wonder if Winnie might have made an even better scientist than politician. Churchill also reported the news from "high authorities" that a new source of power based on the atom was going to make feasible "schemes of cosmic magnitude" (such as moving Ireland into the middle of the Atlantic, he suggested, purely as an example). With such power, "geography and climate would obey our orders," Churchill claimed in classic imperialistic style. Other remarkable schemes ("We shall escape the absurdity of growing a whole chicken in order to eat the breast or wing, by growing these parts separately under a suitable medium," he wrote) loomed fifty years hence, with the world of 1982 to be as unrecognizable as 1932 would have been to folks in 1882.[66]

Those in industry too had high hopes for what science would contribute in the years, decades, and centuries ahead as bigger brains were put to good use. Speaking at the annual sessions of the American Chemical Society in 1935, Thomas Midgley, vice president of the Ethyl Gasoline Corporation, made some rather startling predictions for the next 100 years, all of them "probabilities which do not overstep the boundaries of accepted natural laws." Midgley, who had discovered ethyl fuel, foresaw a host of scientific breakthroughs ahead, including interplanetary travel, age reversal, the cure of cancer, and "dream pills" (the latter allowing the swallower to choose the dream of his or her, well, dreams). Midgley also envisioned chickens as large as pigs and cows as big as mastodons that would be milked by stepladder, not unlike Woody Allen's satirical vision of the future in his 1973 film *Sleeper*, which also included gargantuan fauna and flora.[67]

As Midgley's rather hyperbolic vision of the future made clear, science between the wars was viewed as something that would improve and extend our lives, a reflection of the era's dominant trust and faith in modernity. Looking ahead fifty years in 1938, Arthur Train, Jr., in *Harper's* also envisioned science leading us to a significantly better world. An array of devices and synthetic materials in use in 1988 would only improve upon the natural world, he thought, transforming how we would eat and breathe and what we would wear, live in, and even sit on. Houses would be constructed not with wood, bricks, and plaster but with panels of beryllium and magnesium alloys, low-grade silicas, and glasslike materials, Train felt confident, while furniture also would be made not of natural materials but of plastic and magnesium alloy and filled with synthetic upholstery. Air-conditioning would not only eliminate dust, germs, and sound from the outside but supply lungs of the future with "air as invigorating as that of the seashore or the mountains," Train believed. At night we would inhale indoor air whose chemical composition had been "calculated" for maximum refreshment, he continued, while during the day we'd take in air that was continually and automatically rebalanced in order to avoid "the soporific effect of monotony." (Even "synthetic air" was going to be close to becoming a reality by 1988, Train forecast.) Our food supply also was not going to be left in the hands of unpredictable, fickle nature. Vegetables and fruit would not be grown in soil but chemically produced in a factory in order to permit "an efficient control of the food supply," with clothing as well made mostly of synthetic textiles. The only disappointing news that Train seemingly had to pass on was that we would not yet have a synthetic substitute for sleep at our disposal.[68]

Rather than predicting the future, Alexis Carrel of the Rockefeller Institute for Medical Research proposed some ideas on how to best move into it, all of them requiring we reject our less-than-scientific past. Carrel, a winner of the Nobel Prize for his surgical research, believed that the future of civilization should not be based on the dated ideologies of the eighteenth century but rather on the modern scientific principles of the twentieth. "If we used scientific concepts instead of ideologies," Carrel told the Rotary Club of New York in 1939, "we might discover a new way of life which would be based on reality." The daring, literally revolutionary ideals of America's founding fathers had served us well but, he argued, a new, more practical age demanded new, more practical ideas. More specifically, Carrel thought the many problems of civilization could be solved by consolidating all of our present knowledge into "a brain pool or a sort of composite Aristotle," one version of the popular fantasy of somehow aggregating all human intelligence into a single reservoir. On the brink of another world war, it would be the rationalism of science, not democratic ideals or musty philosophy, which would save civilization.[69]

A MURDEROUS RAIN OF ROCKETS

Something on the order of a composite Aristotle would have been necessary to forego the natural inclination to develop better methods of destruction as advances in military technology continued throughout the 1920s and 1930s. Predictably, however, the war to end all wars had barely ended before those in the know started to think about what the next one would be like. In 1921, for example, Eugene Debeney, a general in the French First Army during the war, envisioned tanks not only watertight and airtight but capable of traveling "12 or 14 miles an hour over any kind of surface" (about twice their speed at the time). Great changes were in store for the airplane as well, which of course would come into play in the war of tomorrow. "Devices for enabling the airplane to find its way through the air independent of physical vision will permit flight during the hours of darkness and in time of fog," the general foresaw before the development of radar. His fellow Frenchman Henry Farman also saw the plane playing a much bigger role in a future conflict, predicting that "if a fresh war occurs, its issue will be decided beyond all doubt by aerial fighting."[70]

Like others, however, Debeney anticipated the advent of weapons of mass destruction in wartime, perhaps the darkest side of the shape of things to come. "A day will come when some old savant will find a means to harness the electric waves, bind them together in such a way that their power will be multiplied to an undreamed of extent, and launch them from the height of something corresponding to an Eiffel tower, against a city, an army, or a fleet," he wrote, an image eerily close to the effect of an atomic bomb.[71] Throughout the 1920s and into the 1930s, the rocket too became seen as a must-have weapon for armies of the future, no longer considered just a speedy means to one day get around the universe. Hermann Oberth, a Hungarian scientist, saw the rocket as the centerpiece of the next generation of war technology, something that various nations were in fact already feverishly pursuing in the early 1930s. Oberth foresaw the "bombarding from the other side of the earth an enemy country with a murderous rain of rockets carrying poison-gas containers capable of exterminating whole populations in a few minutes," as the *New York Times* put it, a pretty good description of what would be long-range missiles. Oberth also saw a peaceful use of rocket technology, however, a way to send mail between New York and Vienna in just half an hour.[72]

Others in the 1930s, however, saw only peaceful times ahead, that the horrors of the Great War and the emerging technologies to fight an even more terrible one were sufficient cause for future lions to lay down with future lambs. In 1932, for example, Sir Arthur Salter imagined that in 1957 we'd be living in a "world without war," with a technology-equipped Council of the League of Nations in Geneva keeping the peace. Chiang Kai-shek of China and other leaders from around the world would be beamed in via "wireless telephony," another reference to what would become two-way videoconferencing. (Salter also anticipated the cell phone or something very much like it, suggesting that, in twenty-five years, "We may, perhaps, be then carrying our little wireless receiving set in our waistcoat pocket as we now carry a watch.") More important than the technological strides to be made, however, was the major decline in nationalism that would sweep the world by 1957, making us all much more of one big happy global family. "National rivalries and ambitions will still remain, but . . . they will be of the nature of healthy competition rather than of dangerous friction," Salter believed, with the international council keeping things in check by ganging up on any country that violated the agreement. As others believed, Salter was confident that eventually nations would come to their senses and mutually decide to focus on more noble pursuits. "Upon such a securely established foundation of world government," he made clear, "man will at last be able to reap the fruits of nature's riches and of his own increasing skill and knowledge." A war and Cold War would prove Salter quite wrong, of course, his ability to predict future gizmos much better than his estimation of the enduring power of nationalism.[73]

As the winds of war grew increasingly stronger throughout the 1930s, many were interested in what H. G. Wells, the esteemed British novelist and social philosopher, had to say about the future. Already famous for works including *War of the Worlds, When the Sleeper Wakes, The Outline of History,* and *The Time Machine,* Wells produced in 1933 *The Shape of Things to Come,* another must-read within the pantheon of futurism (then and now). The novel portrayed a world in which things would get a lot worse before they got better, as another war (this one decades-long) brought down capitalism and much of civilization as we know it. In a generation or two, however, a utopia filled with peace and abundance would emerge, a world state not too unlike Huxley's, in which universal commonalities trumped nationalism and ideology. Interestingly, Wells located the creation of this society led by intellectual revolutionaries in the 1960s and 1970s, foreshadowing that era's countercultural resistance to the military-industrial complex and utopian dream of going back to an Eden-like garden.[74]

Perhaps even more interesting was that Wells, the leading visionary of the day, claimed to have no predictive abilities at all. "It is not a bit of good pretending I am a prophet," Wells wrote in 1938 after *Things to Come,* a film based on his book in which he portrayed the city of 2055 as a "shining technocentric Utopia," was released.[75] Wells admitted that

> I have no crystal in which I gaze, and no clairvoyance. I just draw inferences from facts in common knowledge. Some of the inferences have been lucky . . . The effect of reality is easily produced. One jerks in one or two little unexpected gadgets or so, and the trick is done. It is a trick.[76]

Asked what life would be like in fifty years, Wells reiterated his belief that big trouble lay ahead in the near future but not the complete destruction of the planet. "There are certainly disasters ahead," he wrote as the German military mobilized, "but not universal disaster." Wells's long-range view of history allowed him to see the approaching war in a way very few other people could. "Millions of people are likely to die violent deaths before they half lived their lives out," he calmly reasoned, "but people must die somehow." Like many more pedestrian futurists, however, Wells thought that eventually humans would figure out that war is ultimately a losing proposition. "Political history is likely to go on being even more insincere, irrational, violent, convulsive, cruel, horrible and destructive for some decades at least," he predicted, "before the obvious common sense of world organization breaks upon the general mind." Given his more than dim short-term outlook, Wells was surprisingly optimistic about the shape of things to come in fifty years, again a result of his historical perspective. "I do not find anything in these present alarms and excursions about us to make me doubt that this secular expansion of the common life will not be equally manifest in 1988," he neatly concluded.[77]

PILGRIMAGE TO TOMORROW

As a celebration of the "secular expansion of the common life" like no other, the New York World's Fair in 1939 and 1940 served as an especially opportune moment to imagine what lay ahead and a fitting way that this era of the future ended. World's fairs typically looked (and continue to look) to the future, of course, but this fair's "World of Tomorrow" was dedicated to a coming utopia just as dark clouds appeared on the actual horizon, even darker ones than those that had hovered over the nation during the early years of the Depression. The 1939–1940 New York World's Fair thus had a much different mission than that of the last major fair in the United States, the Century of Progress exposition in Chicago. That fair had celebrated the growth of science over the last 100 years as a way to remind the world that it was Big Business that had made many everyday miracles a reality, giving consumer capitalism a boost when it needed it most. "Science Finds—Industry Applies—Man Conforms" went the fair's rather clunky motto, illustrating the idea that because of industry's dedication to scientific research, the life of Man was, in a word, better.[78]

The 1939–1940 fair, however, looked forward rather than backward, a declaration of future possibilities versus a celebration of past achievements. As the event approached, it was clear that the fair was assigned the mighty purpose of reinventing the possibilities of tomorrow. "In short," announced officials in 1936, the fair "will seek by reviewing tomorrow and studying today to aid him in charting a better and happier future," an attempt to answer the question "What kind of world shall we build?"[79] The fair was thus a conscious effort to advance civilization, a "gigantic crusade against man's chief foes: inertia, lassitude and chance," as a 1938 publication, *Pilgrimage to Tomorrow*, pronounced. Never before had there been, on such a grand scale, an effort to not just predict the future but make one happen. "Modern life has become so intricate that obviously intelligent planning is essential if social and economic chaos are again to be averted," it stated, proposing the idea that rather than being random, the future can be designed, engineered, and manufactured much like a car engine or skyscraper.[80]

If the two decades between the wars were the period in which modern futurism was born, as I believe it was, the 1939–1940 New York World's Fair was not only the era's climactic moment but a moment of futurism that has likely not been surpassed and likely never will be. The fair was an unequivo-cal future-fest, the first real, dedicated exploration and celebration of the idea of tomorrow. "No previous fair had been so explicitly, so self-consciously identified with the future," Corn and Horrigan wrote, as "everywhere one turned, the future was arrayed in gleaming, confident form." In the Peri-sphere, the huge orb adjacent to its towering obelisk partner, the Trylon, was "Democracity," a futuristic, people-friendly metropolis created by indus-trial designer Henry Dreyfus. Other representations of the future at the fair included the "Town of Tomorrow," Donald Deskey's "The World of the Day after Tomorrow," Raymond Loewy's "Rocketport of the Future," and even a "Drug Store of the Future" and "Soda Fountain of the Future," all of them optimistic views of things to come.[81]

Also holding court at the fair was Elektro, the Westinghouse robot, which delighted audiences with its song-and-dance routine, a tangible sign of the machine-friendly world of tomorrow. Robots had emerged as a ubiquitous symbol of the future in the 1920s, the definitive expression of the cross-pollination between Man and machine. Our ambivalent, tense relationship with automatons could be detected even before Czech playwright Karel Copek first coined the word "robot" in 1921, however, raising the persistent question of whether these anthropomorphic machines would be our slaves or our mas-ters. Members of the short-lived Technocracy movement of the early 1930s definitely believed the latter, but by the end of the decade, Corn and Horrigan observed, robots and many of our fears about them had been tamed.[82]

These were all sideshows, however, to the main futuristic event at the fair, Norman Bel Geddes's Futurama. Futurama was the centerpiece of General Motors' Highways and Horizons exhibit, which offered visitors other peeks into tomorrow like "Previews of Progress" (a stage show revealing "the won-ders of modern research and science"), the "Glass" car (the "first full-sized transparent car ever made in America"), and "Mysteries of Cold" (featuring the "magic of microscopic life").[83] The exhibit as a whole was a means to push forward an autocentric future when the car was under attack for causing both urban congestion and a startling number of lethal accidents. "In presenting Highways and Horizons," a brochure for the exhibit read, "General Motors seeks to show that highway progress will be an even more important factor in the world of tomorrow than it has been in the world of yesterday," an overt attempt to make a car-friendly future a self-fulfilling prophecy.[84]

With its 50,000 scale-model vehicles traveling on a seven-lane highway at constant speeds of up to 100 miles per hour, Futurama was without question the best piece of propaganda for the automobile ever conceived. With no traffic or slowdowns in our automotive universe of 1960, much less any horrific crashes, the future for the car (and GM, of course) looked bright indeed. "This vision of 1960 dramatizes possible highway progress—highways to new horizons of a country's welfare and happiness," GM told visitors, raising the status of the automobile from a means of transportation to something that would advance civilization.[85] "The 'Futurama' is presented, not as a detailed forecast of what the highways of the future may be, but rather as a dramatic illustration of how, through continued progress in highway design and construction, the usefulness of the motor car may be still further expanded and the industry's contribution to prosperity and better living be increased," the company explained.[86] With its "The Road of Tomorrow" exhibit featuring no intersecting streets or traffic light delays, Ford also presented a self-serving vision of the automobile at the fair, yet one more example how Man would harness the power of the machine to forge a better future.[87]

Was the fair a prophetic event, a true pilgrimage to tomorrow? "The fair gave us a spacious, gleaming make-believe future, far preferable to most Americans, who saw their recent past as something to surmount, not celebrate," Sherman Yellen has written, answering the question with a decidedly qualified yes. Although much of the world of 1960 to which the fair looked forward was realized—television, washing machines and dishwashers, the rise of suburbia, and interstate highways—the ugly side of tomorrow—urban decline, continued poverty and racism—was totally ignored. "The fair's architects and industrial designers seemed to suggest that many of the world's ills could be cured by the judicious use of pale geometric shapes," Yellen adeptly put it, "with fountains and lagoons, leading to a new, modernist aesthetic that would assure a just society." The machine-made shape of the future typically could not or would not accommodate major problems of the past and present unless they were envisioned in dystopian terms, one could argue, the basis for the polarized, "all or nothing" paradigm of prediction that was pervasive between the wars.[88]

With the modern fairgrounds in Queens ground central for the world of tomorrow, the event was a catalyst for experts of all types to make their predictions known. One of the many scientists who seized the futuristic day was Robert A. Millikan, the Nobel Prize–winning physicist, who spoke at a dinner at the Waldorf-Astoria on the eve of the opening of the fair. Like many of his colleagues, Millikan believed science would transform the world, but only if civilization could survive "man's present or prospective international wickedness, stupidity and folly." Even with war already waging in Europe, Millikan held "promise that a permanent method of assuring peace may ultimately be worked out," a promise that would soon be proved false.[89]

For centuries the stuff of fanciful whimsy, futurism became a legitimate discipline between the wars, infused with the cool efficiency and rationalism of the times. It was machines that had won the war to end all wars, after all, and it would be machines that would determine the shape of things to come as well. Inspired by two men who had mastered the machine—Edison and Ford—visionaries imagined a world of tomorrow less bound by the constraints of time and space and more tailored to the interests of the masses. America may have lost its innocence, but it had gained the confidence to create an entirely new set of possibilities not tethered to the illogical, folklorist past. Utopia may come at a great cost, some feared, but most believed the brave new world that lay ahead would be a wonderful one. The idea of tomorrow would soon take a major turn, however, and a new era of the future would emerge in the midst of another world war.

CHAPTER 2

GREAT DAY
COMING,
1940—1945

Tomorrow Has Arrived.

—American, 1941

IN 1945, EDDIE RICKENBACKER, ACE FLYER IN THE FIRST WORLD WAR and now president of Eastern Air Lines, was asked why people should be optimistic about the future. Millions were dead and wounded, after all, many European cities were in ruins, and, even though an Allied victory was all but assured, major political and economic uncertainties remained. Rickenbacker, however, was positively giddy about the future, absolutely sure that big things were in store for America and the rest of civilization.[1] "When Japan is licked," he wrote shortly before the end of the war, in an article fittingly titled "I Live for Tomorrow":

> I am going to have the time of my life. So are you. I don't mean a V-J binge. I mean the biggest creative binge in the history of the world—a tremendous release of high-octane imagination and energy which we have been storing up in this country for 25 years. That is one of the things and one of the principal things I live for—Tomorrow.[2]

What was Rickenbacker so excited about? "I don't want to miss anything," he explained:

> I don't want to miss plastic skyscrapers; frozen-food dinners in one package . . . ; wireless transmission of electricity; the chance to live energetically to the grand old age of 150 years. Screwball? Nothing of the kind. All of these things are here already in the minds of men; in scientific possibility; in materials. They just have to be put together.[3]

While Rickenbacker had, like other ultra-alpha types, an especially optimistic view of why to "live for tomorrow," many believed during World War II that the just-around-the-corner postwar years would be a time of bountiful abundance and prosperity. "Tomorrow" was in fact one of the seminal words and ideas during the war, as Americans sacrificed for, as *Time* expressed it in 1942, the "great day coming."[4] This almost messianic vision was articulated most clearly in the promise of "better living," encompassing wonders ranging from super-jets and super-automobiles to the future "dream house." The future of the war years became heavily domesticated and privatized, its arc now largely limited to the coming postwar years versus the centuries or millennia of earlier futures. If the prewar future was abstract, public, urban, mass, and mechanical, the wartime future was warm, family-oriented, suburban and exurban, and consumer friendly. The postwar boom that did indeed follow was in part a self-fulfilling prophecy, as nearly all citizens looked to the future with faith, hope, and confidence in a new and improved American Dream.

FROM SWORDS TO PLOWSHARES

Of course, the postwar future was relying heavily on the much-anticipated conversion from a military-based economy to a consumer-driven one, that is, the turning of "guns into butter." With "the present out of stock," as a popular wartime phrase went, "tomorrowism" thus became a familiar trope in popular and consumer culture. "The deferred future became the central theme of 1940s advertising," Corn and Horrigan observed, "as consumers were promised fabulous prizes for their patience and patriotism." The best-known example of a deferred tomorrow in wartime advertising was the "There's a Ford in Your Future" campaign, in which the automaker located its products as waiting calmly in the wings, ready for action when consumers could once again buy them.[5] Another juicy carrot dangled before home-front Americans was

Libby-Owens-Ford's "Kitchen of Tomorrow" (also called, even more futuristically, the "Kitchen of the Day after Tomorrow"). Designed by H. Creston Doner, the prototype kitchen (actually three of them) traveled in 1943 and 1944 to department stores around the country, where more than 1.6 million people reportedly oohed and aahed over the glass storage cabinets, glass oven, and built-in waffle iron and electric mixer. The low countertops (to prepare food while sitting) and the ability to hide the stove and sink were icing on the cake, so to speak, a dream that would one day come true. The kitchen was also featured in a Paramount movie short (in Magnacolor!), further glamorizing this slice of a future domestic paradise.[6]

Even before America's entry into the war, in fact, the future was very much in the domestic air, largely as a result of the forward-looking, consumer-oriented 1939–1940 New York World's Fair. The "World of Tomorrow" naturally heavily informed futurism in the early 1940s, imagining an America of a couple decades hence as a much cushier place. One writer in early 1940 presented this portrait of "the housewife of 1964—on a winter day":

> Wearing stockings made from coal and a dress of spun glass, she stands in her kitchen. The windows are open, the temperature is only 50 degrees, but she is warm and she cooks her mango-tomatoes (fourth crop since April raised on her water-farm) with infrared rays. And she has plenty of time to enjoy her television set, because dusting the house (whose walls are of plastic, whose bathroom was molded in one piece) is no longer a major chore.[7]

For the moment, at least, it wasn't a given that only women would be running the kitchens of tomorrow. As Rosie the Riveter had proved that women were capable of much more than just tending house, some wartime prophets suggested that their newfound freedom and earning power would extend into the postwar years. "Women will desert their nest for desks," predicted *Ladies' Home Journal* in 1943, adding the paradoxical news that they would also have "more leisure time than they have ever known before."[8] Another feminist of sorts was the aptly named Maury Maverick, a Texan who in 1944 was running the Smaller War Plants Corporation, a major contractor for the federal government. "Women have learned too much to go back" to just being homemakers, Maverick believed, something that would cause a fundamental shift in the American workplace. "Women will either be out hoot-in' it up or doing something constructive," Maverick thought, "so we have to do something to make it so they can work."[9] Blacks also were learning too much during the war to go back to being second-class citizens, although mainstream America was not quite ready to allow them to be as constructive as they could be. The war vividly exposed the contradictions between the nation's democratic ideals and the pervasive discrimination against African Americans, the basis for the 1943 "race riots" in New York, Los Angeles, and Detroit. Gunnar Myrdal's *An American Dilemma,* published the following year, captured the dynamics of race in this country as no book before had, making it clear that the issue was not going to go away simply by patriotic rhetoric.

For those invited to the table, however, there was little doubt that the coming years would be a veritable feast, a just reward for the sacrifices Americans were making. "To-day, we produce to destroy but to-morrow we will produce to build," wrote Charles Stine, vice president for R&D at du Pont, making it clear that the same effort dedicated to winning the war would be devoted to winning the peace.[10] Industrial designer John Tjaarda also believed, like many, that the nation's victory would do nothing less than spark a new and improved American Way of Life. "When the war is over, our spoils will be found in our own backyard," he said in 1943, adding that "Our riches will come from the fertile brains of our own engineering and chemical genius, meeting the great and urgent need for new and better products and more and more production for our national preservation." Based on the standard set of predictions circa the early 1940s—flying cars, plastic clothing, and the throwing out of such old-fashioned mainstays as washing dishes and the proverbial kitchen sink itself—the transformation from a military-based economy to a consumer-based one would be much more than a simple conversion from guns to butter, according to Tjaarda and others, taking on dimensions of truly biblical proportions. "Our total facilities adaptable for producing the instruments of better transportation and gracious living will be greater than anything dreamed of up to now," Tjaarda concluded, "a bolstering thought for the future of America and the world that this gigantic production capacity can be easily transformed from swords to plowshares."[11]

Wartime lessons did not have to be revolutionary to suggest they would improve the postwar quality of life. Food and beverages would be dehydrated, vacuum packed, and bombarded with electrons to produce longer lasting, more convenient, and less expensive products to eat and drink.[12] Butter and chocolate that didn't melt in 120-degree weather had been developed for soldiers in jungles and the desert, perfect for that postwar picnic on a hot summer day.[13] Clothing too would be improved, as a result of newly developed technologies such as synthetic rubber. "Elastic in our shorts won't give way after 10 washings and leave them forever after hanging at half-mast," *Better Homes & Gardens* happily predicted in 1943 when speaking of the latter, "but somehow it makes us kind of sad to think that we'll no longer see the pretty girls hitching up their stockings."[14] New synthetic fabrics used in parachutes offered major opportunities to produce lighter but tougher and longer-lasting clothes after the war. One of these, called Fortisan, was reputed to be three times as strong as silk. "The paratroopers are now gobbling up Fortisan for lighter, stronger chutes [and] its makers jolly well intend after the war to find a market in . . . shirts, women's frocks, underwear, football pants, and summer sports clothes," *Better Homes & Gardens* reported, a perfect conversion of swords into plowshares.[15]

Businessmen, naturally, looked to the end of the war with keen anticipation, already thinking how they would convert their new knowledge from military to consumer applications. Executives such as Charles Stine seemed to be fully aware in 1943 that his company was in the catbird seat when it came to postwar opportunities. "The nation will emerge from this war with capacities for making plastics, synthetic fibers, nitrates, hydrocarbons, high octane gasolines, and literally scores of chemical and other raw materials on a scale that only two years ago was beyond comprehension," he gushed. Among the many new things to spring out of the labs of companies like his were unbreakable glass, nonburnable wood, and fifty-miles-per-gallon gas, the latter something that would "draw thousands of city dollars to suburbs and country," thereby helping "empty the slums."[16]

Edgar M. Queeny, chairman of Monsanto, the chemical giant, was just as enthusiastic about life after the war as his rival at du Pont was. "The possibilities of the future, now that industry has embraced science, are so limitless that only one forecast can be made with certainty—that the most extravagant prophecy will fall short of potential accomplishments," he exclaimed in 1943. Queeny had just published a book, *The Spirit of Enterprise*, which included a number of predictions (e.g., germicidal light and waterproof, stainproof, and flameproof stockings) that not surprisingly drew upon his company's chemistry-based capabilities. But the businessman's book was really about the classic American values of curiosity, entrepreneurialism, and can-do-ism, values that were cast in a new, brighter light as they had been threatened during the war and now served as the foundation for the boundless future ahead.[17]

Other books published in the early 1940s took on wartime technological progress as their subject, all of them proposing that these developments would make the world unequivocally better. In the 1944 *Your World Tomor-*

row, for example, Donald G. Cooley (along with the editors of *Mechanix Illustrated*) predicted that sterilization of dishes via ultraviolet bacterial lamps would make eating a safer affair and that taking out the garbage would become a chore of the past, our trash to be electronically ground up and flushed down the drain. Rather than anticipating the fashion industry's dipping heavily into the chemistry set that was the 1950s, Cooley et al. believed that clothing would be made out of soybeans, milk, and air (disturbingly like the ingredients in a Starbucks soy Frappuccino). Norman V. Carlisle and Frank B. Latham's *Miracles Ahead!*, also published in 1944, too painted a rosy picture of, as the book's subtitle suggested, "better living in the postwar world." In addition to prefabricated houses, prefab rooms would be a popular choice after the war, the authors claimed, fully designed, in stock, and ready for installation in one's apartment. Smokeless furnaces, soundproof buildings, and wall-generated heat would be other miracles ahead, according to Carlisle and Latham, with synthetic chemistry the source of many new products that nature somehow overlooked.[18]

With the nation soon to blossom into a land of milk and honey, the media, in concert with advertisers, appropriated much of the rhetoric dedicated to the future, watering the seeds of consumerism. Voices of the future directed to women presented the postwar home as an almost unrecognizable place, chock-full of new appliances born out of wartime technology. "Let's move the calendar ahead and live for a few minutes in the home of tomorrow," *Woman's Home Companion* suggested in 1943, filling readers with awe at what it considered "facts instead of fancies." One of the "strange and wonderful devices now taking form in steel, glass and plastics," the magazine reported, was a new kind of oven employing technology that wartime steel mills were using to heat and harden metal in seconds. "You open your new induction-heater oven door, put the roast in, close the door and snap on the switch" and, a mere six seconds later, said roast is done, without the oven even getting hot. "This is the miracle of internally induced heat, created electrically by high-frequency radio waves, which have their source in the miraculous electronic tube," the explanation went, mumbo jumbo to most but undeniably impressive if true. The fact that it would take decades for the microwave oven to find a place on most kitchen counters and has yet to produce a roast in six seconds that one would want to actually eat shows that much of early wartime futurism was, despite what the media claimed, more fancy than fact.[19]

Another strange and wonderful device, the automatic washer-dryer, also was not far from reality, according to *Woman's Home Companion*. Like television, the automatic washer had appeared before the war but was quickly squelched as factories turned their attention to more pressing needs. During the war, however, engineers were finding some time to improve the laundry machine, building in a dryer to make the old-fashioned clothesline a thing of the past. "You simply put in soiled clothes and set a control knob [and] an hour later your clothes are automatically dried," the magazine told readers, keeping wartime spirits high with the thought of such future labor-saving, leisure-creating machines. Other good things (only relatively recently brought to life) such as security cameras, 3-D television, and high-intensity lighting too were on the way as military technology was applied to the consumer market to be. "Tomorrow they [electrical appliance manufacturers] won't want to junk their machines, skills and knowledge," *Woman's Home Companion* summed up, "they will make these war-born devices your peace-time servants."[20]

With nothing less than the revival of the American Way of Life at stake, however, this seismic transformation in national identity would not be left simply to chance. Beginning in earnest in 1944, experts took on or were assigned the task of properly educating Americans to help citizens transition from wartime to peacetime, a logical extension of both the government's propaganda campaign and Corporate America's renaissance. As part of a postwar-planning speaking series, for example, Gerald Wendt, science editor of *Time*, told members of the New York Junior League that technical developments made during the war would produce many changes in civilian life of the future. Manufacturers of radar, electronics, aviation, shortwave radio, plastics, and synthetic rubber, Wendt pointed out in his 1944 talk, would pitch their goods to civilians rather than the government soon after the war was won, instilling the ethos of spending versus saving among a group of influential young adults.[21] This kind of formalized planning for the future helped set the stage for the consumption-based consensus of the postwar years, when consumerism was cast as a form of good citizenship, and contributed to what was arguably the biggest change in the idea of tomorrow in history.

A NEW REVELATION OF GREAT LIVING

Lessons in good citizenship could also be found in wartime high school and college yearbooks, offering keen insight into how those in the education arena—faculty, staff, and students—imagined the future. As it became clear that the Allies would ultimately prevail (something few Americans seriously doubted), yearbooks reveal, the nation's ambitious postwar plans became an integral part of everyday conversation. Language about America's postwar future appeared in yearbooks as early as 1942 but rose substantially in 1944, as the tide of the war began to turn decidedly in the Allies' favor. Administrators well knew that more teachers and facilities would soon be required, and excitedly discussed plans for new buildings put on hold during the war. The issue of postwar "reconstruction" began to get serious attention, specifically how and when the nation's military-based economy would revert back to one that produced consumer goods. As well, yearbooks of the later war years included extensive discussion about the retraining, reorienting, and, in some cases, rehabilitating of returning soldiers.

Most important in yearbooks' portrayal of the future, however, were questions about how democracy could thrive in an unstable postwar world. Conferences focusing on this very question became common affairs on campuses, as students and faculty postulated on likely scenarios stemming from the new world order. The University of Minnesota, for example, sponsored a Postwar Conference in the spring of 1944, with much discussion about whether it was possible to achieve a "perfect" peace and, if so, what it would be like.[22] When referring to the postwar peace, yearbooks also often imagined it as "lasting," "for posterity," or even "eternal," a clear sign of the utopian vision that was emerging. As well, there was a frustration that the first world war had not produced a perfect peace, leading to the current situation. "Last time we won the battles," said the president of Drake University, Henry G. Harmon, in the 1942 *Quax*, "yet no one won the war and that was because no one was prepared to implement the victory in the relationships between nations."[23] This time, the consensus was, America would ensure a lasting peace through "international understanding."

Closer to home, school yearbooks also showed that education was being counted on to pave the road for a better world. The 1943 Fresno State *Campus* observed that "Now our studies are not just homework," believing that education was the key to a lasting peace:

> We realize that we must search conscientiously for truth and justice. First we must win peace, but to keep peace we must, through education, guide all peoples to hope and sympathy and freedom of thought.[24]

The role that higher education would play in postwar America became a dominant theme in yearbooks, as schools boasted of their success in preparing students for the weighty challenges that lay ahead. "We expect to find ourselves ready for the post-war challenges which will likely surpass even the demands of war," preached W. R. White, the president of Hardin-Simmons University, in the school's 1943 *Bronco*.[25] The 1944 University of Iowa *Hawkeye* captured the confidence of academia toward the end of the war, tempered by the awareness that there remained many unknowns:

> Sometimes we're not altogether sure what we're going into, but we know it has something to do with freedom and the world of tomorrow. We might have been frightened once, for we are still young and worlds are mighty things to shape. But we're leaving now to do the job, and the fear is no longer there, for here we have half the task done.[26]

High schools too were part of this chorus of confidence, proud to be playing a small role in creating the possibility of a perfect peace. As early as 1943, West Lafayette (Indiana) High School was "adding those studies that prepare for living in the new world that will follow the peace," according to the *Scarlet and Gray*.[27] Even in small-town America, the high school experience was perceived as a wartime acorn that would blossom into a giant postwar oak. "Our education will provide the background music for the huge drama of life as yet unplayed; that of re-establishing and rebuilding a world of peace and freedom," proclaimed the 1945 St. Cloud (Minnesota) Technical High School *Techoes*.[28]

Authorities in fields outside education also agreed that, as long as "international understanding" prevailed, the future had great things in store for the human race. At New York University's 1942 baccalaureate exercises, for example, Reverend Ralph W. Sockman, minister of the city's Christ Church, envisioned "economic plenitude" for the common man, a result of the war's accelerated production. The nation's new industrial opportunity not only "dizzies the imagination," the reverend believed, but would lead to a much more equitable society and "a new revelation of great living."[29] Business leaders like Henry J. Kaiser, the war's leading shipbuilder, too not surprisingly saw good times ahead. Assuming "we use our heads and manage things right, it [the postwar period] will be a time of almost incredible achievement and advancement," said Kaiser in 1943. "I find myself thinking in post-war terms all the time, planning and talking about it with the nation's industrial and business leaders," he continued, a clear sign that, even in the heat of battle, visionaries already had their eye on the postwar prize.[30] Seer deluxe H. G. Wells also was gung ho about the future but with a similar caveat. Speaking in 1943 over the radio from London in a series called "Reshaping Man's Heritage," Wells told listeners that "what our physically and mentally emancipated race will make its collective property dazzles and blinds the imagination," so long as the species could, after the war, "adapt itself and conquer the new world."[31]

Some others were not as bullish on the future as these men, however, reflecting the uncertainty of the times. The newest member of the Supreme Court, Justice Wiley B. Rutledge, for example, had concerns about what he saw in 1943 as "what is becoming more and more a non-Jeffersonian world." Speaking at the annual dinner of the University of Iowa Association of New York, Rutledge believed the principal challenge of the postwar world would be to "find a way to work out in a society so knit and bound together Jefferson's basic ideal of the dignity, individuality and independence of each citizen."[32] Fulton Sheen, then of Catholic University, also saw a much more problematic postwar world ahead, at least where religion was concerned. In a 1944 sermon at St. Patrick's Cathedral, Sheen spoke of "a secularized, technical scientific propagandized barbarism" that lay ahead some twenty-five years, followed by yet another world war (a view, rather oddly, not unlike that put forth by H. G. Wells a decade earlier). "We are passing from an age in which religion is tolerated into one in which religion will not be tolerated," Sheen concluded, with "not the church but the world that is in danger."[33]

The postwar era would actually be a highly religious time in America, of course, part of the more conservative agenda of the Eisenhower years. W. M. Kiplinger, whose Washington-based newsletter was already essential reading for businessmen, was especially prescient about the political and social climate that lay ahead. Kiplinger not only predicted that the war would end in 1945 a full two years before it did ("the beating of Germany is supposed to come in 1944, the cleaning up of Japan in 1945," he wrote in July 1943), but he recognized the shift from the left to the right as the New Deal breathed its last gasp. "The trend is toward conservative ways of thinking and doing," Kiplinger advised in his last newsletter of 1943, believing that "individual initiative, private enterprise, and maintenance of the essentials of what we call 'capitalism'" would soon be the order of the day. "The trend in the United States is away from further growth of government domination and political management of the economy from central watchtower," he told readers, seeing the end of the FDR era and the emergence of another one grounded in Republican values.[34]

THE PRE/ENT WITH THE FUTURE

Kiplinger's political forecast must have pleased businessmen who looked forward to a friendlier climate for industry in the postwar years than that before the war. A prosperous future was a way for Corporate America to repair its reputation caused by the Depression, for which many believed industry was to blame. David Sarnoff, head of RCA, was one such executive determined to make a capitalism-friendly future a self-fulfilling prophecy, not wanting government agencies to interfere with his plan to use communications and entertainment as a way to win the peace after the war. "If American industrial science is to play its destined role in the reconstruction period," Sarnoff told an audience at Franklin and Marshall College in 1943, "government should not unduly restrict private enterprise or enter into competition with industry."[35]

Sarnoff had good reason to be worried about Uncle Sam meddling with his radio and emerging television empire. The federal government, specifically the FCC, was especially interested in how technological advancements made in communications during the war would play out in postwar America, which was concerned about who would control what kind of airwaves. In early 1945, in fact, the FCC published a 200-page report in which no fewer than 231 experts were asked to forecast the future of just a single technology, radio. The report was especially gung ho about future applications of a new kind of radio—the walkie-talkie—which was used heavily during the war between pilots and ground staff and among tank drivers, outlying patrols, and commanding officers miles away. "We are presented with the promise of a service which will enable a central exchange to reach physicians on the road, of business firms communicating with their delivery vehicles, of housewives talking to their husbands as they ride tractors in the field or trucks on the road," the *New York Times* gushed in an editorial about the FCC report, concluding that "Jules Verne prophesied many an invention that is now in daily use, but he never saw a future like this."[36] It would take other communications technologies developed over the decades to make this fantasy real, of course, but with the FCC's blessing of commercial television, Sarnoff would have his dream medium to allow private enterprise to fully recover from its prewar doldrums and fully "play its destined role" in the postwar years.

It was not private enterprise, however, but rather the federal government that played the biggest role in helping the nation as a whole recover from its prewar doldrums. Through its immense war bond program (which many in the media called "the greatest sales operation in history"), the Treasury not only had Americans literally and figuratively buying into the war but also spreading the idea of saving now for a future bonanza. The idea of the future held particular power as a selling point for bonds, with investment in them presented as the key to both national and individual postwar prosperity. In the most literal sense, war bonds represented a financial future, as they approached full value in a decade and, for many, bonds held to maturity in the early 1950s would indeed serve as seeds of personal postwar prosperity. Wanting bonds to serve private interests after the war to fuel the economy, the administration urged Americans to resist redeeming them before full maturity, as suggested by poster slogans like the 1944 "Nest Eggs Won't Hatch Unless You Set On Them! Hang On To Your War Bonds." As well, with most consumer goods unavailable during the war, the bonds' appreciating value made them a worthy gift item, as suggested by the Treasury's 1943 advice to "Give War Bonds. The Present with a Future."[37]

A more compelling way to use the concept of the future to sell bonds, however, was to present them not as a financial investment but as an investment in Americans' lives and in the nation itself. In posters such as the 1943 "For Their Future Buy War Bonds" and "Your Bonds Are a STAKE in the Future," and the 1944 "Protect His Future," bonds were directly or indirectly presented as a way to protect the lives of the ones perceived as most at risk—soldiers and children. Emotional appeals such as these drew upon Americans' personal connections to the war, whether they be a relative in the military or family at home. Although some fears of postwar inflation and depression remained, this orientation toward the future cast the war years with a palpable feeling that prosperity did indeed lie ahead. War bonds were thus instrumental in creating the popular perception among many Americans of an emerging society of abundance, perhaps acting in part as a self-fulfilling prophecy.[38]

Not just the government but also Corporate America, of course, had via war bonds a convenient and patriotic tool to promote future consumerism. Editors of women's magazines were especially keen on presenting bonds as an ideal way to purchase the things of tomorrow's good life, directly tying article content to their purchase. "Thru the smoke of war production we are catching glimpses of postwar America," wrote the editors of *Better Homes & Gardens* just a year after Pearl Harbor, and "here are hints of some of the things you'll be able to buy with dollars you're investing for the purpose in War Savings Bonds now." After citing a litany of potential postwar miracles including luminous paint, glowing doorknobs, and nonporous upholstery, *Better Homes & Gardens* told readers, "Another great product of tomorrow is War Savings Bonds. For, as you mark them today for your purchases of tomorrow's products when they become available, you're making sure of your family's share in these finer things to-come."[39] Six months later, the same magazine linked the future of transportation to war bonds, encouraging the public to directly shape tomorrow by investing in them today. "Today the bonds we buy are building the highways and skyways that will win a war," *Better Homes & Gardens* told readers, and "tomorrow those bonds will pay our way over those same highways and skyways to the goals of fun and business."[40] And finally, a few months later, the magazine again tied the stuff of tomorrow (milk in a cube, boneless spareribs, nonreflective paint) to bonds:

> If you want to invest in this America, if you want the savings with which to buy the superior and more plentiful products of tomorrow, if you want to do your part in bringing our young fighting men home again, and soon, remember you can do it with War Savings Bonds bought today, bought until it hurts.[41]

With some temporary sacrifice, wartime Americans were told and no doubt largely believed, the stage was set for a utopian future to soon become a reality.

WHEN THE STORK'S BEEN AROUND

And where would consumers put all their superior and more plentiful products of tomorrow? Their homes, of course, the heart of the new and improved American Dream. Throughout the war, the postwar home was increasingly imagined outside the city, with pioneers settling down on the twentieth-century frontier of newly blazed suburbs and exurbs. While the between-the-wars future was undeniably "vertical" in orientation, with ever-rising skyscrapers to be built to accommodate more and more people and businesses, the wartime future was distinctly horizontal, with newly constructed flat-roofed houses and industrial buildings in the country. Famed industrial designer Walter Dorwin Teague was an early subscriber to the idea that major changes were in store for the nation's cultural geography as emerging technologies—particularly the private aircraft—allowed Americans to flee decaying cities for bucolic bliss. "The flight from cities has already become something of a mass exodus," he wrote in late 1940, prophesying that "The city will become a place of business, barter, intellectual and artistic exchange, social enjoyment and amusement, rather than a place of residence in our better world."[42]

Many believed definite changes were ahead for the most vertical and crowded of cities, New York, with Gotham epitomizing an increasingly dated and potentially perilous paradigm of the future. In addition to the slums filled with people from across classes and races, the traffic congestion was, according to a "careful" study, costing the city more than $5 million a day. "Authorities say that parking automobiles in the street will soon be entirely prohibited," wrote Bruce Bliven, editor of the *New Republic*, in 1941 (an idea still being batted around).[43] Although it was rarely publicly acknowledged, an imagined mass exodus from cities had a grander, scarier purpose, that of moving millions of citizens away from urban centers thought to be vulnerable to enemy attack during or after the war. "A planned decentralization of industry into beautiful greenbelt communities . . . will be spread, in General [Henry] 'Happy' Arnold's phrase, 'from hell to breakfast' because of the power and reach of the super-bombing plane," explained John Chamberlain in 1941 in the *Yale Review*, one of the few to make note of this darker side of going back to the country.[44]

If the media were interested in where Americans would live after the war, they were obsessed with what they would live in. Many magazines used their editorial space as free advertising for marketers of homebuilding materials, inviting business executives to present their particular vision of the future, which would almost always be self-serving. It was thus during the war years that futurism became for the first time heavily imbued with consumer-based agendas in order to promote a particular industry, company, or product. Using prediction as a public relations tool, corporations scrambled during the war to position themselves for the upcoming postwar consumption frenzy. Asking themselves and a group of industry insiders the tough question "What will our dream house look like?" in 1943, for example, editors of the *American Home* were certain that "Future houses will make our lives happier ones," the magazine's own future of course wrapped up in that happiness. Pushing his own agenda for the postwar home, Vernon F. Sears, research director for the US Plywood Corporation, believed that flexibility was the operative word for the domestic future. "With the aid of mobile walls, any number of space combinations can be achieved," Sears suggested, so that "our rooms will become larger or smaller as the needs of the family dictate." And because "today's wood is temperamental," he went on, "the new wood will be tamed," that wood naturally being flexible, pliable plywood.[45]

In the next month's issue of the *American Home*, Bror Dahlberg, president of the Celotex Corporation, a maker of insulation, had the opportunity to predict his concept of the future home. Dahlberg encouraged those on the home front to save now for the home of tomorrow, which would not only be "colorful, well-proportioned and attractive to the eye" but have "kitchens where mechanical servants take over the housewife's harder tasks." How would housewives of the future be able to pay for things like tamed wood and mechanical servants?, Dahlberg asked, reading readers' minds. Through war bonds, of course, demanding that citizens sacrifice today so they could become consumers tomorrow. "The family that tucks away payments in the form of war bonds for a post-war home will be the envy of less foresighted families who aren't prepared to buy and enjoy a 'Miracle Home' of tomorrow," he told readers, knowing that more nest eggs would translate into more future profits for his company. "So be patriotic and farsighted, too," he advised, adjectives that accurately described how many Americans did indeed serve the nation first so they could serve themselves next.[46]

The most prevalent wartime prophecy when it came to postwar housing, however, was the prefabricated home. Rather than build or buy homes on a fixed spot, many believed, people after the war would buy a prefabricated house and have the ability to move it to a new site whenever they liked. F. Vaux Wilson, Jr., a vice president of Homosote Company, a manufacturer of prefab houses, envisioned department stores as the logical place for consumers to pick out their dream home, available as "a completely equipped package."[47] Prominent architect Whitney R. Smith had another idea, that postwar consumers would head to their nearest "Home Center" to buy a house or create one from scratch. With "plenty of models to choose from and 'extra parts' for later expansion," as the *American Home* described his forecast, the postwar Home Center would be a one-stop shop for all things housing, allowing shoppers to choose from an array of options to make their dream home as dreamy as possible. Select a floor slab, roof, and the desired number of room-dividing panels, "and before you can say 'pre-fabrication' your house is on its way," the magazine reported in 1943, the components ready to be snapped into place like Legos. And when "the stork's been around," as it was tactfully put, the happy postwar family would just head back to the Home Center for more panels to "give junior a room of his own." "With flexible partitions like these, home can take on the excitement of the latest model automobile or airplane," Smith's vision went, the complexities of building a house reduced to a fun recreational activity.[48]

More general-interest magazines like *Woman's Home Companion* agreed that "Industry plans to mass-produce tomorrow's homes as Henry Kaiser builds ships," as it reported in 1943, confirming that soon readers would be able to "make over these homes almost as easily as you make over last year's dress." It was no accident, of course, that the postwar home would be flexible and modular, its design clearly intended to accommodate growing families as the baby boom boomed. "When Miss Postwar Baby arrives, Dad orders a nursery and has it bolted on the house before the young lady comes home from the hospital," the magazine chimed in, the bonus being that, should Dad get a new job in a new city, he could "take along not his family but his home." Within just a few years, the futuristic home as perfect running machine had been tamed, its between-the-wars rationalism redefined as postwar practicality in order to meet the needs of a society headed in a new, more domestic direction.[49]

The most successful futurist of the day, W. M. Kiplinger, recognized that the stork coming around to deliver postwar babies represented a much bigger opportunity for businesspeople than just expanding houses. Kiplinger didn't realize how big the baby boom would be and how long it would last, but he did recommend that his readers immediately capitalize on the growing market for children as well as start planning for the spike of grade-schoolers in the early 1950s, high schoolers in the latter part of the decade, and college students in the early 1960s. This savviest of visionaries, however, expected "a brisk demand for household goods about 1965 as war babies become homemakers," as the *Atlantic Monthly* phrased it in 1945, unable to anticipate that many boomers would as young adults seek a different kind of lifestyle than had their family-oriented parents.[50] Kiplinger wasn't alone, of course, in failing to see how the biggest generation in history would permanently reshape the very character of American culture. "Another boom in babies is expected in the United States about 20 years from now when the stork brings large numbers of grandchildren of the great war," reported M. G. Morrow in 1945 as the war drew to a close, like Kiplinger getting the numbers right but guessing wrong when it came to the values and lifestyle of this future generation. "These babies . . . may grow up in a much more conservative and less exciting United States," he thought, adding the equally off-the-track prediction that "Romance will lead to marriage at a younger age in 1965."[51] With no way to anticipate the countercultural leanings of many young people in the mid-1960s or the feminist revolution, which would lead millions of boomer women to careers first, husbands later, Morrow could only look forward by looking backward.

GOING PLACES SITTING DOWN

"London express leaving in fifteen minutes!" So began *Senior Scholastic*'s 1944 prediction of our transportation future, claiming that postwar Americans would be headed in many directions in many different ways—400-seat airplanes, 100-mile-per-hour luxury trains, buses equipped with two-way radio "to permit passengers to talk to anyone anywhere," and faster, more fuel-efficient automobiles were out there on the horizon, according to the magazine, all resulting from technologies allegedly developed during the war. "The post-war period will be one of *specialized* transportation," *Senior Scholastic* made clear, informing its younger readers that "a new era of transportation will be one of the rewards for our sacrifices in fighting this war."[52]

Other, more authoritative sources were confident that a new era of transportation lay ahead, especially when it came to the automobile. By 1960, claimed Norman Bel Geddes in his 1940 book *Magic Motorways*, "100 miles an hour will seem no faster than the motor speeds we now take for granted and travel certainly will be much more safe and comfortable," making it clear that his Futurama exhibit for GM at the world's fair was not intended to be pure fantasy or just entertainment.[53] As Bel Geddes's claim suggested, however, the world of transportation was particularly vulnerable to what were often literal flights of fancy as wartime imaginations ran wild. Anyone able to put pencil to paper could design a teardrop-shaped car made of plastic that ran on miniscule amounts of fuel, after all, with flying wing attachments often thrown in just for fun. By the end of the war, industry officials were careful to provide a reality check so that consumers wouldn't be disappointed when they went to car dealers. "It is easy to produce such ideas on paper, but motor vehicles, engines and wheels must be made from much tougher material and are much tougher to make," a 1945 report by the SAE warned the overenthusiastic.[54]

Although in fact precious little that was truly revolutionary was even close to rolling off the assembly line, top industry executives agreed that the war marked an opportunity to reimagine what the automobile could and should be. "The war has freed motorcar engineers from the traditions of the past, freed them from the stranglehold of old machine tools and methods," said Fred M. Zeder, chief engineer of Chrysler, in 1942, seeing cars that would be lighter, have better gas mileage, and offer a smoother-than-smooth ride coming down the road. "In the car of the future," he prophesied, "you will be able to read and write with comfort and ease," something not possible in prewar automobiles, which could often be like riding on a roller coaster.[55]

Just a year into the war, Detroit's best and brightest couldn't help but look ahead to the postwar years, knowing full well that their industry was very likely to experience a full revival and then some. Bel Geddes's cold and people-less Futurama was no longer the model of the automotive future, but all could see the prospect of better vehicles driving down better roads. Harley

J. Earl, head of design for GM, saw a new generation of "low, racy styles" on the way, a design approach that would ultimately earn him legendary status in the field. Henry Ford was particularly excited about the prospects of plastics during the war, believing that the next revolution in automobile manufacturing could very well reside in organic chemistry. With steel a precious commodity, one of Ford's top research engineers, Robert Allan Boyer, was in fact busy building experimental vehicles made of plastic, agreeing with his boss that one day the material would produce "a better car at a lower cost." Detroit industrial designer George W. Walker, who had designed many Packards and Nashes, saw another benefit of using plastic in a car. "Plastics which permit the transmission of ultra-violet rays will give the passenger a good tan without the discomfort of sunburn due to the elimination of the infrared rays," he reasoned, consistent with the commonly accepted belief that exposure to the sun was, sunburns aside, purely therapeutic. "The postwar era will see more people than ever going places sitting down and they will go faster, more cheaply and more comfortably in lighter, handsomer motorcars," a reporter for the *Saturday Evening Post* concluded, accurately forecasting America's love affair with the automobile in the 1950s.[56]

Better cars coming down the road didn't preclude the idea that a personal aircraft would also be at one's disposal in the go-go postwar years. "World War II intensified popular expectations that some kind of family flying machine was just around the corner," according to Corn and Horrigan, with "the public exuberantly await[ing] a post-war world in which airplanes or helicopters would become a part of everyday life." Neighborhood "air parks" and the ability to choose between a driving machine and a flying machine (or even better, a combination airplane-automobile) at one's local transportation dealer were each real possibilities in the not-so-distant future, many believed.[57] "Is it 'Buck Rogerish' to expect that the time is not far distant when we will do most of our long distance traveling in airplanes, instead of relying entirely upon trains or cars?" asked *Senior Scholastic* in 1943.[58] George Walker, the industrial designer, had the answer, declaring that "You are going to see service stations along our highways designed to accommodate both motorcars and planes." Whether it be by land or air, Americans were going to be constantly on the move in the future, few would disagree, the freedom of the road extended to the sky.[59]

As Corn and Horrigan noted, some thought it would not be the private airplane but the helicopter that would be at our aeronautic disposal in peacetime. The war only cemented the popular 1930s idea that helicopters—part of the lore of futurism since Leonardo first imagined something much like one—would soon be parked on our flat roofs, an alternative to the family automobile for longer trips. "Ten years after this war is won we shall use hundreds of short-run helicopter bus services," wrote future aviation legend Igor Sikorsky in 1942, adding that "Hundreds of thousands of privately owned direct-lift machines will carry Americans about their business and their pleasures." Sikorsky even believed that it was not the car but the helicopter that by all logic should have emerged as the method of personal transportation of choice, something that would be rectified after the war. "If chance had produced the helicopter for general use before the automobile was invented, people would recoil in dismay at the hazards of a Sunday drive on a modern highway in what would to them be a newfangled dangerous contraption," he argued.[60] William Ogburn, the professor of sociology at the University of Chicago who in the late 1930s had predicted the advent of shopping by television, was similarly confident that the helicopter was in our collective future. "The privately owned helicopter, taking off from a roof or back yard and, after landing, folding its wings to be driven into an ordinary garage, may never be so common as the automobile is today, but it will certainly be in mass production, and there will certainly be airway traffic cops," he wrote assuredly in 1943.[61] By 1944, Raymond Loewy was designing a giant helicopter-bus for Greyhound that would, in theory, take off from and land on the roofs of the company's many bus terminals scattered across the country.[62]

The implications of anywhere, anytime air travel for both personal and professional purposes were, of course, huge. The postwar Air Age would have a huge impact on shopping, for example, making geography and distance virtually irrelevant and creating an industrial marketplace for goods and services. "Today, the women of the hinterland must be content with the purchases of merchants who can go to San Francisco or Chicago or New York but once or twice each year," wrote Gill Robb Wilson for *Nation's Business* in 1942, while "tomorrow, every fashion, every product that advertising imagination can present, will be available through merchants who hop weekly to Paris or Berlin or New York, and return the next day with their purchases." And while better-dressed women in the hinterland were certainly going to be a nice development, Wilson and others saw the opening of markets as much more significant. "Aviation will transport the nations to the greatest prosperity the world has ever known," Wilson boldly claimed, seeing quick and easy globe-hopping as the most direct route to the most bountiful horn of plenty in history.[63] Wilson wasn't the only one to consider aviation as the future's biggest story, as advancements in wartime air travel changed the rules of travel and transportation. "Nobody else in the world is so busy shoving

Today into the past and reaching forward to pull in Tomorrow as the air-man," wrote *Better Homes & Gardens* in 1943.[64]

Like other fields in which today appeared to be rapidly shoved into the past, aviation was subject to some far-reaching and often farfetched looking ahead. In 1943, for example, William Burden, special aviation assistant to the secretary of commerce, predicted there would be 500,000 planes in American airspace by 1950 (which would turn the skies into something like the Long Island Expressway at rush hour).[65] In just four months, however, Burden had changed his tune considerably, referring to such prognostications as from "the Buck Rogers school of forecasting." "If credence is given to only half of the extravagant claims," he wrote in early 1944, "anyone walking either crowded streets or deserted fields is in danger of being bombarded with the remains of picnic lunches dropped carelessly from a sky black with airplanes." Because aviation was "the most American of all achievements of invention," however, Burden did see some amazing strides made over the course of the first postwar decade, including cross-country trips by plane taking less than ten hours and fares thirty percent below those of the Pullman train.[66]

Because the new Air Age was obviously an international phenomenon, aviation leaders around the world were excited about the enormous opportunity that beckoned. J. R. D. Tata, who ran a major airline in India, believed the postwar era would be "one of greater happiness, leisure, and enjoyment [and] when man will truly come into his own, unrestricted by space, unfettered by time, with the whole world as his neighborhood." Tata saw the aerocentric future as not just offering speedier and cheaper transportation but also encouraging greater international understanding and tolerance. "When, in the Air Age, the peoples of the world thousands of miles apart will freely mix with one another, distrust and hostility between them will fade away as differences in their modes of living, in their outlook on life, and in their manners tend to disappear," he told the Rotary Club of Bombay in 1944. Even the very physical laws of the universe would one day be no match for future engineers, according to Tata. "When the problems of distance and time have ceased to exist, adventurous man will begin to think of interplanetary travel," he proposed, foreshadowing the Space Race of the 1950s and 1960s.[67]

GREEN LIGHT FOR THE AGE OF MIRACLES

The felling of space and time—an extreme version of the familiar Man-over-Nature trope—would of course be brought by the cornerstone of futurism, science and technology. The war may have interrupted the wonderful world of tomorrow presented at the 1939–1940 New York World's Fair, but there was a silver lining—the fast-tracking of many technological dreams into practical realities. "A lifetime of progress in physics, chemistry, electricity and every other science has already been achieved in the first few months of the emergency," stated *Collier's* in 1943, forecasting that, "when victory releases this great flood of new knowledge and new techniques, we shall suddenly begin to live in the twenty-first century."[68] It was true that a bevy of scientific and technological achievements were realized during the war, many if not most of them originally designed to help the military cause. Automatic transmission and color television in 1940, napalm and K-rations in 1942, streptomycin and the Mark I electromechanical calculator in 1944, and frozen orange juice and Tupperware in 1945 were just a few things to spring out of university and corporate R&D labs during the war, many of them federally funded.

One seemingly twenty-first-century technology in development during the war was the "automatic telegraph," by which someone could instantly send or receive a letter or drawing without assistance. "You will have all the freedom of a sealed letter transmitted at the speed of the electric current," *Collier's* predicted that same year, although what would be the fax machine would take some forty years to become a common sight in the workplace.[69] The same magazine also anticipated the much later use of DNA in the legal field, including paternity or maternity suits:

> . . . Enigmas of kinship will be quickly disposed of in the courts of the future when a new kind of scientific test is made on the blood of the contending parties . . . Long and costly court actions will become unnecessary. Clever circumstantial evidence will no longer help an imposter gain a fortune, prevent a mother from establishing her right to her fortune or prevent a mother from establishing her right to her child.[70]

Occasionally, however, voices of reason would appear on the scene to temper out-of-control forecasting made in the throes of wartime enthusiasm. Although he was hardly a slouch when it came to making bold, perhaps outrageous predictions (he was responsible for the "Rocketport of the Future" at the 1939–1940 World's Fair, after all), Loewy seemed to have changed his tune by late 1943. After ridiculing those in 1861 who predicted that people would be getting around by pneumatic tube and those in 1896 who foresaw a sea railroad, Loewy had serious reservations about the "wave of predictions about the immediate postwar industrial dream world that makes the writers of 1861 and 1896 look like sissies." The leading industrial designer blamed wartime escapism and the vagueness of the very term "post-war" for what he saw as unrealistic expectations on the part of the American public, and felt the need to put things back in perspective. "The type of design that is being discussed today assumes that American manufactur[ing] can skip over four or five years of gradual development and still produce a mechanically perfect, inexpensive, highly desirable product," Loewy stated, an idea with which he and other smart people had serious problems. Alfred P. Sloan of GM did some major backpedaling from the Futurama exhibit of just a few years back, now saying that "our immediate postwar car will be the 1942 car with such modifications and improvements as can be made without important engineering development or changes in tools," with his research colleague Charles F. Kettering chirping in that "what the car of the future will look like and be like will be determined by the same old trial-and-error methods that mechanics and designers have used in the past." E. F. McDonald, Jr., president of Zenith, was even more sobering, warning his dealers, "Let's not kid the public into believing that they are going to have a combination radio-phonograph-FM-facsimile-television set for $14.92, with 40% off for cash."[71]

Businessmen had good reason to be concerned about excessive optimism during the war. Too-dramatic visions of the future could actually hurt the postwar economy if consumers postponed their buying until the supposed miracle products appeared, some thought. The business community actively debated whether there was a massive "pent-up" consumer demand after a decade and a half of scrimping, not a universally accepted idea, and fears of a postwar depression remained as well. Exactly how and where the millions of returning GIs were going to find jobs also was a source of consternation. Although he conceded that the invention of the automobile had actually created jobs rather than eliminating them, William Ogburn, the sociology professor, feared massive "technological unemployment" after the war, believing that industry had to make sure that newly developed machines didn't replace people in the workplace. "We can't afford the luxury of letting the future take care of itself, or of trying to adjust hurriedly, recklessly to social changes arising from invention," he insisted in 1943.[72]

Despite these don't-count-your-chickens-before-they-hatch kind of cautions, the faith in the ability for science and technology to lead the nation to a glorious postwar era was triumphant during the war. With the end of the war in sight, there was a "green light for the age of miracles," as a 1944 article in the *Saturday Review* claimed, as "science knocks at your door," put *Popular*

Mechanics that same year.[73] "Life will never be the same," wrote Roderick M. Grant for that magazine, raising the stakes of what was or wasn't to be. "The techniques and materials conceived under the impulse of war must inevitably bring vast changes in our ways of living, greater comforts and greater efficiency," he argued, making it clear that the nation was about to embark on something bigger, bolder, and more ambitious.[74] Consistent with the more qualified brand of futurism by 1944, however, Grant was sure to locate his view within a broader context, tempering the wilder predictions made in the early years of the war:

> This is not to say that your p.f.c. will come home to a pink plastic house with dustfree air conditioning and a rear-engine car traveling 50 miles on a gallon of 150-octane gas. But this is a promise that evolution of better living will begin when the war ends for it has begun already on the drawing boards of American designers who are shaping the future for our builders and manufacturers . . . The innovations in store for your new way of living will come gradually as the dreams of the designers prove marketable and economical and sound.[75]

Many of the innovations in store for postwar Americans' new way of living would, not surprisingly, be electric, as a second wave of appliances emerged that would make their prewar ancestors look prehistoric. "The war electronics of today about which as yet little can be said, if given proper encouragement and support, will develop spontaneously into the electronics of tomorrow," believed Irving Langmuir, associate director of General Electric, in 1943.[76] It seemed certain that wartime technology applied to the telephone would result in new and different kinds of communications devices. In addition to the answering machine (defined by *Newsweek* in 1943 as "a telephone that will answer itself and talk back to you when you come home"), one communications idea making the futuristic rounds during the war was a portable gizmo that would let one know when his or her phone was ringing. Described by the same magazine as "a little radio gadget that a subscriber could carry with him and that would signal when his phone at home or office is ringing so he could pick up the call at the nearest public phone," the proto-beeper was a great example of how technological strides made during the war (in this case by Bell Labs) would bear fruit in the postwar future. Some, however, were less than impressed with what eggheads were cooking up. Russell Malone, writing for the ever-skeptical *The New Yorker*, for example, sneered in 1943, "We're going to get what the boy Edisons choose to give us, not what we need, and by 1946 we'll all be lugging about with us a radio gadget that emits a mean little buzz whenever anybody dials up our house or our office." Malone had another idea for the folks busy dreaming up the stuff of tomorrow: "If the Bell Telephone Laboratories really want to make me happy, they can turn their engineers loose on the problem of building a receiver that will register slams [because] as it is now, no matter how hard you bang the receiver down, all the other person hears is a genteel click," he quipped.[77]

One of the principal journalists covering the futurism beat through the first half of the twentieth century, Waldemar Kaempffert, was an early cheerleader for the role military-based science and technology would play after the war. Even if his 1941 declaration in the *American Magazine* that "Tomorrow Has Arrived" was a bit premature, if not downright suspect, from an existential standpoint, Kaempffert successfully envisioned many of the things that we now consider quite current. Freshly prepared meals would arrive promptly with just a phone call (although Kaempffert saw the delivery system as a *Brazil*-like pneumatic tube versus a Fresh Direct truck), wall-size televisions would be commonplace and, shades of Netflix, a subscription service for movies would make going to theaters unnecessary. Like others, he expected technology to meet consumer culture head on, privatizing the public activity of shopping. "Shopping is done by television and telephone," he projected, another accurate forecast that took almost half a century to become realized.[78]

A couple of years later, with the war now in full swing, however, Kaempffert approached the idea of tomorrow differently. Rather than make fantastic predictions about a faraway future, he focused on closer-in opportunities that would materialize in peacetime, reflecting the reeling-in of tomorrow as it got closer to today. Now the stuff of the future was things like lighter cars, synthetic rubber, and color television, all developments that would logically grow out of wartime technology. "War presents the scientist and the inventor with a supreme opportunity to break down resistance to innovation," he explained, believing that "it prepares the mind for seemingly new ideas [and] accelerates a normally slow process and telescopes years into months."[79] The following year, Kaempffert was equally reserved, citing high-octane gasoline, prefabricated housing, and international aviation as a few things advanced during the war that would improve postwar life, rather modestly observing that "inventions that seemed far off before Pearl Harbor are already at work."[80] And in 1945, Kaempffert announced a "revolution in postwar living" that was about to result from some of the advances in science and technology made during the war, but now tomorrow was almost on top of today. Spray fertilizers, cooking by "infra-red rays," and dirt-resistant paint were a few of the innovations he felt strongly were waiting on America's doorstep soon to be unwrapped, all interesting developments to be sure, but none of them close to revolutionary.[81]

Other journalists, like F. Barrows Colton, still maintained by war's end that technological progress made over the past few years would not only reshape the stuff of everyday life but overhaul the very ways in which people related to each other. "There isn't room here to begin to mention all the postwar improvements in prospect," wrote Colton for *National Geographic* in 1945, but he decided to give it at least partly a go anyway. "There are promises of radios you can put in your pocket, stockings that won't run, pants with a permanent crease, and, for tomorrow's glamour girls, artificial eyelashes of nylon with a permanent 'built-in' curl!" It was other, more important developments, however—television, faster and cheaper travel, and, notably, atomic power—that would truly change the world. "It will take time for all of them to come true," Colton wrote, "but I think [of] what they will mean in terms of opening up the world's remote corners, annihilating time and space, getting alien peoples acquainted, putting new life in that overworked phrase, 'international understanding.'"[82] It was ironic, to say the very least, that atomic power was about to annihilate not time and space but rather "alien peoples," marking what was arguably the absolute nadir of international understanding in human history.

Colton's positive spin on atomic power was typical of wartime prophecy, however, with broad speculation about how the ultimate form of energy could be applied within the peacetime economy. Many visionaries anticipated that the discovery of U-235 would usher in a "Uranium Age" in which unlimited amounts of cheap energy would not only power America's postwar prosperity but even eliminate poverty once and for all. "A four-ounce chunk of this stuff may heat your house for thirty years!" exclaimed *Woman's Home Companion* in 1943, adding that "You may never need to worry about gas for your car if you have a small piece of uranium-235 sealed in your automobile engine."[83] William B. Stout, past Ford designer, ex-president of the Society of Automotive Engineers, and research director of the Graham-Paige Motor Corporation in 1945, saw a fist-sized, atomically powered engine running cars one day. "The revelation of the possibilities of atomic power means as much, and even more, to peacetime progress than it does to warfare," Stout said in 1945, a good example of how many believed atomic power would help save the world just as it was destroying part of it.[84]

Bigger than the Empire State Building in the 1920s and 1930s, the future shrank during the war years, contained in a nice, neat (but expandable, if necessary) postwar box. And having only recently been conceived as a public enterprise, intended for mass production and mass consumption, tomorrow was reimagined in the early 1940s as a private affair, grounded in the ideals of a new and improved American Dream. Most importantly, the future that lay ahead was deserved, a reward for surviving more than a decade of scarcities and sacrifices. If less ambitious than futurism past, the wartime view of tomorrow was undeniably cheery, another victory waiting in the wings. Just as we would win the war, we would win the peace, leading visionaries assured Americans, a bountiful feast for all to come. The "revelation of the possibilities of atomic power" would prove to usher in a new era of American history and, with it, a new paradigm of futurism filled with both boundless optimism and major anxiety.

CHAPTER 3

THE BEST IS
YET TO COME,
1946–1964

*"An affluent society, universal education, the welfare state, and a
growing awareness of and respect for world opinion should go far
to bring about a truly classless society in the United States."*

—Henry Steel Commager, Amherst College professor of history, 1959

IN LATE 1956, A GROUP OF BUSINESSMEN MET IN ATLANTIC CITY TO plan for the future, the future being in this case the seemingly far-off land of 1965. The group, consisting mostly of bankers, retailers, and utility executives, was most interested in hearing about ways to sustain and even surpass the phenomenal growth of the past decade, when the United States had enjoyed an economic boom as never before. One speaker at the conference, a vice president of General Electric, had exactly the kind of idea—what he called Americans' "two-of-a-kind urge"—that resonated well with the audience. The GE executive believed that just as American families had wanted "two chickens in every pot" in the prosperous 1920s and now sought two cars in their garages in the good times of the 1950s, they would by 1965 desire two homes, each one filled to the brim with the latest conveniences. The thought of each family in the country owning four telephones, four TV sets, four refrigerators, and four stoves—twice as many appliances in the typical home of the day—made the businessmen virtually swoon with joy as they pondered this opportunity to double their profits in ten years.[1] The next year, *Changing Times* predicted that in twenty-five years, automobiles would multiply like rabbits, even more so than the "two-of-a-kind urge" that was perhaps part of the American character. "Only poor relations will get along with one car, come 1982," the magazine insisted, as "Detroit plans for three cars in every garage"—a large one for long-distance travel, a mid-size one for in-town driving, and a sportster for commuting.[2]

Such was the outlook in postwar America, when many believed that, as the Frank Sinatra song went, "the best is yet to come." As fears of another depression ebbed and citizens started to enjoy the fruits of their victory, the future of the American Way of Life indeed appeared brighter than ever. The possibility to one day work half the time and enjoy leisure the other half was a common theme, with science and technology being counted on to make life as easy as that of everyone's favorite future family, the Jetsons. Builders and appliance manufacturers paraded homes and kitchens of the future before the public (and the occasional Soviet premier), capitalizing on Americans' fascination with the even better consumer paradise that was still to come. And while one probably had no idea what a computer actually did, one was likely to believe experts' claims that these room-sized things were going to revolutionize the business world.

Beneath the shiny, scuff-free surface of postwar America, however, lurked a much darker future, what even the fluffy *Parents* magazine termed in October 1959 "the hazards of the Atomic Age." The looming threat of the Cold War provided a counterbalance to the cheerful tomorrow of everyday life, as apocalyptic visions crept into the discourse of popular culture. The tendency to locate tomorrow in outer space, whether in hobby magazines like *Popular Science*, on TV shows like *Space Patrol* and *Twilight Zone*, or in movies like *Forbidden Planet*, said less about our vision of the future than our fears of the present. And despite all the fabulous inventions and innovations, there was an underbelly to the age that reflected the pressure to conform to consensus thought and heed any and all advice from "experts." The Red Scare, from HUAC in 1947 to the McCarthy hearings in 1950, turned American democracy on its head, while Arthur Miller's 1949 *Death of a Salesman*, David Riesman's 1950 *The Lonely Crowd*, and John Kenneth Galbraith's 1958 *The Affluent Society* each captured the palpable sense of alienation or institutional inequities that coursed through society. As well, protests such as the Greensboro lunch counter sit-in and CORE's Freedom Riders campaign and lightning rods like Lenny Bruce and Betty Freidan suggested we were not as free a society as we liked to think, something that would inevitably catch up to us a little bit down the road.

Likewise, popular culture of the postwar years is often remembered as unfailingly conservative—Norman Vincent Peale's *The Power of Positive Thinking* and Dr. Seuss's *The Cat and the Hat* on bookshelves, *Father Knows Best* and the *Lawrence Welk Show* on TV, and Doris Day maintaining her virginity at all costs in movie theaters might come to mind—but in fact radical change was heavy in the air. The future could be detected in everything from the arrival of Dior's simple yet somehow shocking "New Look," the, well, absurdity of the theater of the absurd, and, of course, the dangerous backbeat of rock-'n'-roll (and especially the dangerous presence of Elvis, Motown, and the Beatles). As well, the debut of *Mad* and *Playboy* magazines pointed the way to a more irreverent and hedonist tomorrow, and the wild antics of the Beats foreshadowed the youth culture revolution that waited in the wings. Finally, the introduction of the birth control pill and VW Beetle, the op-art explosion, and the bursting-on-the-scene of Cassius Clay in the early 1960s were sure signs that something entirely different was bubbling up in the American stew.

A PACKAGE OF APPLIANCES

Even the most prescient of futurists in 1946, however, could not predict the likes of Muhammad Ali or Warhol's soup cans. With the publishing of Benjamin Spock's *The Common Sense Book of Baby and Child Care* that year, the postwar era grounded in everything-but-revolutionary family life was off and running. After a decade and a half of economic, political, and social upheaval, most citizens were more than ready to pursue a traditional version of the American Way of Life based in domesticity and consumerism. The opening of the first Levittown the following year also signaled that a major shift was taking place, as returning GIs and their wives set up camp in the new frontier of suburbia. Bombarded by a constant parade of new products and services—prepared and frozen foods (cake mixes, Minute Rice, instant iced tea, TV dinners, and Coffee-Mate), electronics (pocket-size transistor radios, stereos, the cassette tape recorder, and the touch-tone phone), toys (Play-Doh, the hula hoop, Barbie, and GI Joe), and credit cards (Diners Club, American Express, and BankAmericard—later Visa), postwar Americans enjoyed the just deserts of victory over economic disaster at home and enemies abroad. With such a steady stream of new things to eat, listen to, play with, and buy other things with, all advertised on a new, and the massest of mass media, television, the transformation of American citizens into American consumers became complete, just as promised during the war. "In the 1950s and '60s, when promises of prosperity materialized for many middle-class Americans, advertisements equated the future with present notions of glamour and wealth," said Corn and Horrigan, the icing on the proverbial cake.[3]

The wartime future centered in the home too picked up right where it left off. "The gadgets of domesticity helped put behind memories of the war and Depression," added Corn and Horrigan, with the postwar home commonly viewed as "a package of appliances." Gadgets of domesticity were perhaps best exemplified by the "Miracle Kitchen," a 1956 joint venture between Whirlpool and RCA. The concept kitchen, complete with "planning center," "electronic [microwave] oven," "mechanical maid," and "mood lighting," traveled across the States in 1957, a preview of the most important room in the house of tomorrow. The "Miracle Kitchen" also served as a cultural ambassador for the nation and our consumer-oriented way of life in Europe and the USSR, ending up at the American National Exhibition in Moscow in 1959. Although it would be a different kitchen at that show that served as the site of the famous debate between Nixon and Khrushchev, the Whirlpool/RCA prototype represented a powerful blend of national and corporate propaganda.[4]

General Motors, fully intending to be as big a player in Americans' homes as in their garages, wanted consumers to think of their kitchens not as a collection of piecemeal appliances but rather as a single unit, which could be replaced by something newer and better every year. GM even featured kitchens of the future alongside their new cars at auto shows in the mid-1950s as a way to "domesticize" the idea of annual model changes.[5] Even if it didn't succeed, trying to get consumers to "trade in" rooms in their house for brand-new models as science and technology improved was a brilliant strategy by General Motors. "If a home's design, materials, or even just its name or the advertising employed to publicize it had the ring of science," noted Corn and Horrigan, "this fact helped position it in the world of the future." The most scientific home of the postwar era, few would argue, was the 1957 "House of the Future" at Disneyland. Sponsored by Monsanto and made of plastic, the house represented the radical idea that homes would not roll off factory assembly lines, as most futurists during and after the war had believed, but would rather emerge from scientific labs. "For the synthetic world of the future," Corn and Horrigan posited, "the plastic house was perfect," as pure an articulation of the artificiality of science as one could imagine.[6]

As leisure increasingly became privatized and domesticized after the war, largely as a result of television, the bigger idea of "home entertainment" entered the discourse of futurism. David Sarnoff, continuing his yeoman missionary work for the broadcasting industry as head of RCA, was the principal champion of home-based entertainment in the 1950s. In 1915, six years before the first radio was sold, Sarnoff reportedly foretold a wireless "music box" that would revolutionize the world of electronics, and the future, one could say, was history. Now, four decades later and with automation and other scientific and technological advances assured, there was nothing short of "a God-given opportunity to add dimensions of enjoyment and grace to life," he believed, leading to "a fantastic rise in demand for and appreciation of the better, and perhaps the best, in art, music, and letters." Sarnoff was confident that atomic energy would one day play a big role in his business, his own company having recently tested an atomic battery, but with or without the magic of the atom he had no doubt that the future of home entertainment was bright. "The dominant physical fact in the next quarter-century will be technological progress unprecedented in kind and in volume," he claimed in 1955, fully aware of the goodies that would eventually materialize from his and his competitors' R&D work.[7]

Two years later, in fact, Sarnoff saw on the horizon two devices that would use the most important development of the postwar years, commercial television, as a springboard for an array of entertainment products. "Perhaps within five years television viewers will be able to record programs—picture and sound, in black-and-white and in color—on magnetic tape, to see them again at will," the "General" predicted, envisioning "extensive libraries of operas, plays and other events of permanent interest expertly recorded and made widely available." *Changing Times* (Kiplinger's futurish magazine targeted to a mass audience) echoed this idea the same year, prophesying that "In a few years there will be electronic films of plays, operas, movies which you will buy like phonograph records and play through your television set."[8] In addition to what would be the VCR, Sarnoff believed that someday "a home television camera will also be in general use to take family movies which can be shown on the home TV set," another startlingly accurate prediction in these days of eight-millimeter films projected onto bulky screens.[9] It would take decades for each of the products to become part of everyday life, of course, but Sarnoff's vision of the electronics landscape was unsurpassed.

Other, less well-known individuals also had an uncanny ability to see around the corner when it came to home entertainment, however. "The principal focus of the average person's activities will be the home, built around a 'communicenter,'" claimed Maurice B. Mitchell, president of Encyclopedia Britannica Films, in 1958, an idea much like the media room or home entertainment center that became common decades later. "The householder of tomorrow will have his choice of movies every evening of the week in the comfort of his own home," Mitchell continued, "and it is largely in this fashion that he will attend most of his concerts, sporting events, and 'public gatherings,'" again correctly forecasting the "cocooning" trend that began in the 1980s. Mitchell too was able to anticipate the convergence of various technologies, although he, like others, had no way of knowing that it would be the Internet-enabled personal computer that would make it all possible. "The library in the communicenter may well consist of millions of books [and] as the great public libraries begin to put their collections on microfilm, people with electronic library cards will be able to view them on their television screens and home microfilm readers," Mitchell believed, closely describing the current online construction of a "master" universe of knowledge made up of the collective, digitally scanned libraries of Harvard, Stanford, Oxford, the University of Michigan, and the New York Public Library.[10] By the end of the 1950s, there was little doubt that the future of entertainment would not be in the movie palaces of the prewar years or on the Great White Way of Broadway but rather on tiny screens in the ticky-tacky homes of suburbia. "It is abundantly clear that the next decade will be the great age of Home Entertainment, based on technical innovations in the television industry," concluded *Newsweek* in late 1959.[11]

FINESSE IN LIVING

With clear signs after the war that the American Way of Life would not only be restored but be stronger than ever, the economic arena was quick to confirm that the best was yet to come. Even the Brookings Institution, normally an organization not known for its sanguinity, issued a forecast for the nation not long after the war that was positively chipper. "After a century or more of phenomenal progress," the public policy think tank's 1949 report boasted, "the economic promise of American life remains undiminished." Specifically because of the "imagination, drive and efficiency" of private enterprise, the institution made clear, much more abundance resided in America's future than in other countries with their own more socially oriented economic systems.[12]

The prosperity of the 1950s now in full swing, the Twentieth Century Fund, an economic research foundation, issued a similarly rosy forecast in 1955. Adolf A. Berle, Jr., chairman of the board of trustees, believed that the overwhelming majority of Americans were enjoying "the highest standard of living ever achieved by a great population and the promise that this standard will continue to rise." Berle's colleague, J. Frederic Dewhurst, was even more optimistic about what lay ahead for the average American. "American productivity . . . is increasing so rapidly that, if present rates continue, in another century we shall be able to produce as much in one seven-hour day as now in a forty-hour week," he said confidently. Like the Brookings forecast, Twentieth Century's positioned American-style consumer capitalism against socialism and communism, letting the numbers speak for themselves. "The aggregate real income of the more than 160 million Americans today probably exceeds the combined income of the 600 million people living in Europe and Russia and far surpasses the total income of the more than one billion inhabitants of Asia," the report, issued at the peak of the Cold War, made clear.[13]

Best of all to economic soothsayers, Americans were not only earning gobs of money but spending it. The combination of fat wallets and new technologies would change the idea of shopping as we knew it, some experts thought, as marketers discovered different ways to present and sell their products to consumers. Malcolm P. McNair, a Harvard University retailing professor, believed that shopping would undergo a huge transformation through different kinds of self-service, streamlining the whole process. After (correctly) predicting that things like razor blades, toothpaste, and men's shorts would one day be sold in vending machines, eliminating the need for expensive, inefficient salespeople, McNair anticipated that television would not be just for entertainment but for shopping as well. Housewives would watch a video display of merchandise, McNair proposed in 1950, and then call in her order, "perhaps through robot mechanisms for recording orders" (a *Brave New World* interpretation of QVC, perhaps).[14] Seven years later, *Changing Times* made a similar prediction, that consumers would shop for things like a new chair via a tag team of television and telephone. "Call the store and ask for the chair department," the magazine imagined, and "in a flash, half a dozen will be displayed on the screen in three-dimensional effect and in true color." This was a classic case of visionaries making an essentially accurate forecast but getting wrong the technology that would make it possible, a not uncommon occurrence in the history of the future because of the virtually totally unexpected rise of an online universe.[15]

Consumer Reports envisioned the possibility of a much more efficient way to shop, one that would take the concept of citizen-as-consumer to an entirely new level. "Instead of receiving cash and hence the need to make decisions amongst all the marvels on the marketplace," the magazine considered in 1957, "the consumer may have his income divided at the source so that each industry gets his fair share." Taking the whole messy idea of shopping out of the equation would not only make the wheels of capitalism spin even faster, this most rational of publications reasoned, but would allow consumers to get right to the point—the pleasures of consumption. "All the consumer will have to do is sit back and take the deliveries as they come!" *Consumer Reports* exclaimed, as perfect a scenario for Corporate America as could be imagined.[16] A couple of years later, researchers at Stromberg-Carlson, a division of General Dynamics, were hard at work developing another kind of system that would make consumerism run a lot faster and smoother. By the government's issuing a "lifetime, nonexchangeable, electronic credit card" to each citizen at birth and retailers' debiting his or her bank account with each purchase, Americans could be instantly transformed into card-carrying consumers as soon as they left the womb. What better way to express the American Way of Life than that?[17]

Ernest Dichter, the founding father of motivation research and president of his own Institute for Motivational Research, saw the changes in shopping ahead not in technological terms but in psychological ones. American consumers would soon be looking to the marketplace to satisfy their emotional needs, Dichter told a thousand members of the Toilet Goods Association in 1955, no longer satisfied by practical necessities or even ordinary luxuries. The Austrian emigrant, who would soon become famous by Vance Packard's 1957 bestseller, *The Hidden Persuaders*, was at the top of his game in the mid-1950s, advising Corporate America how to imbue the most utilitarian products—including toilet goods such as Procter & Gamble's Ivory Soap—with emotional resonance. In fact, Dichter's very definition of motivation research (MR) was rooted in consumerism, describing it as "qualitative research designed to uncover the consumer's subconscious or hidden motivations that determine purchase behavior." MR, in other words, "rooted the selling act within the human personality," just what the doctor ordered for companies trying to figure out how they should position their products in the future. Dichter's recommendations to the association were thus heavily steeped in his application of the social sciences to solve problems, his goal to uncover "unconscious" attitudes and beliefs that helped explain why people did the things they did (and how those actions could be changed, especially to marketers' advantage). Through psychoanalytic theory and in-depth interviewing, Dichter not surprisingly often drew Freudian interpretations, focusing on the individual's inner life and in particular their irrational insecurities and erotic desires. For the toilet goods people, Dichter saw consumers moving toward a "finesse in living" by choosing things that "strike an emotional gong," making it imperative that they recognize the operative "psychological climate."[18]

While he was way ahead of the curve in his approach to marketing research (many of his views are considered advanced to this day), Dichter was not the only one thinking that marketers had better develop more sophisticated techniques to effectively reach the consumer of the future. The leading advertising publication of the day, *Printer's Ink*, in fact, believed that Americans were rapidly evolving as consumers, requiring that marketers adopt a more mature approach. By 1980, the magazine predicted in the mid-1950s, "mass taste will have reached a degree of sophistication that will not tolerate some of the current vulgarities and exaggerations," something that of course has yet to happen, to say the least.[19]

Buoyed by the economic boom and consumers' more finessed lifestyles, American business increasingly sought out the services of self-proclaimed futurists who could help them better anticipate and capitalize on the winds of change. Frank A. Anderson, whom *Coronet* considered in 1951 to be "just about the world's hottest citizen with a prediction," was doing quite the business telling clients which way he believed the stock and commodity markets were headed. Ruined by the 1929 market crash, Anderson decided to try to figure out what, if anything, drove what he called "mass psychology," thereby shaping people's behavior. His finding? Lunar motion, of course, although he was quick to declare, when accused of simply "moon-gazing," that "it's not astrology!" Anderson's forecasting abilities, based on his determination whether mass psychology was "ascendant" or "descendant," were not limited to the financial universe, however; he also claimed to know when conditions to make a sale were most favorable, when a teenager was likely to have a successful date, and even when the fish would be jumping.[20] Also making the futuristic rounds in the early 1950s was one Frederic Snyder who, with his brand of "pre-writing," was having considerable success with his "Keeping Ahead of the Headlines" lecture. Although his method of prediction was perhaps not as loony as Anderson's, Snyder's approach too was admittedly less than scientific. "What I do is to sow the seeds of deduction in a garden of reflection," he explained, joining a long line of apparently divinely inspired prophets.[21]

Other prophets of the 1950s found inspiration not in the stars or deep reflection but in actual human behavior. Leo Cherne, head of the Research Institute of America and, according to *Coronet*, a "leading expert in the new science of prediction based on patterns of action," had a lot of good news to report about the future but some not-so-good news as well. While correctly predicting but overshooting some welcome things like solar energy and pay-as-you-watch television (for just $1 per night!) in his 1955 forecast for 1965, Cherne also anticipated "greater suffering from nervous and emotional disturbances due to the increased strain and tension of 1965's faster and more complicated pace." (Cherne actually believed that one child in ten would spend some time in a mental institution in just ten years, the flip side to better physical health for young and old alike.)[22] Four years later, now looking out to 1975, Cherne held that America would be "a consumer's utopia," as *Life* summarized his forecast, having no reason to think otherwise in 1959. "Technology and salesmanship and industry will conspire to make every American's life safer and easier," *Life* reported, a prophecy that fell flat as a recession, energy crisis, and bevy of social problems rained on the nation's utopian parade.[23]

As more futurists appeared in the 1950s, each seemingly with his own book to sell, cultural critics couldn't help but notice this rather new cottage industry springing up. "Any author in search of a good meal-ticket subject, dependable stuff that he can market again and again, year after year, would be well advised to settle down with the World of the Future," wittily observed Charles W. Morton in 1955. "As a field of inquiry, the future has plenty of room," he added, "it is likely to go on for quite a while, and if the author finds that the year 2000 is wearing a bit thin or becoming old hat, he has merely to raise his sights by a few decades and go to work on 2055."[24] As the 1960s approached, futurism as a field of inquiry (or meal ticket) accelerated even further, spurred on of course by the nomination of a man who if elected would be the youngest president in history. "At this turn-of-the-year, 1959 to 1960," Philip Burnham wrote for the *Commonweal*, "the prophecies or, more politely, the 'surveys' and 'projections' published in newspapers and magazines, in newsletters and special reports, and via radio and television, have been more than ever before." Burnham knew that something new and different was in the air, making the time ripe for futurism of all sorts. "This year is a special year, inaugurating the new and already famous Decade of the 60's," he suggested, almost as if he knew that the next ten years would be nothing like the nation had ever experienced.[25] Not only was the sheer quantity of forecasting greater than ever before, but the "speed" of it also seemed to be escalating. "Forecasting ten years ahead now is like forecasting half a century or more ahead in the simpler, slower past," observed Ernest K. Lindley two weeks before the end of the 1950s.[26] "Experience tells one to be chary of those who foretell what will be happening ten, twenty or thirty years from now," added Dorothy Thompson, writing for *Ladies' Home Journal*.[27]

The all-systems-go climate for futurism in the early 1960s was cause enough for figures who might otherwise not notice or care to give their take on the phenomenon. "Psychoanalyzing our grandchildren before they're even born is an increasingly popular sport," noted the esteemed novelist Kingsley Amis in 1962, rather oddly writing for *Mademoiselle*. While Amis understood the increased popularity to predict tomorrow ("although we cannot control the future, to abandon all concern for it is to abandon most of what is involved in being civilized," he observed), he was firmly against our profound desire to know the unknown. "A world in which thought and behavior were entirely predictable would be worse than anything we have imagined," Amis believed, a warning that we should perhaps be careful about what we wished for. The author also had a message to send about what he considered to be "the great superstition of our part of the twentieth century," this being "that machines will eventually learn to do everything for us, even our thinking." Amis had major concerns that there was "the nucleus of a new priesthood ready to exploit our superstition," something that could result in a loss of individuality if we weren't careful, just as Huxley and Orwell had prophesied. "Every time we let a machine or a machine-minder make a decision on our behalf, we make the future of individuality just a little more precarious," Amis cautioned in this time of intense conformity and rapid automation, a potentially perilous combination.[28]

If Amis represented the top of the ladder of celebrities to weigh in on the future, Zolar, considered "the high priest of the cult of astrology in the United States" by *McCall's*, probably fell decidedly lower on the rungs. There were an estimated 5,000 astrologers in the country in 1961, but most were, compared to Zolar, as the magazine put it, "what the corner delicatessen is to Swift & Company." A sixty-three-year-old ex-clothing salesman from Chicago, Zolar (aka Bruce King) reeled in ten million readers with his syndicated horoscopes and "mystical publications," clearly the biggest fish in this most populist form of futurism. Zolar explained the secret to the popularity of astrology in the mid-twentieth century despite its having been discredited 400 years previously, when Copernicus discovered that the earth revolves around the sun rather than vice versa. "Fear still is the dominant emotion in mankind as he wonders about what tomorrow will bring in terms of his security and welfare," he said, and "I try to allay fear by making people understand that possible events that may occur can be avoided, if unfavorable."[29]

Zolar wasn't the only one trolling the seas of lowbrow futurism in the early 1960s. Charles Criswell, alternatively nicknamed "the seer without peer" or "Boastradamus," was, like Zolar, perhaps not the most erudite of postwar futurists but definitely among the richest. By 1963, his weekly column, "Criswell Predicts," was syndicated in a hundred newspapers from coast to coast, telling readers where storms would strike next, which world leader would soon croak, and a litany of other predictions that could be easily mistaken for gossip. Criswell was reportedly right eighty percent of the time, using stockbrokers, the police, and the occasional undertaker for inside information to bump up his hit rate. "People aren't interested in hearing about the future unless it's more exciting than the present," Criswell astutely explained. "You've got to jazz it up a little."[30]

As the postwar era wound down, a new form of futurism, or perhaps antifuturism, played out in the television coverage of state primaries leading up to the 1964 presidential election. By means of a "Voter Profile Analysis" (fancy talk for a survey), networks had begun to "declare" winners of the races soon after polls closed, displacing newscasters' custom to "predict" who would finish first. This new policy irritated at least one person, a writer for *The New Yorker*, who hypothesized that newspapers would soon decide to "declare" the future in their own coverage of events. "The New York Yankees were declared the winners of the American League pennant today in the fourth inning of their game here with the Boston Red Sox," the writer jested, another story beginning, "After watching six minutes of the first reel of the premiere performance of Robert Cudahy's 'Tomorrow and Tomorrow and Tomorrow,' the A.B.C. Drama Department today declared the film the winner of the coveted Oscar award in the 'Best Picture' category."[31] No doubt humorous, but with new analytic tools like the "Voter Profile Analysis," would "declaration" replace "prediction" as the primary goal of futurism, one might wonder?

MEGALOPOLIS

Concerned about their cities' future, there was no doubt that the nations' leaders had made a declaration of war on what it considered to be "slums." Between the wars, authorities of all stripes too had voiced their displeasure with parts of urban life, but now they were more prepared to do something about it. "To some extent, the epic visions of the 1920s and 1930s became the planning realities of the postwar era," wrote Corn and Horrigan, claiming that both the government's and the public's "revulsion" about slums became official policy through urban renewal programs. Experts and local, state, and federal politicians envisioned a day when economically distressed neighbor-hoods were a thing of the distant past, viewing them as a principal source of society's ills.[32] "The cities need physical rehabilitation if we are to come to grips with the disturbing phenomena of racial hostilities, juvenile delin-quency, disordered family relations," wrote Louis M. Hacker, a professor at Penn State, in 1960.[33] When it came to urban planning, one thing was clear: economically distressed neighborhoods would be a thing of the past, not the future. "As for slums," predicted Robert Wagner, mayor of New York in 1962 and looking ahead fifty years, "they will be just a memory of a rot that afflicted the city long ago."[34]

In fact, that city's West Side Renewal Plan, by which "slums" had been transformed into the glistening Lincoln Center, was the very model for the American city of the future. But by removing, replacing, or reconstruct-ing poorer neighborhoods, as Corn and Horrigan have pointed out, propo-nents of urban renewal focused on the effects of poverty rather than its root causes, not prepared to tackle deeply embedded issues of class, ethnicity, and race in a supposed democracy. "Planners embraced the modernist vision of the future, but relied on the image itself to carry it out, slighting the neces-sary underpinnings of real social change," Corn and Horrigan concluded, a missed opportunity that ultimately led to the violent protests in many Amer-ican cities.[35] Even the brightest minds of the day believed that the nation's institutional racism would somehow magically disappear as we became more enlightened. "I think it will not be long before it [racism] has to cease in regard to Negroes," wrote eighty-year-old Renaissance man Bertrand Russell in 1952, firmly believing that "biological ways of viewing social relations are likely to lose their force in the near future."[36]

Much because of the turbulence in urban America, the nation's cultural geography significantly shifted during the postwar years, with a "great migra-tion" from the industrial northeast to the South, West, and Southwest. As well, new suburbs extended the boundaries of cities, increasingly making them bump into each other, and the Federal Highway Act of 1956 further linked previously distinct communities with each other. All this blurring of lines was sound reason for the belief that in the future, gaps between cities would be further filled in, not a bad thing at all to the mid-century mind-set geared toward perpetual growth. "People will live in new 'interurbias' in which cities overlap and fuse with one another," proclaimed *Changing Times* in 1957, not seeing any problem with what would come to be known as sprawl, also happy to report that "today's farmlands will be tomorrow's suburbs."[37] New technologies also would help pave the way for the nation to become decentralized, in part of course a way to spread out the population in case of a Soviet nuclear attack. "There may well be fewer 'central cities,'" announced *Parents* that same year, proposing that by 2009, "imaginative use of television and other media of instant communication may enable large businesses to locate many of their offices in the suburbs."[38]

Naturally, the American landscape of the future would be redrawn as more citizens flocked to these "interurbias," creating fewer but much larger cities. Jerome P. Pickard of the Urban Land Institute, a research organization, saw the rise of ten "super-cities" by 2000, in which a full third of all Americans would live, his 1959 outlook correctly anticipating cluster communities connected by I-95 like "Chesapeake & Potomac City" (Baltimore/Washington) and "Southeast Florida City" (Miami to Palm Beach).[39] *Coronet* too could make out what it called a "megalopolis" on the nation's horizon, its own 1959 scenario for 2000 including a super-city that ran all the way from Bangor, Maine, to Richmond, Virginia. "Old cities have ceased to exist as they once were," the magazine projected, as "with the huge spurt in population they have grown together." Like others, *Coronet* believed these megalopoli were absolutely a good thing, "made possible by improved transportation." "Had it not been for this improved transportation and accompanying spread-out," the magazine explained, "cities as they had once existed would have suffocated under the mounting pressure of traffic."[40]

Other visionaries saw an even bigger cultural shift ahead, that from West to East. British historian Arnold Toynbee believed in 1952 that in just fifty years, there would be a major backlash to the technology-based society championed by the United States and Europe, posing a much different kind of ideological battle than the who-can-build-a-bigger-and-better-bomb Cold War. "The nineteenth century movement in the Western world which replaced religion by technology as the center of interest will be reversed in the twenty-first century by a counter-movement in which mankind will turn back from technology to religion," said Toynbee, anticipating the dynamics of today's fundamentalist movement. Toynbee also was prescient when it came to where this resistance to the forward thrust of "progress" would originate. "The center of power in the world will ebb back from the shores of the Atlantic to the Middle East, where the earliest civilizations arose 5,000 or 6,000 years ago," he proposed, something today's Western leaders probably would not want to hear.[41]

Writing for the *American Mercury* in 1957, Harold Lord Varney also saw a major geopolitical shift ahead, one that did not bode well for the United States of the year 2000. Varney believed overpopulation to be by far the biggest problem of the future, especially for the United States as its own numbers were outpaced by other countries around the world. "The history of the future is being written in the wildly gyrating human birthrate needle," Varney insisted, something to which both the US government and the United Nations were not paying nearly enough attention. Although Latin and South America, with their high birthrates and increased life expectancies, posed a significant threat to the United States as their populations grew over the next few decades, it was Asia that would really upset the apple cart at the turn of the century. "When we contemplate the grim possibilities in Asia, at the end of the next 43 years, our picture becomes nightmarish," Varney warned, "its immense population a time-bomb which threatens the whole future of American security." For Varney, China was not surprisingly "the most frightening spot," the thought of a billion communists almost too much to bear, with India "the other great glacial population mass which threatens to upset all present balances." Together, he insisted, the forecasted population growth of points south and east presented "an acute political challenge" as the nation faced the "prospect of dwindling importance in the world." What could the United States do about this apparent unstoppable tide? "Surrounded by a rising sea of non-Caucasian or mestizo races, it must find alliances among the great new population masses, or pass into a political decline," Varney concluded, sound advice even today.[42]

NEW MEN IN NEW WORLDS

For many in the 1950s, however, there was a bigger, more immediate threat than a rising sea of nonwhite races. Nonhuman races trafficked freely in postwar Americans' imaginations, tapping into both our fears of and our fascination with what may lie beyond this island Earth. Paranoia about a future alien invasion could be seen in movies like *War of the Worlds*, *Invaders from Mars*, and *Earth vs. the Flying Saucers*, all not-so-disguised fictionalizations of the Red Scare, while exercises in space travel, for example *Rocketship XM*, *Destination Moon*, *This Island Earth*, and *Forbidden Planet*, offered viewers escapist fantasy during a time of serious concerns about the longevity of our own planet. Outer space could also be found on radio and television of the postwar years, of course, heavily informing our vision of the future. On radio, alien invasions, flying saucers, humanlike robots, and faster-than-the-speed-of-sound rockets could be heard on shows like *Dimension X*, *Exploring Tomorrow*, and *X-Minus One*, all dramas intended for adult listeners. On television, a new generation of intergalactic cops patrolled the futuristic universe with sidekicks in tow and gizmos in hand, packaging Cold War tensions into politics- and ideology-free adventure. Called "kiddie space operas" by Corn and Horrigan, these very popular shows (including *Captain Video*, *Tom Corbett*, *Space Cadet*, *Space Patrol*, *Rod Brown of the Rocket Rangers*, *Rocky Jones*, *Space Ranger*, and *Commander Cody, Sky Marshall of the Universe*) were primarily a platform for related merchandise such as games, toys, furniture, and furnishings, turning baby boomers' holidays into a frenzy of futurism.[43]

As scientists and engineers worked out the mind-boggling details of how to send a rocket into space and the even more mind-boggling matter of getting it to come back, much of 1950s futurism was directed to when (versus if) Man would land on the moon. Forecasters consistently believed the event of events would take place later, sometimes much later, than what actually took place, very typical of visionaries' historical underestimation when it came to flight. "To the moon? Maybe," mused *Changing Times* in 1957, on the fence about whether Man would get there by 1982, even though it would happen in just half that amount of time.[44] That same year, Frederick C. Durant, president of the International Astronautical Federation, predicted that Man would land on the moon sometime before the end of the century, an especially conservative guesstimate for someone in the field.[45] American scientists should have known better, having been shocked when the Russians launched *Sputnik* in 1957—probably the greatest technological achievement of the decade—and given the time lines of previous aviation milestones. Commercial jet service had developed much faster than most airline executives had expected, and even one of the masters of futurism, Jules Verne, misjudged how quickly the airplane would make his eighty-days-around-the-world trip seem quaint and poky.[46]

For every astronautical undershooting, however, there was an occasional overshoot. "By the year 2000, it is entirely possible that we may have spaceships which can travel at a speed approaching the speed of light," believed H. J. Rand, the president of Rand Development, his 1958 forecast more likely posed by a teenage boy's hobby magazine than one of the world's premier think tanks.[47] Walter Dornberger of Bell Aircraft predicted that same year that rocket-powered commercial airplanes would in the not-so-distant future move along at a zippy 11,000 miles per hour, an idea almost as way off as Rand's.[48] The most sensible predictions about space travel placed less emphasis on the technical obstacles to be overcome, and more on the financial. "Going to the moon is not a matter of physics but of economics," insisted John Rader Platt, a professor at the University of Chicago, his levelheaded view of 1958 recognizing that the future was more about priorities than possibilities.[49]

Regardless of the timing, space travel was apparently something that parents of the future would have to equip their children for, some experts believed, and it wasn't too soon to start planning. "Every child will own a suit for jet, and later on for rocket travel," declared *Parents* in 1957, with "thermo-static fabrics . . . developed for these suits, which can be worn here or in outer space." One fashion designer, Richard Englander, went as far as to sketch out hats that little girls would one day wear in space, his collection of "Solar System" sun hat, "Flying Saucer" two-part hat, "Outer Space Calot" (complete with antenna), and "Space Cloche" (with built-in visor) perhaps the first (half-serious) attempt at interplanetary couture.[50] Werner von Braun, director of the army's Ballistic Missile Agency in the 1950s, also saw "gold in them thar hills" of space. "At some particularly scenic spot in the moon, lavish excursion hotels have been established," said Braun in 1957 of life a century later, "run[ning] the whole gamut from honeymoon hotels to gambling joints."[51]

Way before such a lunar Las Vegas could be established, however, there remained the not-so-simple issue of launching something much bigger than a breadbox into space. A couple of generations later, it's easy to forget how remarkable an achievement this was considered at the time. "In the decade of the Sixties man will finally soar beyond the thin film of the earth's atmosphere in which he and all his ancestors have been imprisoned for a billion years or more," declared *Fortune* in 1959, making it perfectly clear that this event would separate the future from the past like no other.[52] Even for travel within the earth's atmosphere, a switch seemed to have been immediately flicked on as the 1960s began. "History will recall the period leading to the Sixties as the prologue to true world travel," suggested John Houser, VP of American Express, just nine days into the decade, citing prosperity and "the coming supersonic age" as two factors in a new era of globetrotting. And like J. R. D. Tata, the Indian airline executive who believed during World War II that a rise in global travel would lead to greater international understanding, Houser saw the wholesale moving to and fro as a form of cultural diplomacy. "The year 1960 will mark a vast, ever-increasing interflow of peoples of the world," he concluded, "a new and a potent means of communication towards peace and sufficiency for all."[53]

The election of JFK in 1960, of course, assured that many of the aeronautical dreams of the 1950s would come to fruition. By early 1961, in fact, NASA had gone public with its more than ambitious plans for the remainder of the decade, which included no fewer than 260 major launchings, a manned orbital flight, a number of unmanned landings on the moon (both "hard" and "soft"), and an unmanned flight around the moon. At this point, NASA did not, at least publicly, expect a manned landing on the moon until the 1970s, but the president's pledge that year for the United States to get there by the end of the decade was all the agency needed to put a "crash" program in place.[54] The only recently fantastic idea of getting to the moon—perhaps within the decade—now an actual plan, many experts could not resist pondering what lay ahead for Earthlings (and possibly little green men). Science fiction (and science fact, he liked to make clear) writer Isaac Asimov (whose day job was professor of biochemistry at Boston University), for example, posed a number of questions to better prepare us for what we might encounter.[55] "In establishing colonies on the moon," Asimov asked,

> What will happen to sexual mores if only a few women can be sent out there? Suppose an intelligent race of extraterrestrials is discovered? How can contact best be made? How certain can we be that relations will be peaceful? What measures must be taken to ensure safety? What will be the role of religion in a world in which space flight is a reality? What effect on the usual beliefs will result from the discovery of other intelligent beings?[56]

Rather than eroding space travel as a theme of futurism, then, the real march toward it served only to further link the final frontier with the idea of tomorrow in the popular imagination. Space was, of course, the central theme of the 1962 Seattle World's Fair, its Space Needle then and now an icon of our commitment to explore what lay beyond the thin film of the atmosphere. Standard Oil's exhibit at the fair also was a gleeful celebration of the planes, trains, and automobiles that would have us coming and going here, there, and everywhere in the year 2000 (all of them requiring fuel, of course).[57] Although the race to space was obviously infused with the politics of the Cold War, exploration of the solar system was at the same time viewed as an opportunity for the United States to find common ground, so to speak, with the Soviets. "As space science and space technology grow . . . and become more ambitious," said John Glenn at the United Nations in 1962 after his brief orbit in *Friendship 7*, "we shall be relying more and more on international team work." Adlai Stevenson, the US Ambassador to the UN, believed that Glenn and his Soviet counterpart, Major Uri Gagarin, represented nothing less than "new men in new worlds" who could lead us to a "profound spiritual insight [of] the unity of mankind." Perhaps utopia—an idea bordering on extinction on Earth—could be found somewhere else, Stevenson seemed to wonder.[58]

THE MECHANIƧM OF LIFE

Hope was not completely lost, however, that a more utopian world could be created through the miracles of science. The wartime faith in science carried over into the postwar years, giving rise to a virtually complete trust in all things man-made. "In the mythology of popular culture," observed Corn and Horrigan, "science had won the war, not just by developing the atomic bomb but by producing a wide variety of new weapons and synthetic materials."[59] Postwar innovations such as the transistor (replacing the fragile and clunky vacuum tube), Polaroid instant pictures, pantyhose, the first operational laser, the weather satellite, the electric toothbrush, instant replay, Velcro, and the hologram all promised to make the good life even better. New machines such as ENIAC (the first real digital computer), UNIVAC (the first all-electronic computer), and the IBM Selectric changed the way that men in gray flannel suits did business, and power steering and automatic fuel injection made Americans' love of the automobile that much stronger. Medical breakthroughs, including the artificial heart valve, organ transplants (kidney and, later, lung), the Salk vaccine for polio, the heart pacemaker and, without question, Valium, improved the quality of life and raised life expectancies, while defense projects such as the nuclear-powered submarine and nuclear aircraft carrier were designed to prevent the Cold War from getting hot or, if that failed, to get the Russkies before they got us.

Indeed, with atomic and nuclear bombs now a reality, many scientists themselves could not help but couch their belief that their efforts would lead us to a better world in the future with a big "if." A 1957 symposium held in New York, called "The Next Hundred Years," sponsored by, of all organizations, Joseph E. Seagram & Sons, was a prime opportunity for leading scientists of the day to weigh in with their cautiously optimistic predictions. "If man survives," posited John Weir, associate professor of psychology at Cal Tech, "he can look forward to learning more about himself in the next one year than he has in the preceding one million." Herman J. Muller, professor of zoology at the University of Indiana and Nobel Prize winner, felt similarly. "Provided that the world does not fall prey to one of the four dangers of our times—war, dictatorship of any kind, overpopulation or fanaticism," he thought, "the coming one hundred years will revolutionize advances in sciences and their application."[60]

This kind of schizophrenic futurism carried into the early 1960s, with various notables offering their own interpretation of a polarized vision of tomorrow. Erich Fromm, the noted psychoanalyst, for example, saw two very different scenarios for life in 1987 a quarter-century earlier. Either "the survivors of a thermonuclear war will have organized a world dictatorship or a renaissance of united humanity will have begun," Fromm thought, quite typical of the all-or-nothing school of prediction in circulation since the development of atomic weapons. Eleanor Roosevelt belonged to the same school, saying that same year, her last, that "if we have not destroyed ourselves, I hope we will have learned that humanity must be looked upon as all of the same race."[61] Others, however, gave little credence to such naysaying or any kind of questioning of the forward thrust of science. "*Brave New World* and *1984* are surely the most depressing societies that have ever been imagined," claimed Jacob Bronowski, a British scientist and mathematician, who was of the opinion that nuclear energy, automation, and a biological revolution would help make 1984 a very good year. "Science promises a future in which men can lead intelligent and healthy lives in cities of a human size," he told the Royal Society of Health in 1962, "and I think it is a future truly worth living for."[62]

As scientific breakthroughs changed the stuff of everyday life in the postwar years, there was indeed good reason to expect even greater things ahead. Hopes were especially high for medicine, a field benefiting from huge sums of money being spent in university and corporate labs. A cure for polio was accurately predicted in 1950 by Kenneth Maxcy from Johns Hopkins and his colleague Jonas Salk at the University of Pittsburgh, the former justifiably confident that a vaccine would be developed in "the not too far distant future."[63] Technology also was being counted on to usher in a new era of health care. Alfred N. Goldsmith, a founder of the Institute of Radio Engineers, believed medicine would greatly benefit from our promising "electronic future," a perfect cross-pollination of scientific fields. "Electronic microscopy and its successors, exquisitely fashioned and informative instruments, accurate diagnostic devices and physiotherapy may contribute greatly to the health, comfort and length of man's life," he told an audience of 1,000 at the Waldorf-Astoria in 1954, accurately predicting the state of advanced health care a half-century hence.[64]

With the best yet to come, it was easy for some to get carried away with future advances in medicine. Looking back on the progress made in heart disease over the past forty years, for example, an editor for the *New York Times* wrote that same year, "In view of what has been accomplished it is safe to predict that, when another forty years have elapsed, what to us are hopes of cures will be realities."[65] Equally overoptimistic were predictions made five years later by George B. Stone, general manager of the J. B. Roerig Company, a division of the pharmaceutical maker Pfizer. With huge sales and profits through the 1950s and millions being poured into research, Stone saw on the horizon the development of drugs that would cure cancer by 1965 and—a mainstay of futurism—an effective vaccine for the common cold.[66] Not at all overoptimistic, however, were expectations for the new "mood-inducing" drugs to become more and more popular as scientists linked brain chemistry with emotions. "I think the day will come when people will be taking mood pills like they take aspirin today," said Dr. George Mangun of New Jersey in 1959, a pretty accurate assessment of the Prozac Nation four decades later.[67]

Much of the excitement surrounding future possibilities in medicine was steeped in attempts to chart the course of biology over the truly long term. With new tools like the electron microscope, scientists came to the full realization that God could indeed be found in the details. "As man learns to control the mechanism of life, he undoubtedly will begin to control the biology of his own species," wrote J. H. Rush, a physicist, believing that "this deliberate control of the genetic constitution of his race is probably the most significant and revolutionary of all the innovations that man has in prospect." Rush thought that it would take Man thousands of years to realize such "control" (taking place now, of course) but had his sights on even greater possibilities much further in the future. "The apotheosis of *homo sapiens* may come in 1,000,000 years or so when man liberates his soul from his body—that fragile retort of flushing chemicals and psychic shocks," he proposed in 1958, something that also may take place a lot sooner if the pace of change in the past holds true for the future.[68] Herman Muller too believed that something potentially transcendent resided in the human body's genetic material. "By working in functional alliance with our genes, we may attain to modes of thought and living that today would seem inconceivably god-like," the Nobel Prize winner said in 1962.[69] Peter Ritner also visited this theme in his 1961 book *The Society of Space*, seeing in a very distant future the possibility of the "ultimate freedom," the liberation of the mind from the body. Through such a process, Ritner proposed, Man would truly defeat the laws of time and space, marking the full and final triumph over Nature.[70]

ATOMVILLE

Until such a triumph, Man's manipulation of the building blocks of Nature, the atom, made do. Within and outside the realm of futurism, the fascination with atomic energy continued after the war but now, after Hiroshima and Nagasaki, it was a double-edged sword. The reality of atomic weapons deeply shaped the arc of the future, something readily apparent in pop culture and specifically in movies. "Around 1950 the future returned to the movies, but the innocent optimism of the 1930s had vanished, obliterated by the horrors of global war and nuclear destruction," according to Corn and Horrigan. Whether the premise was a postapocalyptic future (*Five, The Day the World Ended, On the Beach, Panic in the Year Zero*), or atomically radiated critters (*Them, Godzilla*), many science fiction films of the postwar years reflected and probably helped to vent some of the anxieties of the Cold War.[71]

With much of the dark side of atomic energy safely channeled into B-movies and pulp fiction, its potential to make the world a better, even more beautiful place spread like kudzu across the American landscape of the 1950s. At its most powerful, the atom was imagined as the core of a tomorrow that had none of the ugly blemishes of today. "Suppose it's a sunny Saturday in 2004 A.D. and you're on your way to visit the Smiths in Atomville, one of America's completely new communities," began a 1954 article in *Popular Mechanics*, this imaginary city of fifty years hence perfect in every way, save the occasional colliding of "converti" (helicopters) that filled the skies. "Laid out along strict radial lines" and "its homes all look-alikes," Atomville was a technological wonderland with no unsightly telephone poles or apartment buildings. And even though the homes were "hidden under earthen shells," just in case Atomville became literally so, terraced lawns and gardens made the place as pretty as any town in America. Conceived by architect and interior designer Paul Laszlo, who believed that such communities would "make Bucky Fuller's Dymaxion house and his geodesic dome appear old-fashioned," Atomville showed that the Atomic Age was not something to fear but rather a simple fact out of which a new way of living would have to emerge.[72]

The idea of Atomic-Age-as-fact-of-life served as the backdrop for much planning for the future in the 1950s, something that would be approached as both a challenge and an opportunity. One of the topics discussed at a 1953 meeting of the Society of Automotive Engineers, for example, was if and how to design a car that would be resistant to A-bomb blasts. At the conference, a special committee presided over by H. L. Goodwin, director of atomic test operations at the Federal Civil Defense Administration, examined test cars that had been exposed to atomic explosions, musing over what the automobile industry could do to make it more likely passengers would survive such an attack.[73] Mathematician John von Neumann believed that rather than talking about the weather, somebody—an imaginary Atomic Weather Commission—would one day do something about it. "A flick of the nuclear switch, and presto!—the North Pole melts, the vast continent of Antarctica thaws into productive use, Greenland grows bananas, Vermont grows oranges, and everybody's heating bill vanishes," *Life* reported von Neumann's 1955 prediction, seeing no problem at all with such intentional, atomically generated global warming.[74]

There seemed to be no limit to what the atom could do in the trusty hands of scientists. That same year, William F. Libby, head of the Atomic Energy Commission, predicted that doctors of the future would give their patients "radioactive pills" to better diagnose causes of pain, just one way knowledge of the atom would be used for peace rather than war.[75] "The atom will do everything," *Changing Times* put it more simply that same year, claiming that "we are still in the dawn of atomic research and development."[76] Although atomic energy was viewed as the skeleton key to the future, its cost and practicality were sometimes questioned by the more skeptical (or simply better informed). Atomic-powered appliances and cars, for example, which were rather familiar ideas before and during the war, began to lose some steam. "[Uranium] is too precious to use to operate electric toasters and vacuum cleaners or automobiles—even if we could," wrote L. A. DuBridge, president of Cal Tech, in 1952.[77]

Despite some reservations among those brave enough to question the possibilities of the almighty atom, experts in all fields viewed atomic energy as a sort of one-stop shop for the future. Rounding up fifteen experts in 1955 to propose their views of life in these United States in twenty years, Prudential found that most roads led directly to the atom. The group, which consisted of college presidents and professors and heads of companies like General Mills, Chrysler, and Dow Chemical, came up with some respectable futuristic stuff—automatically piloted cars, videophones, cures for the common cold—but it was the applications of atomic energy that clearly stole the show. In 1975, atomic energy would not only create electricity but also sterilize food, fight disease, and serve as a fuel supplement, the experts agreed, a kind of miracle tonic for whatever was ailing society.[78]

Similarly, "the atom loomed as the biggest thing in the crystal ball" at a 1957 gathering organized by the Wharton School, as reported by *News-*

week, which included heavy hitters like H. J. Rand and Robert D. Calkins, president of the Brookings Institution. By 2000, believed attendee Charles H. Weaver, head of Westinghouse's nuclear program, "nuclear energy will be the dominant factor in our power economy," with coal, oil, and gas no longer sufficiently able to fuel the nation's needs.[79] The ways in which the atom would be used in the future were truly diverse, however, with postwar visionaries using it essentially as the default setting for tomorrow. In 1982, claimed *Changing Times* a quarter-century earlier, "breakfast will consist of bacon and eggs that you've kept around the house for weeks (fresh as ever, thanks to atomic sterilization)," but that was just the beginning as "electrons and protons shape[d] the future." "Changing matter will become almost child's play for the scientist when they perfect their atomic tools," the magazine declared, with "new plastics, paints, textiles, metals, medicines, building materials and chemicals [to] result from experimentation and atomic processes." Even "the factory or office you work in or the apartment house you live in may be heated by a low-pressure atomic reactor," Kiplinger's editors thought, something that might have made those upstairs a bit edgy had such progress been made.[80]

Of course, in the Nuclear Age, the potential existed that atoms would not be used just for peace but also for war. Herman Kahn's 1961 book *On Thermonuclear War* was a perfect example of how futurists have not only predicted what may come next but at times, to their credit, have attempted to shape outcomes. As one of the top futurists of the day, Kahn was uniquely qualified to present the potential consequences of what were some very dangerous times, the book's quantitative analysis of the Cold War military situation based on RAND research dedicated to the noble goals of "anticipating, avoiding, and alleviating crises" and "decreasing the probability of catastrophe." Without such kind of thinking, Kahn warned, "we are not going to reach the year 2000—and maybe not even the year 1965—without a cataclysm of some sort."[81]

PUSH-BUTTON PARALYSIS

Definitely making some postwar Americans edgy about future technologies was George Orwell's 1948 novel *Nineteen Eighty-Four*, his dystopian vision of a totalitarian world state a warning about unchecked nationalism (and repressed sexuality). Echoing Aldous Huxley's own concerns that humanity might be heading to places it should not go in a brave new world, *Nineteen Eighty-Four* tempered the otherwise firm faith in science and technology during the postwar years. In particular, rather than a miraculous device of entertainment or education, Orwell's two-way television of the future meant that Big Brother was watching and listening, something considered very much within the realm of future possibilities in the Wild West days of the medium. Also making some mid-century folks nervous were future scenarios for the always controversial robot. Early forms of industrial robots were already eliminating some manual, repetitive jobs, triggering fears of rampant unemployment as they further developed. "It is certain that robots are on the way and that some kind of cushion for their impact upon society is essential," wrote Edmund C. Berkeley, a "thinking machine" expert and designer, in 1950. "If we are not to be displaced by robots we must establish social control over them," he argued, suggesting perhaps the creation of a Robot Machine Commission whose oversight function would be analogous to that of the Atomic Energy Commission (and von Neumann's imaginary Atomic Weather Commission).[82]

As with many if not most emerging technologies, however, the new generation of thinking machines would also create jobs, many recognized. The details were certainly hazy, but it was clear that there would be a big future in computer-related fields. "Mathematics sharks . . . will be in great demand in the future," *Changing Times* forecast in 1954, as "they are the only ones who can figure out what to feed the new electronic brains and calculators."[83] Three years later, the same magazine again urged readers to consider technology-oriented careers as an "automated society" became real. "A new breed of workers will develop," *Changing Times* predicted, "both in offices and factories, and those who can truly be masters of the machinery will be the ones who move ahead," wise words that many in the next couple of decades probably wished they had heeded.[84] Visions of there being plenty of opportunity to be "masters of the machinery" were in part a result of the general expectation that the computer would be in the 1960s what the transistor had been in the 1950s. By 1959, in fact, both GE and RCA had developed solid-state electronic parts, ushering in a new era of "micro-miniaturization" that would lead to much faster and, thankfully, much smaller computers.[85] The writing now clearly on the wall for those not afraid to look, sources as unexpected as *Cosmopolitan* suggested its readers think about careers in the emerging field of automated machines. "A particularly promising field for women college graduates will be jobs as 'programmers' or 'systems personnel' with firms using big new computers," the magazine advised in 1960, feeling the need to explain that "it is necessary to have people devise 'systems' [or] 'give instructions' to the computer, preparing it to do a specific job."[86]

Women opting for careers as homemakers, something a bit more common than computer programmers in postwar America, also would benefit from rising automation. "Housewives may get push button paralysis," *Changing Times* joked in 1957, but they were dead serious about the automated possibilities to come in a quarter-century. "They will push a button to cook, to raise or lower shelves, to get a recipe, to draw the coffee or cocktails, to get rid of wastes," the magazine predicted, but it would be a "kitchen-sized Univac" that would literally take the cake. "The housewife will insert a coded card, push a button, and presto, the food for the meal will be prepared," all this button-pushing making things much more convenient but also raising big questions about the very identity of women in the future. "Will all this produce feelings of absolute frustration in housewives, making them fear that no one needs them now?" *Changing Times* asked, adding that psychologists of the day were pondering that very question.[87]

In fact, some readers of this very *Changing Times* article too were pondering this very question, not too sanguine about the prospect of being replaced by a set of mechanical switches, knobs, or other thingamajigs. Three months after the article appeared, the magazine published a follow-up with questions reportedly from readers, along with "additional council on how they [readers] can best apply our look-ahead to their personal lives."[88] One question, and even more so its answer, spoke volumes regarding gender roles circa 1957 and those imagined for 1982:

Q: As a housewife, I am honestly worried about all those push buttons to do my housework. Isn't there anything I will have to use my brains and imagination for?

A: Don't fret—you'll have plenty to do. Planning recreation, for example. Spare time will be more abundant, and it will be up to you to see that it is used intelligently by your family. Community needs (schools, hospitals, play facilities) will cry out for volunteers. The growth of adult education will give you opportunities that you may have long been yearning for. In other words, you'll have more time to live outside of the house—and what housewife won't welcome that? And it will still take plenty of planning—and time—to run your house.[89]

There were bigger social implications of push-button paralysis, with entire industries perhaps endangered species as they became increasingly automated. "Clothes will be cleaned quickly and efficiently within the home merely by hanging garments in a closet wired with supersonic sound [and] at the touch of a button, all soil will be released, caught in a floor trap," predicted *Parents* in 1957, a possible death knell for dry cleaners.[90] Food service employees also might find themselves in long unemployment lines if things went the way that most experts were predicting. "In restaurants, full-course dinners are prepared and served without a soul in sight—except the button-pushing patrons," *Coronet* envisioned in 1959, as automation "set in with a vengeance" in another half-century.[91] Would even fine dining become a Horn & Hordart experience, one could ask? Such fears of unbridled automation continued throughout the early 1960s, with some experts in 1964 forecasting that in just a decade, automation could take over the jobs of half the workers in the country. Interestingly, almost as great a concern as widespread unemployment was the thought of having a surplus of leisure time as various kinds of thinking machines improved our quality of life. In the 1920s and 1930s, some believed that the Machine Age would lead to a three- or four-day work-week, causing a minor crisis regarding how more leisure time could be used productively (versus "sinfully"). Now, in the early 1960s, with automation already beginning to "set in with a vengeance," similar concerns were raised about what to do with all this extra time. "The fundamental problem will be represented by the ability of people to make productive use of their time," emphatically stated Norman Cousins, editor of *Saturday Review*, in 1964, echoed by Dennis Gabor, author of *Inventing the Future*, published that year. Gabor in fact considered "the approaching age of leisure" as nothing short of one-third of a great "trilemma" that threatened tomorrow, the others being the apocalyptic duo of nuclear war and overpopulation. Because of automation and other achievements, science and technology would "interfere with the fate of man as never before," Gabor thought, something to think seriously about as we invented our future.[92]

The best minds of the day too were obsessed with this idea of abundant leisure as automation inevitably rolled on into the twenty-first century. Marshall McLuhan, the postwar king when it came to the dynamic between Man and machine, proposed that in an automated world, people in the future would have to "learn a living" as opposed to just earning one, a concept described by Barbara Ward in *Saturday Review* as "a fuller development of the spirit in esthetic and contemplative training."[93] Buckminster Fuller believed that more automation, specifically that made possible by new computers, was nothing less than a key turning point in the history of mankind. "That the machine is to replace man as a specialist, either in craft, muscle, or brain work, is an epochal event," he thought, something that would redirect the trajectory of our species. Fuller was right, of course, but in his enthusiasm misread what they could and could not do. "The computers will soon eliminate war as an evolutionary function by providing enough wealth to supply all mankind," he rather ridiculously wrote in 1964, just as the conflict in Vietnam escalated to full-fledged war.[94]

Much more prescient about the future relationship between computers and war was someone in the business of the latter, one Lt. Col. Robert B. Rigg. "Any war fought after 1974 will have some strange proportions," he predicted in 1957, foreseeing a "pushbutton soldier" firing long-range missiles from faraway, underground military installations. Likewise, the army officer believed there would be "no bloody beach assaults" in the wars of tomorrow, made obsolete by "secret, sudden, and strategically subtle" air attacks by an all-powerful "Futurarmy." Rather than encourage future wars, however, such advanced technologies would help discourage them, Rigg argued. Because these techniques were "ultra-swift and responsive," he maintained, they would "invoke the minimum of destruction and provide the best basis for a peace," like Fuller falling into the wide-open, utopian trap of technology.[95]

FUTURAMA II

It would be, fittingly, a technological utopia that would serve as the final hurrah of futurism in a time when the best was yet to come. But how could a world's fair out-tomorrow one held on the very same spot called "World of Tomorrow"? That's a question officials of the 1964 New York World's Fair might have asked themselves, knowing full well that the 1939–1940 fair remained a powerful, beloved memory for many. Not only did the previous New York fair carry the definitive futuristic theme, but many of the predictions made by exhibitors—rockets, air-conditioned homes, a national network of superhighways, and others—had come true. When it came to tomorrow, the "World of Tomorrow" would be a tough act to follow, permanently engrained in the public's consciousness as one of the seminal symbols of the future in the twentieth century. With postwar America's worship of science and technology as a cultural backdrop, however, officials and many exhibitors eagerly embraced the idea of the future, sprinkling visions of tomorrow all over the grounds. Most of these visions were, like the fair as a whole, heavily commercial attempts by exhibitors to, in effect, brand the future. From General Cigar's Hall of Magic, where one could take in "the magic of the future," to the "Futorian" upholstered furniture in the Pavilion of American Interiors, to the fair's aluminum, prefab Atomedic (for Atomic Age Medicine) hospital, which the *New York Times* considered "as futuristic as a flying saucer," the world of tomorrow could be found in Flushing Meadows almost everywhere one looked.[96] "The common man is being given a splendid opportunity to stand in awe at what he can do and comprehend, now and in the future," Barbara Tufty wrote in the *Science News Letter* shortly before the fair opened. "The New York World's Fair offers many brief vistas into secrets of the earth and universe which science is probing and technology is using," she reported, a sentiment many visitors shared after their journey to Queens.[97]

The biggest, most popular, and most commercial presentation of the world of tomorrow at the fair was, of course, GM's Futurama, its utopian view of transportation a ringing endorsement for its unique style of corporate colonialism. Under its clunky umbrella theme of "General Motors— Many Minds and Many Hands Serving the Needs of Mankind," the company made the case that "mobility" in all its forms was the solution to the world's problems.[98] Although Futurama's fifteen-minute ride and "Avenue of Progress" included plenty of futuristic eye and ear candy, like demonstrations of laser light and the sound of stars as "heard" by radio telescope to warrant their names, GM chairman Frederic G. Doner had told the exhibit's designers he wanted "no fantasies, nothing that can't be backed up with hard facts as a definite, practical possibility." What Doner did want was for his company to be perceived as the future solver of many of the world's present problems, a messianic messenger that would deliver a better tomorrow through incredible leaps in transportation-based technology. If Man could only devote all his energy and know-how to peaceful purposes rather than to war, Futurama told visitors, a more prosperous and more leisurely society lay ahead for all. Family farms, for example, would not only survive but thrive in the years ahead, a result of (GM-produced) push-button controls allowing farmers to plow, seed, cultivate, and harvest the land without taking a step outside. Traffic congestion, a problem GM had of course helped create, through its aggressive dismantling of many cities' very efficient cable-car systems, would be solved by adding another level of highways in the air. By being extremely entertaining, easily understood, and overtly optimistic of the future, Futurama, with 70,000 people a day moving through it in 463 three-passenger Fiberglas cars, became the most popular exhibit at the fair and, probably, in world's fair history.[99]

While the company can't be blamed for presenting a self-serving, auto-centric vision of tomorrow, how GM planned to achieve its utopia was, even for the times, myopic and ignorant. The 1964 version of Futurama was rooted in the missionary-style conquest and exploitation of various natural environments—jungle, desert, ocean, Antarctica, and outer space—for the expansion of Man, an idea whose popularity had peaked in the nineteenth century or even earlier. "Everywhere you go," a brochure for Futurama stated, "you will see man conquering new worlds, to a large degree because he will have available to him new and better methods for transporting machines, materials and people." The ocean floor would be drilled for oil and mined for diamonds, GM proudly announced, while the ocean floor in the ride was "composed largely of coral removed by divers from deep beneath the Caribbean Sea." Even Antarctica would be "probed," its "frozen wastes" turned into "resources needed by a growing world population." In one segment, giant machines of the future invaded a primordial jungle, taking down ancient trees with red laser beams right out of *War of the Worlds*. The machine proceeded to gobble up the trees and undergrowth and then, miraculously, extract a four-lane highway from its rear. Cities would then arise out of this "wasteland" and resorts (Hotel Atlantis, naturally) be built under the sea, each a solution to the growing population explosion as Man established outposts in the most remote regions of the world.[100]

Futurama, like most exhibits at the fair, was designed first and foremost not for education or even entertainment purposes but commercial ones, intended to pave the way, so to speak, to make a favorable future a self-fulfilling prophecy. With Nature now conveniently out of the way, GM explained, "an extensive freeway network [would] speed traffic to a park-like industrial sector or to festive recreational and cultural areas" (despite the less than speedy scenario actually taking place on the expressways right outside the fairgrounds).[101] Rather than offer solutions to the growing problems of pollution or the destruction of thriving urban neighborhoods due to continued encroachment of highways, GM proposed that the introduction of the automobile into virgin land was the path to a better tomorrow.[102] As well, despite the blossoming of the 1960s ecology movement (Rachel Carson's *Silent Spring* had been published in 1962), Futurama was completely blind to the role of jungles in creating oxygen or to the "ozone effect." Ironically, Futurama was not progressive but regressive, an all smoke-and-mirrors spectacle that looked backward versus forward in order to promote a way of life centered around and dependent on the combustion engine. The exhibit was in fact as dated as its name, an anachronism grossly out of touch with not only the future but the present. Still, visitors loved Futurama, more so than any other exhibit at the fair, precisely because it solved major problems with a quick flick of its magic technological wand. The future of Futurama was, although fantastic, somehow comfortable and reassuring, just the thing visitors wanted to experience and feel before returning to the much more complex and challenging real world.

Ford's centerpiece exhibit, the Magic Skyway, on the other hand, was a harmless piece of Disney fluff, geared toward promoting its new models and moving product after or even during the fair. Hoping to hear a resounding yes from visitors after posing its advertising question, "Is there a Ford in your future?," the company featured advanced research projects in progress at its labs as well as at those of its subsidiary Philco.[103] Like GM, which displayed experimental cars such as the Firebird IV, the GM-X (which looked like a cross between a Jaguar XKE and a rocket), and the Runabout (a three-wheeled vehicle designed specially for the woman of the house by incorporating a removable shopping cart), Ford offered dream cars up for inspection to position itself as a company with big plans for the future. Ford's star dream car was the Aurora, which Gene Bordinat, vice president and director of styling for the company, pointed out meant "beginning or rising light in morning." A "luxury lounge" station wagon (and forerunner of today's tricked-out minivans), the Aurora included a children's compartment, which could be "sound-isolated" from the rest of the car with a flick of the power-operated glass switch. The rocketlike car also had a communications console with a TV set, "sound recorder," and bar, the latter presumably for passengers versus drivers. Also built into the auto of the future were a swivel armchair and a curved sofa that could accommodate no fewer than four adults, turning the vehicle into a living or rec room on wheels.[104]

The day before the exposition closed, VIPs gathered in Flushing Meadows to put this world's fair to rest. Just ten feet south of where a similar ceremony had occurred a quarter-century earlier, guests signed their name in a special book that was then put into a time capsule to be opened in 5,000 years. The capsule was a replica of the one buried in 1940, when officials of that fair, along with executives from the Westinghouse Electric Corporation, buried circa 1930s artifacts and microfilmed records to document their time and place for the benefit of those finding themselves in Queens in the seventieth century. Such things as a woman's hat, a slide rule, and an assortment of newspaper and magazine articles describing the (mostly sorry) state of world affairs at the turn of the decade were sunk into a fifty-foot steel shaft, not to be opened until the year 6939. Dozens of experts also deemed that the Lord's Prayer (in 300 languages), a newsreel of a Miami fashion show, and a copy of the book *Gone with the Wind* were worth preserving for 5,000 years. The location (in longitude and latitude) and a description of the time capsule's contents were recorded in a "Book of Records," hundreds of copies of which were scattered around the world to help humans (or others) in five millennia to find the thing and decipher what was inside.[105]

Time Capsule II, also sponsored by Westinghouse, included twice as much material as the first, reflecting how much had occurred over the past twenty-five years. "In a quarter of a century," stated Westinghouse in its brochure for Time Capsule II, "man split the atom, danced the twist, ran the four-minute mile, scaled Mt. Everest, fought another World War and began to probe space and the seas." The eighty-plus items were selected by a fourteen-person committee led by Leonard Carmichael, VP of research and exploration for the National Geographic Society, with input solicited from fairgoers. Included in the 7-1/2-foot-long, torpedo-shaped, 300-pound metal (a new "super" alloy called Kromarc) capsule were what could be considered the greatest hits of the postwar era—credit cards, a bikini, contact lenses, birth control pills, tranquilizers, a plastic heart valve, a pack of filter cigarettes, an electric toothbrush, and a heat shield from the *Apollo 7*. The arts too were represented, with such items as photographs of an Andrew Wyeth painting (Wyeth was a member of the selection committee) and Henry Moore sculpture, a microfilmed book of Ernest Hemingway's and poetry by Dylan Thomas and Robert Frost, and a tape of a Danny Kaye television show. Records by the Beatles, Joan Baez, and Thelonious Monk were also part of the capsule, as were photographs of important cultural figures of the 1940s and 1950s (including the rather odd triumvirate of Joe DiMaggio, Errol Flynn, and Adolf Hitler).[106]

With much of the great day coming envisioned during the war realized during the postwar years, there was an opportunity to imagine even greater possibilities for the distant and not-so-distant future. Our horn of plenty was already spilling over, but a consumer utopia lay ahead, its sheer abundance capable of solving all of our social ills. Brought to us by those twin towers of tomorrow, science and technology, postwar futurism was, in a word, limitless, fueled by the unsurpassed power of atomic energy. Fears that we wouldn't be able to consume as much as we could produce, that we would become overautomated or, much worse, that atoms would be used not for peace but again for war haunted this era's paradigm of the yet-to-be. Overall, however, the best was yet to come, whether it be in outer space or right next door, the American Way of Life bigger and better than ever before. With the literal burying of the future's past at the New York World's Fair in 1964, a new tomorrow was born, one that even the most sharp-eyed visionaries of the postwar years could not come close to imagining.

CHAPTER 4

Future Shock, 1965—1979

We cannot go on letting the future just happen to us.

—Edward Cornish, president of the World Future Society, 1975

I N 1967, FREDERICK POHL, ONE OF AN INCREASING NUMBER OF FUTUR-
ists on the lecture circuit, addressed an audience of businesspeople at the
Palmer House in Chicago. Pohl, by trade a writer and editor of science fiction stories, told a group of "insurance men" that they had "expanded [their]
market as far as possible through selling pensions plans, annuities, and the
like," and they should now focus instead on the "$30-trillion market of the
future." What market did Pohl have in mind? Cryonics, of course, the freez-
ing of a body after death and its revival once a cure is discovered (now called
cryogenics). Writing policies to cover the storage of frozen bodies waiting
for a cure would be a huge business in the future, Pohl thought, something
the insurance industry should now take seriously (the first cryonics customers had just begun their big chill). Even death—one of only two proverbial
sure things—would no longer necessarily have its way, because of emerging
scientific possibilities, Pohl and others believed. Soon Pohl was off to speak
to executives at Dow Corning, a maker of silicone products for industrial
applications. Liquid silicone, Pohl told the men, would one day be used for

cosmetic purposes, "injected into the body to swell curves or wipe out wrinkles." Basing his prediction on San Francisco's topless "go-go" dancers, who were the first to use silicone this way and were apparently delighted by the results, Pohl went on the record that "Silicone injection apparatus is going to be as common in a girl's make-up kit as the eyebrow pencil and lipstick are today."[1] Given the popularity of nips and tucks in the early twenty-first century, Pohl still may be proved right on this one.

Pohl's predictions were an inkling that Americans were in for quite a shock as the future unfolded in the mid-1960s. As America's postwar triumph faded, so did much of its faith in a future defined by unlimited progress, a leisure-based society, and urban utopias. In its place, a new future emerged in the late 1960s that reflected the social, economic, and political turmoil of the times, specifically, a growing generational divide and the loss of two of tomorrow's most promising leaders. Alvin Toffler's 1970 *Future Shock* became a poster child for this era's dominant narrative of tomorrow, as concerns about the economy, the environment, energy, and, of course, the Vietnam War became dark clouds on the horizon of our collective tomorrow. For the first time in American history, it became apparent that the future might not be as good a time as the present—a sharp break in the previously ever-progressing idea of tomorrow. Dystopian voices in the crowd were nothing new, but now with an unpopular, perhaps unwinnable war, major racial unrest, and the power to do serious damage to the planet in any number of ways, the American future was an increasingly perilous place.

Given the upheaval of the late 1960s, pundits not surprisingly viewed the 1970s with trepidation. *Fortune* announced in 1969 that it was the "end to hyperprosperity," *Time* predicted that the 1970s would be characterized by "dissent and discovery," and *Business Week* anticipated a "bumpy decade with a social sense," all prophetic visions of what lay ahead. As concern about the destiny of Spaceship Earth accelerated during the 1970s, futurism became much more of a legitimate discipline, popularized by various so-called prophets (Toffler and Isaac Asimov), methods (the Delphi technique), professional organizations (the Institute for the Future and the World Future Society), and specialized publications (*Futurist* magazine). With the mainstreaming of futurism, however, it lost much of its prewar and postwar magic, the idea of a coming age of miracles deflated by growing skepticism and cynicism. Unlike the previous, utopian paradigms of the future—the between-the-wars "shape of things to come," wartime's "great day coming," and postwar America's "best is yet to come"—a dystopian world was lying in wait, according to the future shock of the late 1960s and 1970s.

NEW FUTURI*S*M

Popular and consumer culture of the period reflected and reinforced the feeling that something was happening here, even if what it was wasn't exactly clear. The countercultural revolution had at least as much impact on style as on politics, some have argued, redirecting the trajectory of everything from fashion (mini- and midi-skirts and the Mod look) to furnishings (the waterbed, the lava lamp, and the curiosity that was the beanbag chair). Television (*Laugh-In, Saturday Night Live*) and theater (*Hair, Jesus Christ Superstar*) also embraced the iconoclasm of late 1960s youth culture, of course, and books like Tom Wolfe's *The Electric Kool-Aid Acid Test* and Carlos Castaneda's *The Teachings of Don Juan* expanded readers' consciousness much like the works of the Beats had done for a previous generation of hipsters. As well, upstart magazines like *Rolling Stone* and *Ms.* challenged the traditional rules of journalism, and public television and FM radio gave viewers and listeners an alternative to mainstream media, the beginning of the fragmentation of the communications universe that continues to this day. And while rock music went psychedelic with trippy albums like *Sgt. Pepper's*, *Surrealistic Pillow*, and *On Her Satanic Majesty's Request*, movies such as *The Graduate, Bonnie and Clyde, Butch Cassidy and the Sundance Kid*, and *Midnight Cowboy* blurred the previously reliable lines between Hollywood hero and villain.

Films of this era located in the future confirmed the palpable feeling that tomorrow was now entirely up for grabs, recast as a Darwinian struggle for survival of the fittest. From the soft-core porn universe of 40,000 A.D. in *Barbarella* (1968) to the predator-filled *Mad Max* and *Alien* (1979), the cinematic future was one in which the id ruled, these movies essentially over-the-top reflections of the nation's pre-AIDS sexual climate and high crime rate. *Soylent Green* (1973), *Rollerball* (1975), *Logan's Run* (1976), and *Silent Running* (1977) vented (or perhaps intensified) our fears of nuclear apocalypse, rampant pollution, and the population explosion, establishing dystopia as its own creative genre. Stanley Kubrick's *2001: A Space Odyssey* (1968) was a lightning rod for the growing ambivalence toward technology, a clear sign that our blanket faith and trust in the machine was over, should there be any doubt. And while the blockbuster *Star Wars* (1977) took place a "long, long time ago," the history of that far, faraway galaxy looked a lot like our future, one that made our two world wars seem like minor skirmishes. The television series *Star Trek* (1966–1969) too implied that even the final frontier would not be a safe haven should we destroy our own little island in the sky.

111

Utopia—a staple of futurism for millennia—had disappeared, reduced to a naïve memory of simpler, more innocent times.[2]

The turmoil of the present and the nail-biting for the future drove many Americans to want to believe that life wasn't as random as it seemed, considerable comfort in the notion that there was some sort of grand design that provided a kind of safety net. Jeane Dixon was now the pop futurist of the moment, her 1965 biography *A Gift of Prophecy* by Ruth Montgomery a very hot item in bookstores. In addition to her syndicated newspaper horoscope columns, Dixon was best known for her new year's predictions, her brand of futurism unapologetically psychic. Dixon also appeared frequently on late-night TV talk shows, making her perhaps the twentieth-century equivalent of the Old World court astrologer.[3]

Spurred on by the Broadway show *Hair* in 1968, astrology swept through the New World, many fans hoping that it really was the dawning of the Age of Aquarius. People from Norman Mailer to Marshall McLuhan ("I'm a Moon child, born under Cancer") seemed to be writing or talking about the planets and the stars in the late 1960s, looking to the skies to guide their personal futures. Although seeing naked people onstage was certainly an intriguing proposition, the wild popularity of the hit celestial musical had as much to do with the growing ambivalence, to say the least, toward science. "It's [Astrology] . . . a form of resistance to the technological juggernaut," explained Lennox Raphael, a writer for the *East Village Other*, a weekly newspaper run entirely by celestial principles. Interest in the supernatural had throughout history always risen during periods of crisis, and this was just one more sign, so to speak, of the times. Looking up was hardly the only method the more anxious used to try to get a little inside information on what might be coming next. Parker Brothers sold more Ouija boards than games of Monopoly in 1967, an indication that mysticism had, for the moment at least, trumped capitalism in popularity.[4]

The spike in more woo-woo forms of futurism had, of course, a very long history, something made crystal clear in Justine Glass's 1969 book *They Foresaw the Future*. Glass traipsed through 6,000 years of prophecy and clairvoyance, her mystical travelogue including everything from ancient Egyptian divinations to the latest utterings from contemporary soothsayers like Dixon, Edgar Cayce, and Maurice Woodruff. You name it—oracles, druids, saints, seers, astrologers, and witches—have taken a shot at prophecy over the centuries, Glass made clear, arguing that recent research in the areas of ESP, precognition, and the unconscious was raising the legitimacy of what had been, during the Scientific and Industrial Revolutions, reduced to myth or fable. "Prevision belongs to the spiritual sphere in which we live, as science is demonstrating and proving," she claimed, convinced that "once again prophecy is important."[5]

It was, however, the "new futurists" who emerged as the power players of prediction in the 1960s, a group awarded almost rock star status even beyond their bread and butter, the military-industrial complex. "Men in business, government, education and science itself realize that they must look at least two decades ahead just to keep abreast, must learn to survive under totally different conditions," wrote *Time* in 1966, explaining the hot demand for the services of this elite group. Although its leaders were generally acknowledged as four men—Henry Rowen, the new president of Rand; Daniel Bell, the Columbia University sociologist; Bertrand de Jouvenal, a top French intellectual and journalist; and Stephen Graubard, editor of *Daedalus*—new futurism was spread out among a wide variety of organizations in all sorts of directions. With its TEMPO (Technical Management Planning Organization) based in Santa Barbara, General Electric had 700 scientists, sociologists, economists, and engineers divining the future at a cost of $7 million a year, while IBM was partnering with Harvard on a ten-year, $15 million program focusing on the relationship between technology and society. In addition to having its own team trying their hand at scientific prediction, the Air Force was also paying the Rand Corporation a cool $15 million to ponder the future via its query-based Delphi technique. Both the University of Illinois and the University of Southern Illinois were in the future business (the latter partnering with Buckminster Fuller's World Resources Inventory project), as was the Hudson Institute, a nonprofit research center headed up by Herman Kahn. The Academy of Arts and Sciences was working with Bell's Commission on the Year 2000 program, and the Ford Foundation was funding a group called Resources for the Future as well as de Jouvenal's Paris-based organization (*Les Futuribles*, naturally).[6]

The proliferation of futurists in the late 1960s, along with their more disciplined, focused approach (so that, as Bell insightfully put it, "our society has more options and can make a moral choice"), was rapidly turning the art into more of a science.[7] "It seems to me that the real usefulness of crystal-ball-gazing lies in the fact that it provides a frame of reference, a set of guideposts," suggested Edward E. Booher, president of McGraw-Hill, in 1967, quite a different perspective on futurism than that of just a decade earlier.[8] In his introduction to Herman Kahn and Anthony Wiener's 1967 *The Year 2000*, Daniel Bell made clear the scientific nature, even sobriety, of this new school of futurism. "We have begun to assemble statistical time-series both to plot trend-lines and to extrapolate likely developments," Bell dryly explained, and "begun to construct 'models' or likely combinations of trends and developments in order to uncover the connections and causal relations between variables."[9] The sea change in the world of tomorrow did not go unnoticed, especially among those with a particular interest in being in the right place at the right time. "Suddenly 'the future' is a subject that we can, with some confidence, know something about—a province no less worth exploring than, say, the past," declared *Fortune* in 1967, excited about the implications for its readers in the business world.[10]

Unlike past genres of prediction, what soon became known as "new futurism" more consciously acknowledged that tomorrow was up for grabs and could be shaped by those who did the grabbing. "Mankind lurches along in an unquantifiable mix of historical determinism, human will and accident" while "futurism is by definition deterministic—an attempt to marshal the perceived forces of the age and cast them forward into probabilities," *Newsweek* said in 1973, in its coverage of the mini-movement.[11] Just as history was written by winners, in other words, so could be the future, an idea that more people and more institutions were cleverly embracing in order to further their own agendas.

New futurism could actually be traced back to World War II–era "operations analysis," out of which the Rand Corporation was founded after the war. The decision-making techniques used by Rand for the Defense Department spread throughout the federal government during the Kennedy and Johnson administrations (especially by Robert McNamara in his management—or mismanagement—of the Vietnam War) at the same time that business schools and corporate planners were developing similar methods based on a systematic assessment of alternative futures. The Hudson Institute and Stanford Research Institute were other key players in postwar futurism, also focusing on Cold War–related scientific and technological arenas such as arms control, weapons development, automation, and space exploration.[12] Although heavily freighted with the layers of 1960s-style bureaucracy from today's perspective, the impact of new futurism upon problem solving among the intellectual elite of the day cannot be overestimated. "By 1977 this new way of dealing with the future will be recognized at home and abroad as a salient American characteristic," boasted *Fortune*, something that would only further the United States's identity as the most forward-looking nation in history.[13]

The idea that the future could now be managed was, of course, especially appealing to Corporate America. Many American companies were by the late 1960s hiring staff economists and marketing specialists to plan for the short range and, increasingly, using scientists for medium- and long-range projects. "You just can't sit still," said Carlos A. Efferson, manager of organization planning at Kaiser Industries, seconded by his colleague Robert W. Roth, director of corporate planning, who felt that "If you don't know what's going to happen, it's like sitting with blinders on."[14] Rather than be concerned with specifics, companies like Kaiser were interested in identifying probable scenarios and then making decisions to prepare for those likelihoods. As Pierre Wack subsequently described in a pair of articles in the *Harvard Business Review*, a team (of which he was a part) at Royal Dutch Shell in Europe developed in the late 1960s and early 1970s the technique of scenario planning, its analysis of the global business environment helping them prepare for the 1973 oil crisis and 1981 oil glut.[15] Rand's Delphi technique, which brought to the surface a wealth of ideas and information from multiple rounds of intensive interviews with experts in a given field, was also ideal for this kind of corporate futurism, as was gaming or role-playing in which participants developed strategies and tactics for hypothetical developments. That most of these techniques had their origins in military maneuvers—a legacy of Rand's defense roots—was no coincidence, a clear expression of the intimate relationship between the federal government and Corporate America within the military-industrial complex of the 1960s.

Despite all these brilliant minds and millions of dollars, the unpredictability of the future would, in retrospect, often win the day. Rand, continuing its overaggressive forecasts in space exploration (no doubt keeping its Air Force client happy), believed in 1966 that there would be a permanent base on the moon well before the year 2000 and that man would have landed on Mars. Rand also thought that marriages in the future would benefit from the wide acceptance of personality-control drugs, which would be used in interesting ways. "If a wife or husband seems to be unusually grouchy on a given evening," as *Time* described the company's prediction, "a spouse will be able to pop down to the corner drugstore, buy some anti-grouch pills, and slip them into the coffee." TEMPO claimed that with computer automation, "there just won't be enough work to go around" by 1984, and that "moonlighting will become as socially unacceptable as bigamy," predictions as old as Grandpa's rocking chair. Equally creaky was Buckminster Fuller's argument that because of universal prosperity, all politics would simply go away, while other pie-in-the-skyers looked to the emergence of a homogenous global culture (referred to by some as "the culture bomb") as the deliverer of world peace. Most acutely and absurdly expressing such utopian imaginings, however, was the prophetlike-named Emmanuel Mesthene, executive director of the IBM-Harvard project. "My hunch is that man may have finally expiated his original sin, and might now aspire to bliss," Mesthene thought, proving that even the biggest brains in the room were swayed more by mythology than by history.[16]

Despite such thinking, which could have more easily been gleaned from a Magic 8 Ball, the adoption of futurism by American businesses continued unabated into the 1970s, as companies tried to get an edge on tomorrow. "'Futurism,' the systematic endeavor to anticipate developments and thereby control our destiny, particularly the effects of technological change, has become a new industry in the past four years," observed Edward T. Chase in the *New Republic* in his 1969 review of Peter Drucker's new book, *The Age of Discontinuity: Guidelines to Our Changing Society.* Chase considered Drucker to be a "super-futurist," citing this and his previous books— *The New Society, America's Next Twenty Years,* and *Landmarks of Tomorrow*— as a seminal body of knowledge, exploring technology and its social impact. Drucker's prediction of the rise of knowledge industries, as well as his understanding of how quantum leaps in new technologies made extrapolation of trends a dangerous exercise, separated him from the rest of the futurist crowd, Chase believed.[17]

Still, Rand's Delphi technique remained the hottest approach to futurism for Corporate America, with more than fifty companies employing it in 1970. Introduced to the business arena only six years earlier, Delphi (after the home of the Greek oracle) was now being used by McDonnell Douglas to forecast commercial air transportation, by Weyerhaeuser to plan for what might happen in construction, and by Smith Kline to explore the future of medicine, illustrating the tremendous range and flexibility of the method. TRW was probably the biggest fan of Delphi, juggling no fewer than fourteen panels with an average of seventeen interviewees on each. The Japanese also had discovered Delphi, something that American companies would have been quite alarmed about had they included "major foreign competition" as one of their hypothetical future scenarios.[18]

NORMAL, STODGY PEOPLE

With futurism (also called futuristics and futurology, the latter term coined in the 1940s) having gained the attention of the media and general public by the mid-1970s, the time was ripe to do what every field does when it reaches a certain critical mass—hold a conference. The Second General Assembly of the World Future Society (WFS) in 1975 in Washington, D.C., could be considered futurism's coming-out party, the adolescent field ready to show itself off to the world. The Society, which was formed in 1966 and published the *Futurist*, a semimonthly journal, had had a first assembly in 1971, but this one made it clear that futurism had grown up. About 2,000 of the society's 18,000 members—a disparate mix of academics, businesspeople, government wonks, and the just curious—rubbed shoulders with the likes of Herman Kahn, Daniel Bell, and Alvin Toffler, a dream come true for both professional and amateur futurists. The conference was decidedly less spacey than the previous one (organizers passed on an astrology booth this time), reflecting both the changes in American culture in the past four years and the infusion of what Constance Holden called "the normal, stodgy people, the bureaucrats, and people responsible for injecting thought into government." The conference also revealed that futurism was gradually broadening its base, its practices being applied not just in high-technology but in more "low-technology" arenas such as retail.[19]

In 1977, Edward Cornish, head of the WFS, published *The Study of the Future*, the most definitive guide to the art and science of predicting tomorrow up to that point. "If anything is important, it is the future," Cornish convincingly argued in the book's preface, if only because that's where all of us would spend the rest of our lives. Although the future was dismal (section titles included "The Elusiveness of Happiness," "The Scarcities of Abundance," and "The Death of Hope," and that was just Chapter 1), futurism was doing gangbusters business, the angst of the late 1970s sparking huge interest in the field. "The future is smashing into all of us so forcefully that it can no longer be ignored," Cornish felt, the "maelstrom of social change" demanding new and better methods of forecasting. Like Herman Kahn a decade and a half earlier with his *On Thermonuclear War*, Cornish believed that futurists had to do more than just ponder the possibilities of tomorrow. "The study of the future may well be the most exciting intellectual enterprise of today," he wrote, "but it is more than an exciting adventure: it is an awesome responsibility." Interestingly, Cornish, like many futurists of the time, believed that affecting change in the short term was difficult at best—the causes of major social and economic problems like poverty too deeply rooted—while virtually anything in the distant future could be achieved. "A seed of change planted today can become a mighty force in the years ahead," he thought, the role of the futurist not unlike a modern-day Johnny Appleseed.[20]

The government too was getting more into the futurist act in a number of ways. Congress had recently passed a measure that each of its committees had to have a "foresight" component, and Senator Ted Kennedy was pushing a bill that would establish an "experimental futures agency" to guide policy in energy and transportation. As well, a number of states and cities were creating commissions on the year 2000—California Tomorrow, the Commission on Minnesota's Future, Alternatives for Washington, and Goals for Dallas—to figure out where they wanted to be in another twenty-five years, more evidence of the spreading tentacles of futurism.[21] Trends in pop culture also bore out the rise in interest in all things future. In 1945, just thirty-five science fiction books—the most popular form of futurism at the time—had been published, while there were a whopping 900 such books published in 1975. With both sci-fi fans and "normal, stodgy people" having a heightened interest in the new possibilities of tomorrow, futurism had, it appeared, gone mainstream.[22]

Reinventing futurism for the demands of a new age required this generation of practitioners to reject the predictions and approaches of their predecessors, however. "Notably missing from . . . forecasts are the science-fiction fantasies often associated with the 'world of tomorrow'—intergalactic pleasure cruises, vast cities built underground, robots doing the work while humans live in idle luxury," observed *US News & World Report* in 1974, reporting that now "practical forecasts come from hard-headed economists, scientists, psychiatrists and other experts [who] are in the serious business of examining future probabilities based on what is happening right now—and searching for ways to avoid the worst of those potential developments."[23]

Based on this kind of superior, left-brain thinking, some believed, even catastrophes might be able to be averted. "Research now underway is concentrating on development of new techniques for analyzing and forecasting international crises," reported *Science Digest* in 1977, quite an amazing achievement if at all true. Robert P. Burton, a computer science professor at Brigham Young, felt that "continuing trends are only one dimension of the future" and, by anticipating what he called "discontinuities," events such as Pearl Harbor, the Cuban missile crisis, and the North Korean attack on South Korea might not have happened. Burton's research was based on "catastrophe theory," something mathematicians were especially excited about (and something that perhaps could only have been developed in the catastrophe-obsessed 1970s). With his "Parabolic Umbilic Catastrophe" model, which he described as "a two-dimensional perspective projection of a three-dimensional orthogonal projection of a four-dimensional cross-section of a six-dimensional surface," Burton believed that even wildly aberrant futures might be able to be detected before they occurred.[24]

Not surprisingly, especially given the alternative current that ran throughout the 1970s, there was an inevitable backlash to this decidedly square style of futurism. Completely on the other side of the futurism fence were people like William Irwin Thompson, an ex-MIT professor who abandoned his faith in technology to create Lindisfarne, a commune-like retreat in Southampton on Long Island. Thompson considered Lindisfarne (after the sixth-century Irish monastery) to be, as a visitor in 1977 described it, "one of several pulsating points of energy spread out across the globe from which [a] new culture would soon emerge," having detailed his unique vision in his 1971 book *At the Edge of History*, which was nominated for a National Book Award. Another utopian community trying to chart a different kind of future in the 1970s was New Alchemy Village in Woods Hole, Massachusetts, its prophets also subscribing to the central belief that technology was a doomsday scenario. Likewise, Doris Lessing's 1971 *Briefing for a Descent into Hell*, which she described as "inner space fiction," was an alternative kind of futurism that countered official versions promoted by the "establishment." With technology continuing to advance within an era subscribing to the ethos that, as the popular margarine commercial of the day put it, "it's not nice to fool Mother Nature," there seemed to be room for everyone in the future-friendly 1970s.[25]

In addition to the small but compelling group of visionaries offering countercultural interpretations of tomorrow, new futurism was also subject to close scrutiny by the mainstream. As futurism got more "scientific," expectations for predictions to be more accurate than in the past grew, the cost, you could say, of doing more business. The maturation of the field thus opened it up to much more criticism, with some going so far as to actually look back to see if futurists had gotten it right or wrong. Americans, at least, had rarely taken the time or effort for such trivialities, something that played a significant role in the field's mixed, at best, success. As often as not, futurists had to date gotten it wrong (or, more precisely, just missed it), giving the field a less than stellar reputation as the 1970s drew to a close. "Plainly, though everybody is obsessed with divining tomorrow, no one on earth can yet reliably do it," argued *Time* in 1979, claiming that "economic prophecy even at its most serious level is not, even with its computer printouts, all that far off from tea-leaf reading."[26] "Their visions of the future compare in subtlety to the plot of *Star Wars*," remarked Lewis Lapham that same year, after attending what he appropriately called "one of those convocations at which augurs on loan from the literary or academic professions peer anxiously into the mists of time future and make dismal guesses about the shape of things to come."[27]

Other brainy people too considered futurism, despite (or because of) its new popularity, more sizzle than steak. Economist Lester Thurow called it "the intellectual's version of going to the palm reader," while even Robert L. Heilbroner, one of the stars of the field, admitted that "there's an awful lot of chic in this thing" and that "people take long-range forecasting much too seriously." Roy Amara, head of the Institute for the Future, one of the top organizations in the field, conceded that "the more important the study of the future becomes, the harder it becomes," in effect blaming greater and faster change (and its more serious consequences) for the industry's spotty record. Despite their occasional success, most futurists continued to look for the Holy Grail of futurism—a method by which to truly understand the laws of change in order to predict it. Amara himself was busy working on something he called a "unified field theory," described by *Saturday Review* in 1979 as "an all-encompassing explanation for human events equivalent to the laws that Einstein hoped would explain physical events." Amara had yet to locate his skeleton key to the future, just more evidence that, as the ancient Greeks expressed it, "Fate is too strong for thee and for the gods."[28]

Increasingly fragmented, held accountable, and in the public's eye, the field of futurism was experiencing classic growing pains. Even within the field, divisiveness seemed to be growing, with "old school" futurists not particularly impressed with the new kids on the prediction block and their computer printouts. "There's no way in which it [futurism] can allow for the unexpected—except by guessing," pointed out Isaac Asimov in 1979, the result being that "prophets almost never see what, later on, turns out to have been obvious."[29] Few, if any, in the late 1960s saw the energy crisis or spiraling inflation coming, for example, just the kind of "discontinuity" that was wreaking havoc with futurists' best-laid plans. More amazingly, very few had predicted the en masse arrival of women in the workplace, equivalent within the universe of futurism to somehow overlooking the proverbial elephant in the room.[30] For some, understanding the laws of change resided less in complex theory than in common sense. "The best prophets will always be those who have just the serendipitous combination of knowledge, hunch and imagination to ask the right questions," wrote Merrill Sheils, in his 1979 essay (titled "The Cracked Crystal Ball") for *Newsweek*.[31]

Critics aside, there was little doubt that new futurism had put the once-fledgling field largely populated by eccentrics on the map. In just twenty-five years, 200 organizations offering futurism research services had arisen, the phenomenon driven by the new, scientifically grounded belief that the history of tomorrow was not fatalistic but deterministic. The cultural backdrop for the rise of futurism as a business had been, of course, the Cold War, as the American defense industry strove to keep (at least) one step ahead of its communist superpower counterpart. By 1979, futurism had reached a state of intellectual promiscuity, its proponents not particularly choosy about what they did and with whom. "Nothing that is human is alien to the futurologist," wrote James Traub that year, "he will study the future of anything." As well, clients could now choose from a wide variety of futurist methodologies generally falling into one of three camps—the analytic, quantitative approach based in the social sciences, the "Big Picture" designed to provide cultural context, or the metaphysical school offering an alternative (some would say flaky) vision of tomorrow. Companies with fat wallets like General Electric or Exxon might contract out for all of the above, using futurism as an essential part of their operations. "We use long-term forecasting as a starting point for all strategic planning," explained Ian Wilson of GE in 1979, the information plugged into the company's new, "interactive multilevel planning system." If nothing else, bringing in such experts opened up a dialogue about where the company should direct its resources, "forc[ing] everyone to spell out their assumptions about the future," said Wilson, something well worth $20,000 or so a pop.[32]

CAN WE AFFORD TOMORROW?

The rise of new futurism not only expanded the field but, not coincidentally, made it decidedly darker. A utopian future seemed to start evaporating with the assassination of President Kennedy, the slide only compounded by the plethora of other major traumas of the 1960s. In 1965, a full five years before the release of *Future Shock*, Alvin Toffler wrote an article for *Horizon* magazine in which he spelled out most of the ideas that would go into his landmark book that captured the anxiousness of the times. Fittingly titled "The Future as a Way of Life," the piece explained the origins of the concept of future shock, a riff on the "culture shock" or disorientation many Americans reportedly experienced as they increasingly traveled abroad in the mid-1960s. The "premature arrival of the future may well be the most important disease of tomorrow," he argued, a kind of culture shock in one's own backyard that all Americans would suffer from and that, more importantly, was not going to go away. "Change is avalanching down upon our heads and most people are utterly unprepared to cope with it," Toffler maintained, citing a host of factors—the shift away from an agriculture-based society, rising urbanization, the array of scientific and technological achievements in the twentieth century, and exponential growth in population, information, and energy consumption—for this break in history equivalent only to "the shift from barbarism to civilization." Even more radical change ahead—the blurring of the lines between man and machine, the cracking of the code of aging, the overthrowing of the occupational structure of society, resulting in a much different kind of workplace—would bring about an era of "postcivilization," placing "unendurable stress on a great many people."[33]

Rather than leave readers hanging with such a heavy message, something that other visionaries soon would, with their own ominous predictions, Toffler had some remedies for future shock. "We need to begin by creating a stronger future-consciousness on the part of the public, and not just by means of Buck Rogers comic strips and articles about the marvels of space travel or medical research," he argued, believing that the personal and social implications of the future were at least as important as the technological. Toffler envisioned an interest in the future equal to that of medievalists' belief in the afterlife, a nonsupernatural faith in what tomorrow might bring. Creating a future-centric society, he insisted, with unrestricted speculation encouraged, courses in possibilities and probabilities taught at universities, and science fiction elevated from lowbrow literature to sociology, represented actionable ways to minimize the inevitability of future shock. Successfully "travers[ing] the passage to postcivilization" was possible, he concluded, but only if we "form[ed] a better, clearer, stronger conception of what lies ahead."[34]

With most Americans stunned by the events of the 1960s, the idea of "shock" was an especially compelling way to imagine the future. Toffler actually wasn't the only one to use the word "shock" to describe the future that appeared to be taking shape in the later part of the century. John Rader Platt, who a few years earlier had recognized that getting to the moon was more a matter of priorities than anything else, also believed that by the mid-1960s the world was in the midst of what he termed a "cultural shock-front," a reference to the physical cause of an aerodynamic sonic boom. "I think we may be now in the time of most rapid change in the whole evolution of the human race, either past or to come," the University of Chicago professor of physics boldly claimed in 1965, seeing civilization at the peak of exponentially rising technical achievements.[35] Michael Harrington's 1965 *The Accidental Century* was almost Huxley redux, a warning that material abundance was coming at the very high cost of an overautomated, soulless culture.[36] And while *The World in 1984*, a vast British collection of the outlooks of no fewer than 100 authorities published that same year, certainly had some good news (artificial body parts, climate control, robot servants), it also foresaw rampant pollution, the demise of wildlife, and a common need for behavior-influencing drugs to control "neuroses" in just twenty years' time.[37]

As with the turning of every decade, the beginning of the 1970s was cause for a spike in futurism, an opportunity to look back on the past ten years and make predictions for the next ten. For the first time, however, less would be more when it came to the future, as the concepts of limits and constraints crept into the conversation about tomorrow. Americans' "two-of-a-kind" urge, so prevalent in the postwar years, seemed to be a relic of the distant past as the American Way of Life trimmed its sails. "Ownership is obsolete," declared Buckminster Fuller two weeks before the end of the 1960s, echoed by Princeton sociology professor Suzanne Keller, who believed "we are at the end of an era when the measure of all things is a material measure." B. F. Skinner thought "the idea of redesigning a way of life is going to be a dominant theme of the 70s"—a perspective that few people just a decade earlier could have even deciphered—while others saw a bad moon on the rise. Arnold Toynbee, for example, predicted "the present worldwide discontent and unrest will become more acute, and will express itself in worse and worse outbreaks of violence," not at all something that most futurists of the past, filled with dreams of international harmony, would have imagined.[38]

What had gone wrong? Automation, after all, had not caused rampant unemployment as feared during the postwar years (it had in fact created more jobs), and widespread famine due to overpopulation also had yet to come to pass (people were actually less hungry because of the development of new grains).[39] The simple answer was that "Faith in science and technology has given way to fear of their consequences," as *Time* succinctly put it in late 1969, the clearest explanation of why the future would never be the same again.[40] Even the normally perky *Life* noticed that scientists were now the bearers of bad news. "All of a sudden they [scientists] seem to be going out of their way to scare us," the magazine fretted in 1970, as "just over the horizon, we are told, such cataclysms as earthquakes, radiation storms, mass famine and even a new Ice Age lie in wait." Even worse, few men or women of science were coming forward with ways to avoid such nightmare scenarios. "There is *no*, I repeat, *no* conceivable technological solution to the problems we face," said Paul Erlich, a Stanford biologist who was about to drop his own whopper of a bomb on an increasingly bummed-out public.[41]

For some, in fact, it was time to start completely fresh, an idea that postwar futurists would have considered beyond credibility. "Americans have lost control of the machinery of their society, and only new values and a new culture can restore control," wrote Charles Reich in his 1970 bestseller *The*

Greening of America, adding that "we seem to be living in a society that no one created and that no one wants." Rather than pursue science and technology purely because we could, Reich seemed to be saying, it was time to approach them quite differently. "Today's emerging consciousness seeks a new knowledge of what it means to be human, in order that the machine, having been built, may now be turned to human ends," he concluded, proposing we chart a new course in the voyage of the future.[42]

Drawing on his theories that had by now been percolating in the zeitgeist of the late 1960s, Toffler reached essentially the same conclusion in his 1970 bestseller *Future Shock*, a work that elevated futurism into the stuff of watercooler conversation. Everyone seemed to be reading the 505-page book—even President Nixon, who had his Science Advisory Committee buy copies to see if there was anything in it they should know about. "Alvin Toffler . . . may become this season's Marshall McLuhan," thought *Fortune*, a fitting development given that McLuhan had provided a quote for the book ("*Future Shock* by Alvin Toffler is 'where it's at,'" his groovy blurb went). Toffler's key message was that "we have broken irretrievably with the past," the reason so many Americans were suffering from "the disease of change" (one of his seemingly multiplying definitions of future shock over the years). Whether alternatively defined as "the dizzying disorientation brought on by the premature arrival of the future" or, more simply, "the response to overstimulation," future shock was in essence the result of a toxic society. "Alvin Toffler's thesis is that 'too much change in too short a time' is already responsible for widespread stress and disorientation, and that unless the rate and direction of change are controlled, psychic and physical illness on a massive scale is inevitable," summarized *Saturday Review* in its review of the book. How could we avoid being, in Toffler's words, "doomed to a massive adaptational breakdown"? We had to "humanize distant tomorrows," he believed, that is, evict the ghost from the machine by resurrecting the soul of the nation and the world, an idea similar to Reich's own call for a higher, deeper form of consciousness.[43] Although panned by many critics who viewed the book more as self-help fluff or pseudo–social science ("future schlock," Robert Claiborne called it in his review for the *Nation*), *Future Shock* would go on to earn a place within the pantheon of twentieth-century future lit alongside works by Wells, Huxley, and Orwell.[44]

Although Toffler made most of the headlines as the 1970s kicked off with a thud, he was hardly the only one to pronounce that the future was virtually unrecognizable from that of a decade past. "I do not think any other generation of Americans would have asked the question 'Can we afford tomorrow?'" remarked J. Irwin Miller in 1971, astutely recognizing how this future differed from all others. Miller, a businessman, was part of a 200-person Committee for Economic Development whose charge was to answer that very question in order to guide public policy by helping organizations set priorities and allocate resources. Miller believed that we had achieved what he termed a "first American dream"—the conquering of the wilderness, creation of modern cities and roads, material affluence for many, and active participation in both education and politics—but had by the early 1970s somehow become an uncertain and fearful people with no second dream in sight.[45]

Others also assessed the state of the union by comparing the current future to that of the recent past. "Everything that science fiction once imagined was coming true, and nothing—if we really put the best brains to the task—was beyond achievement," Peter Schrag wrote that same year, remembering the golden days of postwar-era futurism. "We were offered a future of robot maids, commercial space travel, effective weight and appetite control, human hibernation, weather control, genetic manipulation, direct electronic communication with the brain, and all the rest," he continued, making it clear that this kind of tomorrow was now part of yesterday. With the nation's postwar balloon deflated by an unpopular war, stagflation, Japanese competition, and the ecology movement, the future, up to this point infinite, now had clearly marked boundaries. "There remain fatal limitations in a future where the horizon can be enlarged only at exorbitant expense in resources and personal alienation," Schrag concluded, suggesting that the nation may very well not be able to afford to invest either financially or psychologically in tomorrow.[46]

The parade of Chicken Littles proclaiming the sky was falling—maybe literally—continued throughout the early 1970s. Jay W. Forrester's 1971 *World Dynamics* not only challenged the historic foundation of futurism—perpetual growth—but proposed that American culture could actually soon be heading downhill, a radical idea after a couple of centuries of economic and social progress. "The question is only a matter of when and how growth will cease, not whether it will cease," wrote Forrester, a professor at MIT, arguing that the industrial world as a whole could be embarking on a new age of declining expectations.[47] More than one critic could not help but think that we had made a kind of Faustian bargain, gaining a rich scientific future at the expense of a moral one.[48] "If 1971 is the future of 1961, who wants futures?" asked John Thompson in *Harper's*, a reasonable question given the plethora of doomsday scenarios in circulation at the time.[49]

Also from MIT in 1972 came "The Limits to Growth," a forecast seeing catastrophic problems ahead in the areas of population, natural resources, hunger, and the environment.[50] Funded by the Volkswagen Foundation and sponsored by the "Club of Rome" (a group of thirty prominent European businesspeople dedicated to "the predicament of mankind"), the MIT study was virtually a death sentence for the planet, decreeing that "the limits to growth on this planet will be reached sometime within the next 100 years [and that] the most probable result will be a rather sudden and uncontrollable decline in population and industrial capacity." The founder of the Club of Rome, Aurelio Peccei, posed a question that many people around the world, even Americans, were beginning to ask. "What is so magic about continuous growth?" he wondered, thinking that "a new generation will say 'To hell with prosperity, survival is what matters.'"[51] Wanting others to ask that question, Peccei and his colleagues published "The Limits to Growth" as a book in 1973 and promoted it heavily with news conferences and by giving away thousands of free copies to influential people.[52]

With *The Limits to Growth* now the state of the art of futurism, the mid-1970s marked the nadir of the future in the twentieth century, as the global community wallowed in despair. Once mostly about how to create a better world, futurism was now mostly about how to possibly avert a worse one, a 180-degree shift in just twenty years. The wake of the ships-passing-in-the-night of futurism and the future—the former moving at maximum speed, the latter barely chugging along—could be most felt in the tomorrow-will-always-be-better-than-today United States. Predominantly progressive, optimistic, and even utopian for the first three-quarters of the century, tomorrow was now something not to look forward to but rather to dread, perhaps for the first time in American history on such a mass scale. Nothing short of the nation's jeremiad appeared to be in jeopardy, its special, divinely ordained mission on the brink of crumbling as self-doubt crept into the country's collective identity.

Indeed, it was becoming hard to find anyone who had anything positive to say about what would come next. The Institute for the Future, a San Francisco–based nonprofit formed in 1968 and "dedicated exclusively to systematic and comprehensive studies of the long-range future," issued a report in 1973 called "Project Aware" that rivaled "The Limits to Growth" in pessimism. Commissioned by a group of corporate heavy hitters—du Pont, Lever Brothers, Monsanto, Scott Paper, and Chase Manhattan Bank—the report reflected the bad vibes of the times and predicted even worse vibes to come. "Government incompetence, corruption and disregard for the law are judged to be largely permanent features of the political system," the Project

Aware report read, with citizens to experience a growing "sense of power-lessness" over their own lives. While there were some things to be cheerful about—sex discrimination would decline, hair transplants would be greatly improved, and the "throwaway clothing" business looked very promising—Project Aware went on to say, the overall quality of life for most would be lower in a decade, as social problems worsened.[53] Was it any surprise that Hollywood, with its read on the American public's mood, was now begin-ning to churn out disaster movies like *The Poseidon Adventure*, *Towering Inferno*, and *Earthquake?*

Absolute rock bottom was, however, Robert L. Heilbroner's 1974 *An Inquiry into the Human Prospect.* In the book, Heilbroner could come up with precious few ways to get out of the hole America had dug for itself, amazed at how quickly the hopes and dreams of just a decade earlier had evaporated. In his 1963 *The Making of Society*, Heilbroner had prophesied the spread of democracy, general abundance, and "new areas of fulfillment—education, the arts and sciences, recreation and personal cultivation, the beautification of the environment," making just minor revisions to the book in a 1968 edi-tion. In his new, pithy (150 pages) book, however, Heilbroner, an economics professor at the New School for Social Research, believed that "the outlook for man is painful, difficult, perhaps desperate, and the hope that can be held out for his future prospect is very slim indeed," a complete reversal that cap-tured the sentiment many felt as the ideals of JFK's New Frontier and LBJ's Great Society became distant memories. "In a single decade since the early 1960s we have compressed a lifetime's transformation from youthful exuber-ance to the gloom of a disillusioned maturity," wrote Melville J. Ulmer in his review of the book for the *New Republic*, blaming the long list of late 1960s and early 1970s trials and tribulations—fears of overpopulation, depletion of natural resources, urban crime, Vietnam, Watergate, airplane hijackings, the energy crisis and, to boot, the generation divide—as the reasons for the nation's fall from grace. Melvin Maddocks, in his own review for *Time*, put it a bit more simply. "This short, urgent essay on the world's chances for sur-vival has all the cheerfulness of a medical warning delivered to a middle-aged man after a bad checkup," Maddocks wrote, but he also observed the deeper currents that ran through the book. "What Heilbroner may express most clearly in this essay is the present fatigued mood of a generation of intellectu-als who began, like good Americans, by believing that they had nearly all the answers and have come to despair that they have any," he thought, consider-ing the book, in a nutshell, an "epitaph for liberalism."[54]

Two events in the mid-1970s, the quarter-century mark in 1975 and the

Bicentennial in 1976, however, served as opportunities to reinvent the idea of tomorrow and begin the long climb back to an optimistic future. "We've lost all idea of what Americans are and what America stands for," thought Richard B. Morris, a professor at Columbia and president-elect of the American Historical Society, but "with the Bicentennial, there should be an opportunity to go back to what we were."[55] "During this Bicentennial year many people in many places are peering into crystal balls trying to extrapolate the future," agreed Sol Linowitz, former US ambassador to the Organization of American States, also seeing the beginning of America's third century as a chance to "remember who we are and what we are."[56] Fluffier takes on the future during the Bicentennial showed that it might not be all doom and gloom, that America might be able to afford to invest in tomorrow after all.

Musing over what clothes might be like when the country celebrated its Tricentennial, for example, Bonwit Teller asked twenty-two leading fashion designers to put together a collection for the year 2076 to be displayed in the department store's New York, Los Angeles, and Chicago windows. Bill Blass, inspired by actual styles of the 1960s, went with silver sequin pants and a white jersey poncho, while Calvin Klein came up with a stretch jumpsuit equipped with a bag in which one could carry necessities. Donna Karan took an innovative approach with her piece of fabric lined with a rope that could configure the garment into a variety of shapes, but it was Diane Von Furstenberg who pushed fashion—or the lack thereof—the furthest. Simply painting a mannequin in "jungle colors," Von Furstenberg predicted that people wouldn't wear clothes in 2076, choosing instead to paint their bodies, probably not an idea that would have occurred to visionaries who had not lived in the late 1960s.[57] Such events centered around the Bicentennial, while no doubt silly, served as important symbolic reminders that America could and should look forward to a third century, something many eggheads were seriously suggesting was not worth doing.

Finally, Herman Kahn's new book, *The Next 200 Years*, was almost a 1970s-style happy face, a solid argument that Americans of the future would have many a nice day to look forward to. Not only would world population growth slow down, Kahn believed, but widespread affluence, plenty of food, and "virtually eternal energy sources" also were out there on the blue horizon. Even the Club of Rome, whose 1972 "The Limits to Growth" report was deemed by *Time* to be a "suicide pact," had apparently changed its tune, now in 1976 saying that growth, when managed appropriately, could actually narrow the gap between the world's haves and have-nots. Futurists had definitely turned a corner, looking to a new century and new millennium for a fresh start. "A.D. 2000 has now replaced 1984 as the favorite year for specula-tion," wrote Stefan Kanfer for *Time,* with prophecy "the most extreme form of curiosity and a vital part of all Western societies."[58]

THE POPULATION BOMB

Before these rays of sunshine burst through the clouds, however, com-mon thought was that the storm would only get worse. Much as Reverend Thomas Malthus in the eighteenth century had predicted that too many people would one day be roaming the planet, dystopians of the later twenti-eth century argued that the world was becoming dangerously overpopulated. Despite the increasing popularity of the birth control pill in the West, fears of there being too little food to support billions more people was a big chunk of future shock, along with the prospect of our being packed in like sardines. Continued advances in the various sciences also posed major changes ahead in reproduction and birth control, possibilities made only more disconcert-ing by the upheaval in gender relationships and sexual politics. Dramatic steps had to be taken to avert or at least control this scenario, some leading futurists believed. By 1990, Isaac Asimov thought in 1965, for example, "gov-ernmentally organized measures for birth control will be taken for granted over almost all the world," practices that would make some areas of the world very child-centered and other areas exactly the opposite. "The recognition of the population explosion as the prime danger to man may make children unpopular and parenthood seem vaguely antisocial," he maintained.[59]

The birth of the nation's 200 millionth citizen in 1967 only served to throw grease on this fire, reflecting Americans' new concerns about the idea of growth. "The arrival of the 200 millionth American seems to have revived the Malthusian panic which periodically overtakes so many of our thinkers and planners," observed Richard M. Scammon, former director of the US Census Bureau, reminding *Life* readers that population anxiety was hardly a new thing. Scammon believed that late 1960s fears of overpopulation were alarmist, at least when it came to the United States, and used the event to make clear there'd be plenty of space for everyone for a very long time. (Even a billion Americans would create a population density roughly equivalent to that of Switzerland, he explained, a country that seemed, if anything, under-populated.) "Perhaps because our big metropolitan areas are genuinely in the midst of crisis, or perhaps because we are all Jeffersonians at heart, we seem to be victims of a sort of demophobia—a fear of people," Scammon surmised, hitting the nail on the head.[60]

Voices of such reason were few and far between, however, or at least weren't as interesting as those predicting scary consequences for an overcrowded nation and planet. "Far-ahead thinkers say that by the time the United States has 400 million people, men may have to forego determining on their own where they will live," fretted *Nation's Business*, concerned that such a kind of zoning would naturally lead to a loss of personal independence and individual freedom.[61] A birth control pill for men, some believed, could be a partial solution, although further advances in genetics could take us down some strange paths. After returning from a genetics conference in Tokyo in 1968, Charles Birch, head of the Sydney University School of Biological Sciences in Australia, envisioned not only oral contraceptives for men but pills that "husbands" could take to decide the gender of their offspring. As more work was done in a new field, molecular physics, Birch felt, it was not unreasonable to think that people one day could even reproduce asexually, not unlike plants.[62]

With some predicting there would be 11 to 12 billion people on Earth in just half a century, overpopulation became a national concern and, resultantly, a marketable property. Reprising the legendary, ominous prediction made by Malthus in his 1798 *Essay on Population* but packaging it within the framework of new futurism, Paul Ehrlich had quite a hit with his 1971 book *The Population Bomb*. "In the 1970's the world will undergo famine [and] hundreds of millions of people are going to starve to death," he wrote, reinforcing the belief among many that troubles of biblical proportions were upon us. Erlich toured college campuses throughout the 1970s, preaching to the choir about the threat of overpopulation and its evil twin, Western overconsumption.[63] Fears of overpopulation could be found in less erudite places as well. On the 1965–1968 television show *Lost in Space*, for example, which took place in the far-off world of 1997, the space family Robinson had left Earth, a "desperately overcrowded planet," for the wide-open spaces of Alpha Centuri.[64] Interestingly, birthrates in the 1970s were actually declining in the West but increasing pretty much everywhere else, a sign that the population bomb had less to do with a shortage of food and other resources and more to do with how the coming tidal wave of other-skinned people around the world would make white-centric America a smaller player on the global stage. The Cold War was one thing—one superpower versus another—but the thought of the nation competing with perhaps dozens of countries with bigger, browner populations was (and remains) extremely frightening to many.[65]

Fears about how much food it would take to feed an overpopulated population were driving some Americans to take drastic measures, not unlike how, a generation earlier, many had built bomb shelters to survive disaster. Preparing for a great famine in the United States, thousands of people in 1975 were buying large amounts of "survival foods"—dehydrated or freeze-dried grains, fruits, vegetables, meats, and meat substitutes stored in specially designed containers. "No one likes the idea of world food shortages increasing," said Ronald G. Whipple, president of Dixie Beehive Foods, one of the leaders in the "insurance against disaster" business, as some preferred to call it, "but we're doing our best to help people to prepare." Another company, Rainy Day Foods, was a little more blunt, telling potential customers, "Remember, it wasn't raining when Noah built the ark," while a distributor of the foods was including a newspaper story with the headline "L.A. Police Training for Food Riots" in its promotional literature. The biblical reference was not coincidental, with both of these companies and most purchasers of the products Mormons, who were following the church's guideline to always have a one-year supply of food on hand in case of famine. Mormons weren't the only ones wondering if there'd be enough food on the nation's table, however. "Will there be riots in the streets over food? Is the U.S. going to become the next Biafra?" asked *Science Digest*, questions to which most if not all experts responded with a resounding no. The simple possibility for such a worst-case scenario was revealing, however, another reminder that the metaphoric American horn of plenty was no longer spilling over.[66]

EARTH DAY

Like overpopulation, late 1960s and 1970s urban angst was woven into future shock, with some believing an entirely new model was required in order to skirt total disaster. Postwar urban renewal had not been a success, to put it mildly, and the crime, pollution, and racial unrest of the late 1960s furthered white flight to the suburbs. Even those in the business had few signs of hope for American cities in the early 1970s. "We *could* build great cities today, but I don't think we have the will to do it," wrote Harvey S. Perloff, the dean on architecture and urban planning at UCLA, in *The Future of the United States Government: Toward the Year 2000*, a 1971 collection of essays he edited.[67] Another authority thought in 1974 that in twenty years, large cities would be mainly populated by "the young seeking excitement and the old who have nowhere else to go," a scenario bringing to mind the dystopian worlds increasingly imagined in books and movies of the times.[68]

Rather than try to reinvent the city as urban renewal vainly did, a new generation of planners dreamed of creating entirely new communities from scratch. Three alternatives to the broken city of the past arose, each a self-contained universe where residents would live, work, shop, play, and learn. The first was the concept of brand-new "instant communities" built near major cities but not dependent on them like suburbs of the past. A dozen such towns, including Reston, Columbia, and Germantown, were part of Washington, D.C.'s "Year 2000" plan, each one promising a perfect balance between urban and small-town life. "We are going to produce a beautiful city with a rich culture and green valleys which will grow better, more creative people," promised James Rouse, the developer of Columbia, Maryland. Another idea was to create "megastructures," massive buildings that would serve as cities unto themselves. Whether giant high-rises like the planned John Hancock Center in Chicago, linear cities that would stretch as much as twenty miles such as the proposed Jersey Corridor Project, floating-in-the-sky buildings like those imagined by Buckminster Fuller (ideal for Harlem before destroying the slums underneath, he believed), or dome-topped, weather-proof communities, megastructures suggested that architecture (and architects) could pave the way to utopia. The third concept of mid-1960s futuristic urban design was platform cities, whereby buildings would be erected on stilts and automobiles would travel on underground roads, creating a much more people-friendly environment. Backed up by some of its principles actually being implemented in Hartford, the American Institute of Architecture (AIA) saw the platform city as the best chance to build a better urban community. "The Platform City will give architects free rein to strive for esthetic marvels," claimed AIA president Morris Ketchum in 1965, believing this model to be the road to "gemlike cities, surpassing any before seen on earth."[69]

Within what could be considered a countercultural paradigm of the future, however, it would not be the city, but rather nature, that dominated visions of a utopian landscape. The ecology movement of the 1970s, combined with the emerging fitness craze and growing interest in all things natural, proved to be a worthy challenger to the previously unstoppable force of science and technology, the first time the latter was seriously questioned as the logical path to a better future. Americans' relationship to Earth was also fundamentally altered by seeing images of their blue planet from the perspective of the moon, something that humans had dreamed of since they could look up into the sky. "The sense of oneness that crystallized when we saw the first pictures of our earth from space will be nurtured by our working together on this earth and beyond this earth to provide a broadening future for all," wrote Theodore Taylor, head of the International Research and Technology Corporation, in 1974.[70] Starting small—the publication of the *Whole Earth Catalog* in 1968, the first Earth Day in 1970, the founding of Greenpeace the following year, and the EPA's banning of the insecticide DDT in 1972—the movement soon became a national cause with the energy crisis of 1973 (and the forming of the Department of Energy). Similarly, a series of relatively modest events throughout the 1970s—the Endangered Species Act, the setting of the fifty-five-mile-per-hour national speed limit, the introduction of the catalytic converter, and the banning of Red Dye #2—set the stage for a momentous one, the near meltdown of the Three Mile Island nuclear reactor (whose impact was compounded by *The China Syndrome*, which happened to be playing in movie theaters at the time).

The new, rather radical idea that the environment was not to be conquered but rather preserved was a complete about-face within the history of the future. "We have all but conquered our environment, bent it almost to our own design," argued J. J. Starrow, Jr., ex-publisher of the *Nation* in 1965, exactly what visionaries of the past few decades had dreamed of doing. Rather than create the utopia that these visionaries had imagined, however, Starrow saw a much different outcome. "The fact remains that we are no longer seriously threatened by anything on earth save the consequences of our own actions," he thought, seeing the best hope for civilization in the hands of students, of all people. "We have given them a world which is a working model of insanity [and] they quite rightly reject it," Starrow believed, but "if there be a way out of the trap we are in, it is they who, given time, will find it."[71] Some in the late 1960s recognized "the consequences of our own actions," seeing major trouble ahead due to environmental neglect and abuse. "Forward-thinkers say that in 10 years there will be the problem of an unnatural warming of the earth's atmosphere merely by the existence of myriads of heat-belching machines," reported *Nation's Business* in 1968, prophesying the future problem if not exactly its cause.[72] Almost four decades before Al Gore's *An Inconvenient Truth*, an anonymous technician the magazine used as a source had a particularly good read on what would crystallize as the central issue of global warming:

> Will heat poured out by billions of air-conditioners and every other kind of friction machine you can think of warm the atmosphere so much that the ice caps will be affected? Even a slight melting would raise the ocean's level, change the contour of every nation that borders on an ocean and restructure the world's business. Low-lying cities like New York and low-lying states such as Florida would disappear under the sea.[73]

Warnings about coming environmental disaster became even more clamorous in the early 1970s, as the ecology movement moved from the margins into the mainstream scientific community. Kenneth Watt (a "systems ecologist" at UC Davis) was an especially loud voice reporting the damage being done to the environment, believing that because of automobile exhaust raising nitrogen levels, "it's only a matter of time before light will be filtered out of the atmosphere and none of our land will be usable."[74] Barry Commoner's 1971 *The Closing Circle* linked the ecological crisis directly to postwar technology, believing it to be inharmonious with nature and that "the vaunted 'progress' of modern civilization is only a thin cloak for global catastrophe." A 1972 study called "A Blueprint for Survival," released by UK-based *The Ecologist,* was as depressing as its name, the authors (thirty-three distinguished British scientists) believing that the depletion of natural resources would lead to "the breakdown of society and the irreversible destruction of the life-support systems on this planet, possibly by the end of the century, certainly within the lifetimes of our children."[75]

Picking up more steam, ecology soon became a cause célèbre among the intellectual elite who recognized it as a key component of future shock. The environment was a main topic at a 1972 summit of brilliant minds, including the critic Alfred Kazin, the author Irving Howe, the sociologist Daniel Bell, and the composer Aaron Copland, for example, the idea being that putting some of the best thinkers of the day in a room together for a few days could perhaps solve a few of the world's biggest problems. Although the distinguished invitees could agree on very little, many had come to the conclusion that "growth" was not necessarily in the best interests of our collective future, an idea that would have been considered anathema by previous generations of futurists. "After 20 years of obsession with growth we discovered it is not a miracle—that it brings pollution and deterioration of the environment," believed French philosopher Raymond Aron, one of the participants, adding that we would ultimately be living "under the shadow of disaster." Another participant, the geneticist H. Bentley Glass, also thought that the postwar obsession with growth was no longer a good model for the future. "We must pass from exploitation to management," Glass argued, "we must shift from growth, which is a sign of immaturity, to a steady-state system."[76]

Official authorities too suggested that Americans had better brace themselves for the less-than-red-white-and-blue concept of shortages. Even many in "the establishment" had, by the mid-1970s, concluded that the postwar idea of unlimited resources was over. Not only did *US News & World Report* think that in twenty years "pollution controls will be stiffer" but also felt "there may be curbs on private use of automobiles," about as un-American an idea as one could think of.[77] "Many face the prospect of a series of shocks of varying severity as shortages occur in one material after another," read a 1975 National Academy of Sciences (NAS) report, "Mineral Resources and the Environment," "with the first real shortages perhaps only a matter of a few years away." Oil would be an even greater problem in the future, the NAS believed, making America more dependent on foreign nations for its fuel needs, a prophecy that more recent administrations perhaps should have taken more seriously.[78]

AN ALMOST ENDLESS STREAM

Regardless of the many branches leading to and from future shock, the "technological juggernaut," as the Greenwich Village hipster put it, continued to whir in the late 1960s and 1970s. In fact, it was science and technology—the heart and soul of futurism—that were most responsible for the cultural vertigo that most Americans were feeling. As usual, an amazing parade of innovations streamed into the marketplace from the halls of corporate R&D—soft contact lenses, Aspartame, Astroturf, the jumbo jet and SST, the UPC code, disposable razor, CB radio, VCR, and Sony Walkman, to name just a few. Unlike previous eras of the future, however, there was a growing sense that society was becoming more of a disposable one, that our nest was being fouled with all of the good things brought to life. As well, the continual flow of information technologies like the microprocessor, floppy disk, microchip calculator, home computer, and even Atari's very cool new game, Pong, were demanding the use of a different kind of thinking, cause for some dogs to wonder if they'd be able to learn these new tricks. Both science and technology became, in short, scarier notions in the late 1960s and 1970s, increasingly perceived by many as threats to a natural and healthy way of life, both for oneself and for the planet as a whole. The way things were going, to paraphrase Yogi Berra, it was clear the future wasn't going to be what it used to be.

Whether or not it was inharmonious with nature, electronic media continued to advance as engineers figured out how to make components smaller, faster, and smarter. As color television became widely popular in the mid-1960s, emerging technology was naturally expected to take the medium to new places. Richard Pinkham, senior VP of media and programs at the advertising agency Ted Bates, saw size as the next frontier, thinking in 1965 that viewers of the future would watch on both "a two-inch portable in a teen-ager's pocket or an eight-foot screen hanging on a living-room wall" (a crystal-clear forecast of the televisual landscape forty years hence).[79] The future could also be seen on television on *The 21st Century*, a CBS series on Sunday night, hosted by Walter Cronkite, which ran from 1967 to 1970. During the first season, Cronkite "traveled 33 years into the future—to the year 2000 and beyond," getting a medical checkup by a "mechanical doctor," copiloting a hovercraft, listening to signals from outer space, and eating artificial foods used in the space program. As the first documentary-style television series about the future, *The 21st Century* told a mass audience not just "that's the way it is," as Cronkite's news broadcast signoff went, but the equally important message of "this is the way it might be."[80]

Television and other media would no doubt benefit from the increasing number of satellites being launched into orbit, many believed, creating a technological wonderland a few decades out. "I am sure that by [the year] 2000 people will wonder how the world ever managed without communications satellites," said Wernher von Braun, NASA's chief planner, in 1971. The now iconic scientist might have been right on when it came to the satellites, but he missed the boat when it came to what would be going on deeper in space. "I am absolutely convinced that by the year 2000 we shall have permanent research stations on the moon," von Braun firmly stated, with "crews assigned to the moon labs . . . quite coolly put[ting] in for permission to bring their families."[81]

Despite some contrary voices (the creepiest being HAL's in the 1968 film *2001: A Space Odyssey*), most felt that computers also would make people's lives better in the years ahead as their potential gradually became clearer. "In computer storage systems there is the opportunity for an international electronic reference library," wrote Jack Gould of the *New York Times* in 1965, just one example of how prescient some were in what was the Paleolithic Age of the technology. "Tomorrow's student may be able to insert into a machine an inquiry as to where he can learn about a given topic [and] in seconds," Gould prophesied, "back would come appropriate references listing the available material in the libraries of the world."[82] (The idea that the actual answer to the inquiries of "tomorrow's student" could be found in this electronic reference library could not even be imagined.) A dystopian world might be lying in wait, according to the future shock of the late 1960s and 1970s, but something incredible too just might be lurking out there somewhere.

It was these years, rather ironically given the Luddite undercurrent of the times, that the phenomenal possibilities of the computer became at least partly clear. Some were able to recognize that a revolution was in the works, something that would alter the dynamics of everyday life. "If any single item of hardware is destined to take command of the look and lilt of urban life over the next 35 years, as the ubiquitous automobile did during the past 35, that item almost surely is the electronic computer," said *Life* in 1965, foreseeing that the device would be "the central nervous system of municipalities, businesses, libraries, and other storage centers for information" by the year 2000. The magazine, like an increasing number of sources at this point, could see that the computer might even be more ubiquitous in the future, much more than a Selectric on steroids. "Later, for better or worse, its nerve ends at least will invade the home," the magazine claimed, seeing possible domestic applications for a thinking machine. Experts in the industry also saw parallels between the automobile business of a generation earlier with their own of the mid-1960s. "Right now we face the same problem as General Motors did back in 1939," thought I. M. Gottlieb, a manager for IBM, believing that most of the electronic technology to create robots for the home already existed but that people were not quite ready for such change.[83]

Consumers may not have been ready for a Rosie (the Jetsons' robotic maid) in their homes, but Big Business was more than ready to move into the future via computers as they progressed. "Every business that wants to stay competitive will have its own computer or will rent time on a 'public utility' computer system," reported *US News & World Report* in its coverage of a 1967 private corporate seminar led by Herman Kahn of the Hudson Institute. And while the thought of an android domestic might be a bit off-putting, for the moment, at least, there was no reason to completely shun computers in one's household. "Homes will be tied to computer networks for instant information," the magazine continued, with "many common household chores 'run' by computers, freeing the housewife from routine." (That Kahn, like every other expert, could get the technology so right but completely miss the idea that many women would very soon forego even computer-run household chores for full-time careers is one of the most striking and puzzling themes of twentieth-century futurism.)[84]

By 1968, 44,400 computers were being used by American businesses, enough for some of their problems, all too familiar today, to become readily apparent. "What to do about 'forgery by computer'?" wondered *Nation's Business* that year, coming to the realization that "computers will stand as open invitations to dishonest programmers to create a new set of books, run off a batch of bad checks, put something in company files and records which should not be there, or take something out of the records which should be there." To thwart such transgressions, the magazine proposed, "computers of the future will have to be kept in vault-like rooms or guarded by security offi-cers so that only 'cleared' people can get near them," not quite able to foresee the much sneakier ways tomorrow's "hackers" could access their systems.[85]

Future forgery aside, there was little doubt at the end of the 1960s that computers would be essential technology for twenty-first-century executives, perhaps the very pulse of the workplace of the future.[86] "A typical office three decades hence will look pretty much like a sophisticated military control center," Auren Uris imagined for *Nation's Business* in 1969, with executives steering their corporate ships a little like Mr. Sulu in *Star Trek* guided the starship *Enterprise*:

> Display boards indicating key factors in operations, everything from cash flow to material movements, will be graphically represented. Computer terminals will supply an almost endless stream of in-line, real-time data, and the executive ensconced on a command chair at a control center will make his moves with the aid of secretaries, assistants, expert advisers.[87]

Less prophetic, and much more bizarre, was Uris's forecast of how secre-taries would be aiding their computer-enabled executives. "As a result of the changing standards and far-out styles in female dress in the world at large, chances are that some secretaries will be topless before the Twenty-first Cen-tury," he seriously believed, citing commonplace nudity and "the aura of pre-eminence that will surround the executive" as the reasons for the emergence of truly personal personal assistants. Uris went even further with his wacko vision of sexual politics at the office of the future, predicting that secretaries would be doing much more than typing and taking steno for their preemi-nent bosses because they, unlike the men's wives at home, would be inter-ested in their work. "The need of the executive for two women in his life will not go unnoticed," he reasoned, maintaining that "legislation will enable the executive to have two legal wives, one at home and one at the office." For Uris, a respected author and editor (and ex-business executive!), to choose this kind of future shows how far off the radar the idea of equal rights for women was, even as the feminist movement gathered steam.[88]

Five years later, however, mainstream futurists began to comprehend that the women's rights movement was not a countercultural fad like the Nehru suit, and that tomorrow's workplace would be more gender neutral than the Playboy Club. By 1994, "women and members of minorities are expected to be spread throughout the work force in roles ranging from ditch diggers to investment bankers," wrote *US News & World Report* twenty years earlier, an accurate prediction of the much more even playing field that emerged over those two decades. "Traditional roles of women as mothers and home-makers are likely to dwindle in importance," the magazine continued, with "husbands [to] share more household chores" and, prophetically anticipating the nanny culture of the 1990s, "youngsters increasingly reared by professional child-care attendants." Besides having a good read on the family of the future, *US News & World Report* was prophetic regarding home technology. Not only would there be "widespread use of tape cassettes for home viewing" in 1994, the magazine forecast in 1974, but also "computer hookups on which people may obtain information, place merchandise orders and pay bills without leaving their homes," a crystal-clear picture of the online universe that entered the American mainstream exactly when the magazine predicted.[89]

Well before the idea of convergence began to be kicked around, futurists could see television and the computer engaged in a sort of rivalry to be the king of information technology. Isaac Asimov, like others, saw computers as the path to the dream of a universal library ("we will have access by computer to a central computerized library in which will be contained the mass knowledge gathered by all humanity through all of time," he wrote) but also had high hopes for the possibilities of television. "I foresee a twenty-first century . . . where it will be possible for each person to have his own private information channel," he predicted in 1978, so "just as we can now . . . each have our own telephone number, we can have our own voice and picture channel." Again, if the future was more about ideas than a particular technology, as Arnold Toynbee claimed, Asimov anticipated the desire to personalize and customize our lives wherever possible, a key theme in American culture over the next few decades.[90] Others envisioned that a "two-way" cable system was the future of television, with sets hooked up to a central computer (such a thing called Qube was actually being test-marketed in Columbus, Ohio, in 1979). Viewers could not only order movies or sports events via two-way cable but "talk back" by voting in polls, something that seemed unsettling as the computer stored all the information (including the watching of what *Saturday Review* called "dirty movies"). "The 'Big Brother' prophesied by George Orwell to arrive in 1984 appears to be on schedule," thought the magazine, believing that in ten years many might "long for the good old days of simple-minded networks putting on simple-minded shows for no purpose other than exploiting the captive television market."[91]

As technology-driven future shock made many look to tomorrow reluctantly or with trepidation, a longing for the good old days seemed like the most sensible and comforting thing one could do. As the 1970s went into the books, the voltage of the future would be reduced considerably, impetus for Americans to recast their future once again. "A new decade yawns before futurologists . . . and they are meeting its challenge by strip-mining the prairies of Potentiality," wrote Mark O'Donnell in 1979, seeing a glimmer of hope in the yet-to-be-explored terrain of the 1980s.[92]

Up to then our best friend—the possibilities of tomorrow thought to be inherently greater than the realities of today—the future became our worst enemy in the late 1960s and 1970s, the first time in the nation's history that what would be was not as good as what was now. With tomorrow more up for grabs than ever, the floodgates to futurism swung wide open, turned into pop-culture fodder and a thriving cottage industry. As the postwar consensus broke down, so of course did its progressive view of the future, replaced by a slew of alternative scenarios that were truly countercultural in thought (and almost always bad news). Science and technology were not only not the magic bullets we thought they were but a big part of the problem, vivid proof that there really were limits to growth. The radical idea that less could be more became mainstream during these pivotal years, ensuring that the American future would never be quite the same. True to form, the twists and turns of tomorrow would make prediction an ambitious and elusive pursuit.

CHAPTER 5

The Empire Strikes Back, 1980–1994

While I take inspiration from the past,
like most Americans, I live for the future.

—Ronald Reagan, 1992

IN JULY 1980, MORE THAN 5,000 FUTURISTS FROM AROUND THE WORLD got together in Toronto to attend the First Global Conference on the Future. Most of futurism's all-stars were there, naturally, and for the opening ceremonies goodwill messages were sent by Helmut Schmidt of Germany, Pierre Trudeau of Canada, and Indira Gandhi of India, all hoping that the visionaries there would find solutions to the world's major problems. Among the 400 or so workshops, seminars, and panels, the most intriguing had to be the one that put Herman Kahn, the director of the conservative, pro-capitalism Hudson Institute, alongside Timothy Leary, legendary countercultural guru and psychedelic pioneer. Leary, now calling himself a "neo-technological pagan," was at the conference to push his own agenda for the future, which he was calling SMI²LE, or "space migration, intelligence increase, life extension." While the two men did not, for the most part, see the sky in the same color (undoubtedly blue for Kahn, unknown for Leary), they did, rather remarkably, find some common ground on the panel they shared. After Leary proposed that progress and growth be redefined in terms of how much money and time people spend on self-indulgence, that is, "breaking away from the productive situation," Kahn agreed that "this is one of the waves of the future," also seeing an era of conspicuous consumption ahead as a result of broader prosperity. Although the specifics were different, to say the least, Kahn and Leary each held optimistic views of the future (the former expressing it in economic terms, the latter feeling that "We are lucky to have been ovulated in this era"). While odd, to put it mildly, the dialogue revealed that despite the continued splintering of the field, futurists of wildly divergent backgrounds agreed that for many if not most people, happy days might very well be here again, and that the era of future shock was officially over.[1]

With America's confidence restored under President Reagan's red-white-and-blue leadership, it did indeed seem to be a new morning in America's tomorrow. As free-market capitalism flourished and the nation flexed its global muscles as a modern-day version of ancient Rome, much of the doom and gloom of the 1970s would evaporate, replaced by the traditional American jeremiad proclaiming our special place as a "city on the hill." Another age of miracles lay before us as we drew closer to a new century and new millennium, and this time, having learned from our past mistakes, we would get the future right. Much like the (evil) Galactic Empire did in the 1980 blockbuster, the American empire was now striking back, given a new chance to fulfill its own destiny as a land of milk and honey in the New World.

As in the 1950s, however, there was an underbelly to the cultural beast, as fears of an impending dystopia or even apocalypse upset the futuristic apple cart. Over the course of the next decade and a half, New Agers and Christian fundamentalists each prophesied in messianic terms while survivalists in the nation's backwaters prepared for the end of days. Pop culture also offered scary views of what might be in store, with movies like *Road Warrior, Brazil, Blade Runner,* and *Escape from New York* depicting an Orwellian, post-apocalyptic future. Uncertainty about tomorrow could be seen even in usually happy-go-lucky advertising, with Apple's incredible "Big Brother" commercial of 1984 suggesting that Orwell might prove to be right after all, despite the introduction of the liberating Macintosh computer. Reagan's "Star Wars" defense initiative and the development of space stations only confirmed that we had better have a backup plan if a Russian rogue state let loose one of the thousands of unaccounted-for Cold War–era atomic bombs. As well, the spread of AIDS throughout the 1980s made many think that a plague reminiscent of the Dark Ages might be upon us, raising our collective paranoia considerably. "Scientists cannot predict how many more will develop AIDS or other ailments that might be caused by the virus," reported the *New York Times* in 1985, "nor can they say whether the disease pattern of this sexually active group of homosexuals [in San Francisco] accurately foretells that of others."[2] As if that weren't enough, concerns about global warming or the "greenhouse effect" were picking up steam as new evidence supported the theory that the planet was gradually heating up, probably because of our burning of fossil fuels. Which narrative of the future would prove more accurate, experts and ordinary folks alike wondered, the triumphant one or the one in which we would self-destruct?

THE COMING BOOM

For a small but growing number of "survivalists" preparing for some kind of disaster in the early 1980s, the answer to that question was definitely the latter. The survivalist movement was not unlike the postwar bomb-shelter craze in some respects, but this time the threat could come from any number of places, including our own backyard. Whether the cataclysmic event was man-made (toxic spill, nuclear war, economic collapse, racial revolution) or "natural" (famine, flood, plague), survivalists had every intention to emerge from the disaster safe and sound by equipping their fortresses with freeze-dried foods, water purifiers, generators and fuel, weapons, and even radiation suits and concrete bunkers. The movement, which was distinctly rural and skewed toward the West Coast, started to kick in 1973 during the Arab oil embargo, sparking some to convert their cash into gold as the dollar fell. By 1980, *Time* estimated the number of survivalists as "perhaps a million or more," definitely a bigger, broader group than just Mormons hiding grain under their beds. "I get everybody from the madman who wants to pack a machine gun to a lot of upper-middle-class professionals who financially have a lot at stake," said Ron Burns of Napa Valley–based Packaway Food Company, one marketer of nonperishables that was doing quite the business as the movement spread.[3]

As with all things apocalyptic, a thriving cottage industry of guidebooks, newsletters, and "survival schools" supported the movement, with former stockbroker Howard Ruff's *How to Prosper During the Coming Bad Years* and the *Ruff Times* newsletter the pessimists' Bibles. Ruff had sold 2.5 million copies by 1980, and had launched *Ruff House*, a half-hour weekly syndicated TV show advising readers and viewers to invest in precious metals, diamonds, and real estate as well as keep a grocery store's worth of cans of tuna and rolls of toilet paper around in case the Big One should come. Believing that "major social and political disruptions in the country's urban areas" and "the most difficult times since the Civil War" were on the way, Ruff found a captive audience and, of course, an attractive business model, allowing him to prosper very nicely during the present good years. Even more radical advice came from Kurt Saxon, whose *The Poor Man's James Bond* (a handbook of "improvised weaponry and do-it-yourself mayhem") was considered a must-read by the average paranoid in the early 1980s. The book recommended that readers learn a trade, have nineteenth-century technology backup—firewood and kerosene lanterns—around if the twentieth-century electrical grid went down and, oh yes, know how to make teargas and a flamethrower should an angry mob appear on your doorstep. Saxon's first rule was for those who thought like him to get the hell out of cities, something that suggested (if his name already didn't) that there was a strong racial dimension to his particular view of the world.[4]

Fortunately, the survivalists of the early 1980s did not represent the majority opinion when it came to the outlook for the American future. One survey showed that the average guy or gal on the street in fact believed that the nation was recovering from the bad trip that was the 1970s, and that things would get even better in the future. In 1981, *Psychology Today* asked 1,600 Americans how they envisioned the nation's future, comparing the findings to those from previous studies, and found that things were definitely looking up. "By the spring of this year, the vision we have of our nation showed a heartening degree of improvement," the magazine happily announced, adding that "We are not yet back to the era of good feeling that existed in 1964 [but] there is renewed optimism in the markedly higher future rating given this year than in 1974."[5]

With President Reagan now in the White House, Corporate America had become especially gung-ho about the future as it became very clear very soon that the early 1980s, at the very least, would be, more than anything else, probusiness. "If the actions of the first two months of the Reagan administration are any indication, business can look forward to far more support for the things it wants from Washington," *US News & World Report* observed early in 1981, seeing less regulation on the horizon, especially related to the environment.[6] "Last year everyone was down in the dumps, but this year there is more jubilation," proclaimed George E. Field, senior VP of Planters National Bank & Trust, one of many businessmen elated that the hard economic times of recent years appeared to be over.[7] Reagan's proposed tax plan allowing companies to write off part of their R&D costs also was cause for joy in Corporate America, perhaps the spark the nation needed to reassert its leadership in the global economy.[8]

Not surprisingly, the most positive (and, at 350 pounds, almost certainly the heaviest) of professional futurists, Herman Kahn, saw prosperity and abundance in our near future, his 1982 *The Coming Boom* making a strong argument that the empire would indeed strike back. As cofounder of the conservative think tank the Hudson Institute, Kahn not surprisingly saw Reagan's economic policies and sheer confidence as the solution to what he considered the "low morale and antigrowth ideologies" of recent years. "Many opportunities are open to an affluent and technological society," Kahn wrote, "opportunities which will continue to expand not only because of innovations and advances, but also because of the elimination of many recent restrictive conditions to innovation." While his clearly politically tinged vision would prove largely correct, Kahn fell right into the utopian trap that so many others before (and after) him also had. "By the year 2000, poverty, as defined by current criteria, except as pathology or voluntary choice, should have disappeared in the United States," Kahn predicted, unable to see that the trickle-down (aka "voodoo") economic policies he so endorsed would result in an increasing divide versus a bridge between the haves and the have-nots.[9]

In addition to a rosier economic picture, the mainstays of futurism in the early 1970s—famine, overpopulation, and ecological disaster—too had rather suddenly faded away. With his 1981 book *The Ultimate Resource*, University of Illinois economist Julian L. Simon made a convincing case that rumors of Earth's death were greatly exaggerated. "The fact is—at any point in the next 50 years—global resources will be more plentiful, and their real costs will be lower than they are today," Simon argued, believing that "man's ingenuity," that is, science, would literally save the day.[10] A few years later, Simon and the eternal optimist (but now recently deceased) Herman Kahn published *The Resourceful Earth*, reaffirming the idea that technology was not a cause but the solution for growing population and environmental problems. "If present trends continue, the world in 2000 will be less crowded, less polluted, [and] more stable ecologically . . . than the world we live in now," the coauthors insisted, a view to which more people were coming around as a progressive orientation toward the future came back into bloom.[11]

To a casual observer, it appeared as if within just a few years, a paradigm shift (forecasters' favorite phrase at the time) had taken place within the realm of the future, a major directional change if not a complete reversal in the idea of tomorrow. "A decade ago, doomsayers painted a chilly picture of a planet ticketed for disaster," wrote *US News & World Report* in 1983, Earth to be done in by nuclear war, famine, or pollution. Now, however, "what lies ahead could well be a renaissance for the U.S. in political prestige and technological power," the magazine felt, with superdrugs, genetic techniques, space colonies, programmed cars, and, of course, robots to make life in fifty years a wonderful time to be alive. A female or minority president, a multi-career work life, and "the highest standard of living ever known" were all now waiting in the nation's wings, a wholesale rejection of the future shock that Toffler and others were predicting not that long ago. Fantastic stuff that seemed all but extinct—floating cities, levitating trains, and "exotic new energy sources"—was suddenly back on futurists' radar, as was the standard idea that science and technology would be the deliverer of a new age of Man. "Freed by technology from much of life's drudgery, people will at last have the time to allow their creativity to flower," *US News & World Report* stated, something more likely to have been written a half-century earlier, before the nightmare of another world war and the cultural burnout of the 1970s. It was, like the 1985 movie, back to the future, a revival of a utopianlike tomorrow that few if anyone could imagine.[12]

MEGATRENDS

Spurred on by a reinvigorated economic climate, the business of forecasting and prediction continued to pick up steam in the early 1980s, moving the idea of the future further from the margins into the mainstream. While a new generation of gurus would soon achieve almost folk-hero status as secular theologians, it was a 1980 piece of fluff that signaled a new, more populist era of the future had begun. Compiled by the same folks responsible for such less-than-weighty works as *The People's Almanac* and *The Book of Lists*, *The Book of Predictions* was the first major exercise in what might be called, to use what was becoming an increasingly popular term, future "lite." Whether it be flushless toilets that composted wastes, optional menstruation, guiltless sex, or the end of communism in Russia, the collection was chock-full of upbeat prognostications by so-called experts. The book did as well have the requisite doomsday predictions involving nuclear accidents or war between the usual suspects (Pakistan and India, Iraq and Iran), but it was the other visions of the future—Muhammad Ali getting fat, Brigitte Bardot having less-than-successful plastic surgery—that, ironically, made the book significant. Futurism had, in current parlance, tipped—no longer the province of social misfits, brainy eggheads, or newspaper gossips but rather turned into a disposable literary commodity intended for consumption by general-interest readers.[13]

The continued popularization of the future could be seen in many fields, sometimes making tomorrow seem more important than today. Journalists especially were becoming attracted to the future like moths to a flame, seduced by the almost irresistible force of anticipating things to come. "The press could cover better what has happened if it were not so preoccupied with trying to guess what is going to happen next," thought Thomas Griffith of *Time* in 1980, seconded in the same magazine two years later by Frank Trippett, who believed that "Society spends so much time looking ahead that the present sometimes seems forgotten."[14] For serious journalists, their colleagues' near-obsession with the future was not just damaging the credibility of their profession but distracting readers from what was really important. "Taking too much thought for the morrow can, in fact, insulate a person far too much from the reality of the present—and the real nature of the future," Trippett argued.[15]

Other journalists were critical of the sheer volume of futurism, peeved that it had become such a big part of what constituted "news." "I have seen the future and I'm tired of it," wrote Gerald Nachman for *Newsweek* in 1982, his riff on the slogan for GM's Futurama exhibit at the 1939–1940 New York World's Fair supported by his claim that "about all I see nowadays is the future." "Today has vanished, swallowed up in forecasts of what tomorrow holds," Nachman continued, believing that "nobody likes yesterday anymore and the present bores people." Nachman dated what he called the "Future Age" to the publishing of Toffler's *Future Shock*, which, he argued, "showed that if you said something scary enough about what Life Will Be Like, many people would buy it." Nachman not only thought that the future had become too big, but he didn't appreciate that much of it was just plain wrong. "The things we actually have now, I notice, nobody predicted—Atari games, call-forwarding, lapel mikes, designer chocolates, indoor football, no-fault divorce, snooze alarms," he observed, justifiably asking, "Where were today's futurists then?"[16] Looking back, futurists of the day also might have better spent their time further developing some of the "catastrophe theory"–based techniques explored in the late 1970s in order to have anticipated and perhaps averted some of the "discontinuities" of the 1980s such as Bhopal, the Exxon Valdez oil spill, the S&L crisis, and Black Monday.

Such sniping, however, could do little to slow down the ever-expanding universe of the future. A new magazine, *Next*, entirely dedicated to "future news," popped up on newsstands in 1982, occasionally using the Delphi method to come up with some of its stories. Even more significant, futurism by the early 1980s had reached a point where some experts believed everybody had, to some extent, the ability to predict what tomorrow would bring. David Loye, a UCLA psychologist, called this ability "the gift of prophecy," half of which was logical ("forecasting") and the other half intuitive ("foreseeing"). Thinking Loye was on to something, *Reader's Digest* suggested to its readers in 1982 that they strengthen their own "future-probing capacities" by using both sides of their brain and even applying the Delphi method. Because the gift of prophecy "can help us lead wiser, more productive lives," the magazine told readers, there was no reason it should be the exclusive province of the intellectual elite. Everyone, it seemed, had become or should become a futurist, the idea of living purely in the present about as dated as a Nehru jacket.[17]

The seemingly universal appeal of the future did not go unnoticed by the editors of one of the premier icons of mass taste, *People*. "Social Forecaster John Naisbitt Says He Has Seen the Future—And It Just May Work," the magazine reported in its 1982 story about Naisbitt's new bestseller, *Megatrends*. Naisbitt, who had served on LBJ's staff, hit it big time with his brand of prophecy based on content analysis of hundreds of newspapers, an intelligence-gathering technique first used during World War II and at the time still employed by the CIA. "An information society is oriented to the future, which is why we're so interested in it," he explained, adding that "we're drowning in data, yet thirsty for intelligence and knowledge."[18] By the following year, *Megatrends* had sold more than half a million copies in its nineteen printings, making Naisbitt more popular and, at $10,000 per appearance, pricier than Henry Kissinger as a speaker. The book could be found on the desks or bedside tables of many Fortune 500 executives in the early 1980s, considered almost mandatory reading alongside two other mega business books, Tom Peters's *In Search of Excellence* and Kenneth Blanchard's *The One-Minute Manager*.[19] Part of the appeal of *Megatrends* to corporate types was its very un-Toffler-like, upbeat tone, reminiscent of an overcaffeinated motivational speaker. "It is a great and yeasty time filled with opportunity," Naisbitt wrote in the book, his very last line "What a fantastic time to be alive!"[20]

For anyone selling the future or something like it in the early 1980s, it was indeed a fantastic time to be alive. "If ever a time was right for painting images of the future, it is now," observed *US News & World Report* in 1983, adding that "the desire to know what will happen next year, next decade, next century seems insatiable."[21] The megatrending of American culture also included, one could argue, the new space craze sweeping the nation. *Star Wars* toys, riding on the blockbuster success of the first two movies in the series, were as popular as the space-themed merchandise of the 1950s, and kids were rapidly becoming obsessed with a new recreation—video games—with futuristic names like Space Invaders and Asteroids. The debut of *Omni* in 1978 was further proof that the future had become fully mainstream, the magazine's popular approach to sci-fi-esque topics very much in synch with the time's millennial anticipation. The opening of Walt Disney's EPCOT (Experimental Prototype Community of Tomorrow) Center in 1982 also was a sign of what might be called "futuretainment," the techno-utopian theme park taking Disneyland's and Disneyworld's vision of tomorrow to a whole new, but similarly populist, level.[22]

Futurists themselves, however, were the most direct beneficiaries of tomorrow-mania. In addition to Kahn's and Naisbitt's books, Isaac Asimov's *Change! Seventy-One Glimpses of the Future* also saw unsurpassed prosperity and progress up ahead, something Americans clearly wanted to hear, while *Seven Tomorrows* by Paul Hawken (along with James Ogilvy and Peter Schwartz, his partners in the Menlo Park consulting firm SRI International) presented a set of alternative scenarios rather than make bold predictions, all of them steeped in the team's commitment to a "post-industrial" vision of tomorrow.[23] A scenario-based approach might have been a wiser choice for Marvin Cetron and Thomas O'Toole, whose 1982 *Encounters with the Future* revealed that, despite an unprecedented interest in the future, the tendency for forecasters to often make odd and retrospectively wrong predictions remained the same. "The equal-rights amendment won't even be an issue [as] it will be passed long before the year 2000," wrote Cetron and O'Toole in their book, "simply because older people who oppose it will have died off." The same pair also thought that "because of great advances in computers and robots, the average work week will be just 20 hours shortly after the turn of the century, which will make leisure a huge industry," an idea about as clunky as an Edsel.[24] This wasn't the first time for Cetron to go out on a limb, which would later fall down with a big thud. In 1980, he had predicted not only that there would be national catastrophic health insurance by 1988, but that "prepaid group health insurance for dogs and cats" would be available as well. Cetron also thought then that both eyeglasses and contact lenses would be obsolete by 1990, replaced by vision-correcting eyedrops, and that TV viewers would one day be able to choose from an amazing twenty-five channels.[25]

Despite or perhaps because of his willingness to take a flyer on the future, Cetron, head of Arlington, Virginia–based Forecasting International, slip-streamed in Naisbitt's wake through the 1980s, making an impressive 112 speeches in 1984 alone to organizations hungry for his read on tomorrow.

Versus Naisbitt's low-tech content analysis of newspaper articles, Cetron used mainframe computers to predict the probability of an event taking place in five, ten, or twenty years and then assessed its potential impact by using "sixty-four indicators for stability factors." By 1987, the ex-civilian planner and forecaster for the Navy had consulted with seventeen governments and more than seventy companies, earning him too a feature article in *People*. Cetron claimed his think tank was "batting 95 percent," which, if true, was a lot better than that of other futurists, and especially surprising given his thoughts on the ERA, the future workweek, and health insurance for pets. A look back on some of Cetron's other predictions would, in fact, suggest that his hit rate might have been a bit less. "I haven't got too much hope for our largest cities, especially New York," he said in 1985, advising people not to "put much money" into the city. A couple of years later, Cetron predicted world hunger would be gone by 2006, that Reagan would step down as president, that a Democrat wouldn't be in the White House until 1996 because we "raised our kids to be Republicans," and that a woman would be elected to the top job in 2004. Cetron also argued that "the upper tenth and the lower tenth of the working population are getting closer to make one great big middle class" just as Reagan's economic policies were making the rich richer and the poor poorer, and that drugs would be decriminalized by the year 2000 or soon thereafter (despite the first lady's advice to "just say no"). Furthest off the beam, however, was Cetron's prediction that, shades of the 1940s, the automobile industry would be selling fiberglass prefab houses built by robots and delivered—no joke—by dirigible.[26]

Although Cetron, with his computer-generated predictions, was proving to be a worthy rival, Naisbitt kept his number-one futurist position throughout the mid-1980s, much because of the success of his next book, *Reinventing the Corporation*. With his vision of a kinder, gentler workplace filled with a "confederation of entrepreneurs" in "nourishing environments" pursuing "personal growth" while working for "coaches," Naisbitt furthered his reputation among corporate executives wanting to be on the cutting edge (and learn a new vocabulary in the process). Naisbitt's own rise to success was no less than remarkable. In 1977, he had declared bankruptcy, listing his debts as $117,000 and his only assets as his clothes, a tennis racket, and $5 in cash. (It turned out that Naisbitt also owned some valuable art, and he later pled guilty to bankruptcy fraud.) After heading up the Washington, D.C., office of Yankelovich, Skelly & White and then going off on his own, however, Naisbitt was back in business, all a prelude of course to the publication of *Megatrends*. By 1985, the book had sold six million copies, making him not just a multimillionaire but affording opportunities ranging from dinner with President Reagan to appearing in a Hathaway shirt commercial (with eye patch, of course). *Reinventing the Corporation* was coauthored by his second wife, Patricia Aburdene, who had introduced Naisbitt to the New Age movement, something that clearly shaped his vision for the future. Besides writing the new bestseller together, the futuristic couple spent time meditating, following a whole-grain diet, and visiting with a spiritual adviser who gave them "life readings," activities that no doubt contributed to the granola tone of the business book.[27]

Beginning to steal some of Naisbitt's, Cetron's, and other independent futurists' thunder, however, was the New York–based social research firm Yankelovich, Skelly & White. In 1968, Florence Skelly had begun conducting extensive interviews with hundreds of Americans, identifying thirty-five social trends in the process. By 1985, Skelly's company was tracking fifty-two trends by surveying 2,500 people a year, selling the information to 140 companies at $20,000 a pop. Such opinion-based, quantitative research, because it was grounded in what real people felt about real issues, was rapidly becoming the darling of marketers looking to justify decision making with hard data.[28] Largely because of Yankelovich and its chief rival, Roper, futurism was becoming by the end of the decade a distinctly corporatized and conservative enterprise, recast as one of many decision making tools used as much to minimize risk as to maximize opportunity. The Wild West days of the field seemed to be over as it entered a more mature, less exciting phase, reflecting perhaps the trajectory of Western culture and, interestingly, the lives of most baby boomers.

This turning point in the field was made clear at the World Future Society's four-day "Future View: The 1990s & Beyond" conference in Washington, D.C., in 1989, where 3,000 attendees from eighty countries mused over such topics as the "biosphere," "politisphere," "technosphere," and "econosphere." Despite the futuristic-sounding names, it was clear that, with the year 2000 just about a decade away, a sea change had occurred in the art of prediction, with many futurists now tempering their outlooks as the Jetsonesque world they or their predecessors had once predicted had not quite materialized. "Part of the problem was that futurists of the past sometimes painted an incorrect view of the future," organization spokesman Tim Willard understatedly explained, with Society members—historically among the most imaginative of visionaries—now taking a more conservative view of tomorrow, if only to avoid embarrassment ten or twenty years hence. "At one time, we predicted that people could take a pill or seaweed and wouldn't have to eat anymore," Willard admitted, but now, keeping in mind that humans like to actually eat, people will be "comforted by knowing steak and potatoes will still be around."[29]

Even Marvin Cetron, of the robot-built-plastic-house-to-be-dropped-from-the-sky school of futurism, confirmed the change that was taking place at the end of the 1980s in order to avoid predictions like the all-seaweed diet. "We are discovering things happening across the board, current trends and life-style patterns that are strong indicators of where we will be heading in the future," explained Cetron, now most recently coauthor with Owen Davies of *American Renaissance: Our Life at the Turn of the 21st Century*.[30] Naisbitt also was now grounding his view of the twenty-first century in trends that were already bubbling up, his 1990 sequel to *Megatrends*, *Megatrends 2000*, less a true look at the future than, according to one reviewer, "a useful summary and overview of what's been going on." For a real look at the future, the reviewer advised, one would "be better off consulting a fearless swami," something that those really wanting to know what lay ahead beyond the next bend in the road perhaps should have done.[31] What was probably the first (and to date, the only) nonfiction book about futurism for teenagers too appeared around this time, Robert Gardner and Dennis Shortelle's 1989 *The Future and the Past: 100 Years from Now and 100 Years Ago*, which was just as bland as the grownup books about the future being published. Damage to Earth's ecosystem, nuclear war, and poverty were all certainly problems we collectively faced, junior high students could learn from the book, but they were all very solvable, reflecting the don't-rock-the-boat brand of tomorrowism currently in favor.[32]

A couple of other books presumably about the future but really more about the present, each a bestseller, appeared in the early 1990s, one by a blast from the past and one by a new kid on the block who would soon take futurism by storm. Alvin Toffler's 1990 *Powershift* was the third in his amazing trilogy stretching thirty years, a body of work that captured much of the zeitgeist of the latter part of the century. "Today, exactly as first suggested in *Future Shock* in 1970 and *The Third Wave* in 1980, we are standing the principle of mass production on its head," Toffler wrote, his new book about "new paths to power opened by a world in upheaval."[33] The book's subtitle, "Knowledge, Wealth, and Violence at the Edge of the 21st Century," was more than a hint of what those new paths of power were, his argument trading on three (and, ironically, decidedly time-tested) quotes: Francis Bacon's "Knowledge itself is power," Mao Zedong's "Power grows out of the barrel of a gun," and the anonymous "Money talks." With a media-friendly brand, Faith Popcorn (née Plotkin) and her *The Popcorn Report* exploded on the scene in 1991, "the Nostradamus of marketing," according to *Fortune*, becoming one of the go-to talking heads on any subject whatsoever. Her unique methodology ("we go out into the culture to interview and observe," she explained in 1992, "then we make a leap that is impossible to explain") made hiring her consulting company BrainReserve nothing less than a status symbol within Corporate America.[34]

Following the trail blazed by Popcorn, trend experts began to pop up all over the landscape of American business in the early 1990s. It rather suddenly became cool for advertising agencies and even some corporations to have an in-house trend guru, and a new flock of consultants dedicated to deciphering the emerging zeitgeist appeared on the scene. "My job is pre-empting the future and getting there before anyone else does," explained Laurel Cutler of the ad agency FCB/Leber Katz Partners, although she, like other folks in the nascent trend field, was in truth more interested in helping her clients decode and leverage what was already beginning to bubble up. The rise of the trend business had much to do with the growing sophistication and fragmentation of the mass market, making it vital that companies not necessarily peer into the future as much as be able to intelligently parse the present, or at least break it down into meaningful segments. The increasingly short-term nature of business, in which companies had their eyes on (and much of their resources devoted to) the next quarter, versus the next ten years, also was steering many executives to make trend experts rather than pure futurists part of their teams.[35]

Like futurists, a mystical aura seemed to surround trend experts, with not only businesspeople but the general public compelled by their seemingly prescient powers. And even more so than with futurists, jargon was an important piece of the trend universe, a way to reduce often complex sociological phenomena into pithy sound bites and to brand one's intellectual capital in the process. Because she appeared to be in the Rolodex of every journalist in America, Popcorn's terms ("Cocooning," "Cashing Out," "Down-Aging") entered the popular vernacular, quite an achievement for anyone in the business world. Other high-profile figures in the field, including Irma Zandl of Xtreme, Inc., and Gerald Celente of the much less cool-sounding Socio-Economic Research Institute, also coined popular phrases, their concepts ("Mall Jamming" and "Previewing," respectively) almost a sure way to garner a media blurb and a phone call from a potential client wanting to know more.[36] Bill Strauss and Neil Howe, using their 1991 *Generations* and 1993 *13th Gen* as a platform, also were busy advising companies on their next marketing moves, their take on the future (and the past) viewed through a historical lens. "Before the year 2030, events will call on 13ers to make aging boomers get real—and, perhaps, to stop some righteous old Aquarian from doing something truly catastrophic," went one of their age-based predictions, seeing another generation gap ahead that would rock America's boat. Whether sliced and diced into generations, sociological tropes, or quantitative data, much of the future had been transformed into marketing research, a capitalistic tool designed to improve organizations' bottom lines.[37]

THE AGE OF INSIGHT

Along with the economic renaissance or "coming boom" of the early 1980s was the resurrection of science and technology from the grave of the 1970s. Many scientists who seemed to have been hiding behind their microscopes, their fields viewed as the devil's handiwork, suddenly went back on the offensive as the concepts of "growth" and "progress" came back into favor. "Bearers of the technology flag all share the responsibility to communicate to the American public that technology is indeed alive and well," said George F. Mechlin, VP of R&D at Westinghouse, in 1983, naming fuel cells, coal conversion, solar photovoltaics, microprocessors, optics, lasers, and robotics as some of the things that would change American life by the end of the decade. "People hostile to technology have emphasized the negative significance of the fall of Skylab, DC-10 accidents, and Three Mile Island," Mechlin continued, dismissing them as rare bumps in the long road of social progress.[38] By the mid-1980s, scientists felt sure that two fields, physics and molecular biology, would keep them busy through the end of the century, confident that decoding the secrets of the atom and the gene represented the skeleton key to the future.[39] As well, in its annual forecast of 1984, of all years, the World Future Society delivered encouraging news about our technological future, with nary an Orwellian scenario in sight. In addition to the United States having a permanent base on the moon by 2007, the Society predicted, there was no doubt that robots were going to become a significantly greater part of the nation's demographic landscape, as the population of robots was growing thirty percent a year while that of humans just two percent. The organization did not point out, however, that at that rate it would take a few millennia for us to start making their beds and cleaning their dishes.[40]

While technology was definitely on the rebound, the idea that robots or any other gizmos would liberate women from housework was summarily dismissed by those who knew better. In 1986, Betty Freidan made it clear that it would not be science but rather basic human values that would lead to a more progressive society, seeing parallels between this latest round of protechnology rhetoric and that of the past. In her 1963 landmark book *The Feminine Mystique*, in fact, Freidan explained that it wasn't the introduction of new appliances that was freeing women from their homes but rather the desire to enter the working world, volunteer in the community, or pursue other personal goals. As new, even more high-tech appliances rolled out into the marketplace some twenty years later, Freidan was doubtful about their alleged ability to save women time and energy. "Are these computer-programmed designs going to revolutionize life for the American housewife?" she asked, wondering if "women, 'freed' more and more from housework by sophisticated appliances, [would] abandon their homes to become enslaved to the time clock." Her answer was a curt "I don't think so," noting that many twentieth-century "time-saving devices" (such as the vacuum cleaner) actually added to housewives' workload because they became an excuse for other family members to not help with chores and multiplied their frequency. Women in the mid-1960s had spent four hours cleaning their houses—the same or even more time than their mothers and grandmothers—making Freidan suspect of a new generation of high-tech appliances whose marketers promised even greater liberation from domestic drudgery.[41]

Gender politics aside, the renewed conviction that science and technology would lead us to a better future continued to gain traction throughout the 1980s. Toward the end of the decade, with a new century and millennium in sight, this conviction took on an even deeper resonance. "We'll see a minimum of ten times as much progress in the next 12 years as we've seen in the past 12," believed John Peers, president of Novix, a Silicon Valley software maker, in 1988, quite a claim given the not too shabby stream of innovations that had appeared since 1976. For Peers and others, however, the scientific and technological breakthroughs of the past decade or so—primarily the VCR, CD, and PC in electronics and genetically engineered vaccines in biotech—would pale in comparison to what would be around by the turn of the millennium. "We'll have capabilities no humans ever had," agreed Ralph E. Gomory, senior VP at IBM, thinking that a transformation equivalent to that which had brought forth the automobile, telephone, airplane, television, and atomic bomb would occur by the year 2000. Why were industry experts so keyed up about the relatively near future? "In contrast with earlier decades of invention, man stands at the dawn of the Age of Insight," was *Fortune's* answer, defining this weighty concept as "a new era of understanding how things work and how to make them work better." The

Age of Insight would be a fertile breeding ground for everything from artificially intelligent computers to diagnostic machines much like Dr. McCoy's
in *Star Trek*, the magazine explained, representing a quantum leap in science
and technology because of the evolution of "smart" capabilities. The digitalization of society in the 1990s would indeed bring many of the changes *Fortune* and industry insiders predicted, with all indications being that the first
twelve years of the twenty-first century would produce another exponential
leap in this kind of "insight."[42]

For some at the end of the 1980s, the big issue wasn't whether there'd be
amazing "progress" made in the next decade but how people would cope with
such major upheaval. "If there is anything truly speculative about the '90s, it
may be not what technology will bring," observed *Newsweek* on Christmas
Day 1989, "but rather how human beings will adapt to the most rapid change
the species has ever experienced."[43] If "Envisioning the Future: IFEx89" was
at all a true look at what lay ahead, there was little need to worry. At the
three-day event held at the International Design Center in Long Island City,
Queens, the postwar idea of the home as a domestic paradise brought to us
by science and technology was revived, a new and improved version of the
kind of ideas last circulating during the Eisenhower administration. One
speaker, James W. Botkin, a business consultant, envisioned in the year 2020
larger houses to accommodate extended families, levitating walls that could
be rearranged when company arrived, and new supplies of once-plentiful
woods like mahogany and teak, the latter made possible through genetic
engineering and biotechnology. "Scientists have already made purple lettuce
and square tomatoes," so "there's no reason why they can't make an abundant
forest of mahogany trees in nice shapes," Botkin told the audience, another
idea that would have felt right at home thirty years earlier.[44]

Botkin wasn't the only one at the time still dreaming how food could be
magically transformed in the future, with science decoding its secrets and
improving on Mother Nature's respectable but flawed efforts. The idea of fatless fat flourished in the late 1980s, a scientific alternative to the fat-friendly
scenario in Woody Allen's 1973 film *Sleeper,* in which steak, cream pies, and
hot fudge were considered the health foods of the twenty-second century.
Procter & Gamble and other food companies saw sucrose polyester as the
secret weapon that would take us to the promised land of guiltless indul-
gence, confident they would eventually figure out the curious texture and the
more disturbing "slippage" issue, and turn this dream into reality. As we now
know, this particular dream turned out to be too good to be true, apparently
even beyond the Age of Insight.[45]

There was no shortage of dreams in the early 1990s, however, as we came that much closer to the limitless possibilities of the twenty-first century. In its forecast of the next century in 1992, *Time* was positively effusive about what was to come in science and technology:

> When asked to close their eyes and imagine the shape of technology in the twenty-first century, scientists and industrial planners describe a world filled with intelligent machines, multisensual media and artificial creatures so highly evolved they will seem as alive as dogs and cats. If even their most conservative projections come true, the next century may bring advances no less momentous than the Bomb, the Pill and the digital computer. Should the more radical predictions prove correct, our descendants may encounter technological upheavals that could make twentieth-century breakthroughs seem tame.[46]

Authorities in science and technology, naturally, were as excited as *Time* about the possibilities ahead. "We're at the knee of a course after which all those intimations of the future may actually come true," believed John Holzrichter, director of institutional R&D at Lawrence Livermore Labs, feeling that the twenty-first century could really be the "twenty-first century." If even some of the predictions being made by those with expertise in specific fields came true, the next century could indeed live up to the mythology that had surrounded it for the past few decades. Nicholas Negroponte, director of MIT's Media Lab, foresaw "full-color, large-scale, holographic TV with force feedback and olfactory output," for example, a cross, in short, between Feel-o-Vision and Smell-o-Vision. Steven Levy, author of the 1992 *Artificial Life*, claimed that in the next century "we'll relate to our machines as we now relate to domestic animals," his particular vision a self-replicating, mobile robot that could find its own sources of energy (hopefully not us or Fido). Levy's idea was one step closer to the recurrent theme of merging Man and machine, something that many experts now believed could very well happen within our own lifetimes as artificial intelligence progressed.[47]

Interestingly, television, an icon of the future since its debut almost half a century earlier, was viewed in the early 1990s as something that could very well create a much more tribal society in the next century. "The array of program choices, already so bewildering, will multiply almost to infinity," predicted *Time* in 1992, making some worry that many more channels would lead to much more Popcornesque "cocooning." Already, with fewer than 100 channels to choose from, it seemed that our national community was breaking down, at least in part because of televisual fragmentation. "We have nothing to share now," complained Kurt Vonnegut that same year, believing that "there are thousands of things a person sitting at home can see that nobody else is seeing [and] we have become lonelier because we no longer have a few central works of art to discuss."[48]

Vonnegut wasn't the only one thinking that television was acting as a divisive force, something that would only accelerate as hundreds more channels were made available. "Within today's cultural and intellectual communities there is no longer any consensus about what kind of information one should know," wrote Katie Lynes in the *Canadian Forum*, something that did not bode well for the future, given the number of channels that were being added to cable systems every month in the early 1990s.[49] Writer and social critic Andrei Codrescu worried that a twenty-first-century version of television could lead not only to a loss of community but to the loss of the individual self. "Will people still know where they live, or will they be living entirely in the hyperreality of television, with their memories provided by TV programming?" Codrescu asked, seeing the future of television through quite the Orwellian lens.[50]

Like Codrescu, Neil Postman, chair of NYU's communications department, believed the implications of an infinite media universe were much more than the loss of something to chat over around the cultural water cooler. "Because most public events and entertainment will be experienced privately, people will lose a sense of how to behave in public," Postman thought, with *Time* agreeing that "the couch potatoes of the future, whose every entertainment wish will be granted at the touch of a button, may have trouble interacting with one another in the real world."[51] Postman, a harsh critic of the social consequences of rampant popular and consumer culture, was expectedly not optimistic about the prospects of what would in all likelihood be a much more technology-oriented future. "Public life will have disappeared because we did not see, in time to reverse the process, that our dazzling technologies were privatizing almost all social activities," he bewailed, seeing few reasons for mid-twenty-first-century citizens to leave their homes with all the entertainment options that would inevitably be available (already being realized, of course). Michael Medved, the media critic, also worried about emerging technologies squelching civic life, and that we would be, as Robert Putnam would soon put it, "bowling alone." "Will we live in a 500-channel environment where people never go out of their homes and have their only significant relationships with characters on huge TV screens?" he wondered in 1993, something that would actually begin taking place in less than a decade, not through television but rather via online role-playing games such as Sims, Quake, and Doom.[52]

Extra concern surrounded the art of reading as encroaching technologies threatened curling up with a good book or learning about world events via the tried and true newspaper. Previous revolutionary technologies, for example the telephone, radio, and television, had prompted similar worries, but the computer, with its textual orientation, could very well gobble up the written word, some believed. "The printed word is part of an old order that we are moving away from," thought Sven Birkerts of the *Boston Review*, seeing "a *terra nova* governed almost entirely by electronic communications" on the horizon. Even the redesign of that bastion of print journalism, the *New Yorker*, in 1993 was considered by reading lovers to be a sign of the times, part of the emergence of a "scanning" culture that had no time for detail and subtlety. The rise of audio books too in the early 1990s was cause for some to think that reading would soon be dead in the water, tossed into the dustbin of history like leeching or the horse carriage as we increasingly chose to listen to literature.[53] Author David Halberstam had a different concern about the future of reading at the time, noting that "as the literacy rate declines in this country, more and more people are writing books." "Are we approaching the moment where more people will write books than will be able to read them?" Halberstam asked, only half kidding.[54]

The idea of technological convergence, hinted at in previous paradigms of the future but never really articulated clearly, began to gel in the early 1990s as it became apparent that the computer could and would become linked to other devices. "With the convergence of wireless communications and digital computing, it won't be long until you can sit at the beach with your personal communicator and take part in a video conference anywhere in the world," envisioned George Fisher, chairman of Motorola, in 1993, no doubt excited that his company would be making such miracles possible.[55] The ability for the computer to literally hook up with all sorts of things made some realize how promiscuous it would soon be. "The telephone and radio and television cavort with the automobile and the airplane and the computer, which itself has an astonishing capacity to copulate with every imaginable device from the printing press to the household diary and cookbook," observed Daniel J. Boorstin that same year.[56]

Boorstin, who as a Pulitzer Prize winner in history and past Librarian of Congress had as keen a read on which ways the American winds were blowing as anyone, believed that licentious technological convergence was part of a much bigger cultural shift taking place in the 1990s. With technology becoming in essence the story of our particular time and place, he argued, we were moving from a Darwinian society made up of three proverbial kingdoms—Animal, Vegetable, and Mineral—to a fourth, the Machine Kingdom. "We have been catapulted from the world of knowledge (information gathered and arranged for its meaning) into a world of data (gathered by mechanized observers)," Boorstin argued, the concern being that "we have created and mastered machines before realizing how they may master us."[57] Boorstin would not have been happy to hear Oliver Stone's concurrent idea of the future, which, if realized, would take his Machine Kingdom to an entirely new realm. "Artificial intelligence will replace experience," Stone thought, seeing "imagery and media which go directly into our circuitry" as the next generation of thinking and feeling. "'Experience' will be like having a dream, which after years becomes a layer of consciousness," Stone envisioned, the movie director apparently taking a page out of the Philip K. Dick school of futurism.[58] Regardless of which particular path it took, the Age of Insight was off and running, its future virtually assured in the new frontier that would be the twenty-first century.

THE THIRD WAVE

Should there be any doubt whether there was a single phenomenon that encouraged many to completely rejuggle their outlook for the future throughout the 1980s and early 1990s, it was without question the rapid march of computer technology and, specifically, the introduction of the PC. This was made readily apparent by Alvin Toffler, whose concept of an "electronic cottage" presented in his 1980 *The Third Wave* seemed very much like the next generation of Marshall McLuhan's televisual "global village," with personal computers poised to become the new technological hearth of the home. "As the basis of our economy shifts from material goods to information, wealth and power will be defined in terms of information," agreed Peter Schwartz that same seminal year, believing that new technologies would cause fundamental changes to society over the course of the next decade or so.[59]

With such heavily freighted ideas as a jumping-off point, it was easy to go a bit too far with how the emergence of a truly electronic society would play out. "Widespread adoption of the electronic office will mean the disappearance of the usual pyramids of printed paper," believed *Nation's Business* in 1980, one voice within a very large chorus proclaiming an emerging "paperless society" as we became a nation of screen watchers.[60] As well, the running theme of the universal library was in circulation, this time merging with the idea of instant search capabilities as computers evolved in the early 1980s. "Libraries of the future will store information on giant videodiscs, each one of which can hold the contents of hundreds of books," envisioned *US News & World Report* in 1983, underestimating the memory of "libraries of the future" by a few gazillion gigabytes rather than overestimating the encroachment of computers on everyday life. "No longer will scholars find research a time-consuming endeavor," the magazine continued, seeing in the next century the possibility of someone typing a phrase into a computer "and within a matter of seconds, pertinent information from thousands of discs will be retrieved by the library's computer." Could Sergey Brin and Larry Page, then tykes but later of Google fame, have been reading the magazine in the pediatrician's office?[61]

Work too, of course, would no doubt be reinvented as the postindustrial third wave washed over everything in its path. Through both the actual automation of labor in the early 1980s and the seemingly certain coming wave of telecommuting, computers were expected to do nothing less than eventually revolutionize the workplace. "Labor will become less and less important," claimed NYU economics professor and Nobel Prize winner Wassily Leontief in 1983, seeing the computerized writing on the wall and adding the Orwellian news that "more and more workers will be replaced by machines." Leontief and others saw the emerging technological revolution of the decade much like that of the Industrial Revolution of a century or two past, which had radically transformed a predominantly rural, agriculture-based economy into an urban one geared toward manufacturing.[62] A few years later, however, the telecommuting revolution had yet to arrive, causing some to wonder how long it would take or if it would ever materialize. "This [telecommuting] is not an overnight phenomenon, as much as some people would like it to be," said Jack M. Niles, director of the IT program at USC, in 1986, a rare instance in which the social aspects of computer technology lagged behind projections. Only 3,000–5,000 people were in fact then working by computer at home for employers or clients, according to the Office of Technology Assessment, a research arm of Congress, which now considered the much ballyhooed estimate that fifty percent of the workforce would soon be telecommuting "highly unlikely."[63]

More importantly, the jury was still out on whether computers, like the next generation of television, would have a positive or negative impact on society as a whole. Some were able to imagine what would become the kind of virtual communities that would, just a decade and a half later, heavily populate the Internet, a new way for people around the world to literally connect.

Gene Youngblood, professor of film and video at the California Institute of Arts, for example, saw in 1983 the rise of "communities of consciousness" as computer networks linked people "separated by vast distances but sharing common ideologies and interests," a phenomenon he thought could even replace traditional neighborhoods.[64] The possibilities for the computer to encourage community building were seemingly limitless, the more prescient could foresee, capable of reshaping work, leisure, and everything in between. "Bridge and other card games, social events, and business conducted long distance by computer will change the way people make friends," envisioned *US News & World Report* the next year, also seeing "interactive classes in home repair, dealing with teenagers, the art of negotiation, and health and fitness" as part of the coming revolution. Those in the business naturally believed the technology would in the future change life as we knew it, especially regarding how we exchanged ideas and information. "I predict that the communicating microcomputer will replace the telephone as the predominant means of interpersonal and group communications," confidently stated Kevin Kelly, editor of the *Whole Earth Software Review*, that same year, a pretty accurate forecast of how e-mail would in a decade or so begin to consume many people's waking hours.[65]

Others, however, were less happy-go-lucky about the ever-growing power of the personal computer, viewing the machines not unlike a late twentieth-century version of The Thing, The Blob, or some other sci-fi monster that threatened to gobble up anything and everything it pleased. Some, in fact, were less than enthusiastic about the emergence of computer-based communities, thinking they, like an infinite number of television channels to choose from, could very well fragment society rather than bring people together à la McLuhan's global village. William Kuhns, communications professor at the University of Ottawa, for example, saw on the horizon in 1983 "tiny specialized tribes, interlocked electronically, perhaps faceless to one another, sharing a private language, a private interest, and all the time becoming more solitary and introverted."[66]

Three years earlier, in fact, Peter Schwartz had recognized that electronic tribes could be a source of unity or divisiveness, laying out two very different future outcomes in his classic scenario-based approach. Information technology could be the basis for computer users "retreating into ever smaller, narrower worlds that rule out their former concern for other people" or, rather, lead to the possibility for them to "create new kinds of political networks [and] alliances around issues of concern."[67] Still others, of course, seemed clueless about the revolution on our very doorstep. "Our grandchildren will be using a complex information-set telephone," wrote Newt Gingrich in 1985, then a US congressman from Georgia and (like Al Gore) a practicing futurist as author of *Window of Opportunity: A Blueprint for the Future.* "They will utilize the library by telephone, shop by telephone, send information to and from their workplaces by telephone," Gingrich predicted, like many before him getting the idea right but the technology wrong and overestimating how long it would take for the concept to reach the marketplace by a good half-century or so.[68]

The possibility for the computer of the future to create a world of electronically connected recluses was hardly the worst-case scenario of the third wave. The flip side of their unsurpassed power was the chance they'd be used for nefarious purposes or at least prove to be highly vulnerable to those with such intent, some could foresee. "Computers will become a popular target for terrorists," predicted the World Future Society in 1989, recognizing that "attacks on computer networks, telecommunications facilities, or defense computers could prove a major security threat to nations." The Society also believed that "future wars may be fought on supercomputers" but that the machines could actually save lives because of their own predictive capabilities. "A military leader may capitulate after receiving an unfavorable computer readout, rather than undergoing a bloody battle with real troops," the Society foresaw, an encouraging instance of advanced technology possibly keeping a kind of peace rather than playing its usual role as agent of more efficient destruction and death.[69]

It soon became clear, in fact, that the computer could not only be the ultimate information processing and communications tool but a gateway to an alternate universe. "Computer games will still be a favorite pastime in the 21st century, but a new product—'Virtual Reality'—will dominate the American market," predicted Judith Waldrop in 1991, seeing the technology used not just as entertainment but for educational and therapeutic purposes as well (which it now indeed is).[70] Howard Rheingold, the biggest champion of virtual reality (VR) in the early 1990s, envisioned (quite literally) virtual sex, virtual sports, and virtually (so to speak) anything and everything else, a simulated world that would seem every bit as real, or even more real, than the one bound by time and space. Virtual reality would be just one of many new technologies that would, as *Time* described it in 1992, "put what is now considered pure science fiction well within society's reach," enabling possibilities limited only to one's imagination.[71] Diane English, television producer and creator of *Murphy Brown*, thought the technology would completely reshape her industry by the mid-twenty-first century, backing up her claim with what was sure to be a popular application of the technology. "Virtual reality will give rise, for example, to 'Virtual Stooge,' where you call up any episode of 'The Three Stooges' and become the Fourth Stooge—actually experiencing the sensation of being whacked on the head with a plank by Curly," English imagined, adding the obvious fact that "this will be a hit primarily with men."[72]

FIN—DE—MILLENNIUM

Although little else in the future could be as exciting as that, for men at least, Americans could look forward to other things to come. With many breathing a collective sigh of relief after Orwell's titular year passed with few of his prophecies yet realized, the approach of the 1990s, as in decades past, caused many to muse over what might lie ahead for the next ten years. For this decade, the largest elephants in the room were clearly the graying of America ("Now the boomers are—gasp!—middle-aged and they are taking society with them," remarked *Business Week* in 1989) and the almost sudden recognition of how many Hispanics ("a nation within a nation," according to the magazine) there were and how many more there would be in the future. Market researchers were quick to extrapolate the implications of these demographic bulges, especially the former, because of its vast economic stakes. Thomas Mandel, a senior consultant at SRI, thought America might go through a "collective mid-life crisis" as tens of millions of soon-to-be forty-somethings struggled with physical decline and unsatisfying jobs, while David Meer, senior VP at the Daniel Yankelovich Group (a split-off from what was now Yankelovich, Clancy & Shulman), saw a pervasive "search for community, safety, and meaning" ahead led by aging boomers.[73] Even with their aching joints, career dissatisfaction, and all-encompassing quest for the answers to the big questions of life, many boomers would be in the 1990s, almost unquestionably, loaded. "The United States stands at the brink of the most affluent decade in its history because of the middle-aging of the baby boom," claimed Cheryl Russell, editor-in-chief of *American Demographics* and author of *100 Predictions for the Baby Boom*, knowing that the leading edge of the generation would soon be at the peak of their earning power.[74]

The career success of many women baby boomers during the Reagan years, as well as the once rebellious generation's full embrace of neotraditional values, was cause for some to think that feminism would play a minor role in the future. Gloria Steinem, however, believed that the "second wave" of feminism was not in decline but had just begun, with much work remaining for women to achieve full equality. "By all historical precedent, this wave will last at least a century, too," she predicted, likening it to the first wave, which had been started by nineteenth-century suffragists and had ended only with the 1970s women's movement. Steinem cited reproductive freedom, "democratic families," the redefinition of work, and the depoliticization of culture as goals women still had to work toward, the realization of which would stretch well into the twenty-first century.[75] Another feminist of sorts, Dr. Ruth Westheimer, saw a different kind of liberation ahead for women of the twenty-first century. "Most women will have orgasms" in the year 2053, the diminutive sex therapist said sixty years earlier, an achievement that would be part and parcel of our "more sexually literate" society.[76]

Given the expectation that the 1990s would be a decade oriented toward social consciousness, it was not surprising that many anticipated a revival of the 1970s-era environmental movement. Once-activist boomers, now in positions of power and looking for a cause, would put their money where their mouths were, many believed, making environmentalism again a cultural priority for the future. Polls in the late 1980s in fact already put environmental issues right alongside crime, drugs, and AIDS as a social concern, beating out the historical power trio of the economy, nuclear war, and communism. It was hardly a given, however, that after perhaps the most materialistic decade in history, Americans would adjust their lifestyles, even to create a healthier planet. "It will not be easy for a disposable society to adjust to sorting household trash," thought *Business Week* in 1989, but both local governments and regular folks would indeed adopt recycling during the next decade as the once-fringe movement became mainstream.[77] Ronald Bailey, writing for *National Review* the next year, satirized the power environmentalism held, especially among the liberal elite:

> Doom haunts the end of the twentieth century. Cocktail parties in Georgetown, Santa Monica, and Manhattan are suffused with a *fin-de-millennium* air. The unwary partygoer will encounter fanatics determined to avert the apocalypse through the proper rituals. If only Americans will use cloth diapers, nonphosphate detergents, cosmetics not tested on animals, and eat environmentally sound ice cream (Rainforest Crunch) from Ben and Jerry's, then maybe a few righteous souls will survive the coming holocaust.[78]

Bailey was being tongue in cheek, but some of the environmental dangers he thought were overblown were in fact real. "Global warming during the next 50 years could cause persistent droughts and changing vegetation patterns that may lead to massive forest fires in North America," cautioned the World Future Society in 1992, one of many such warnings that basically went unheeded.[79]

With the Cold War over and stagflation nipped in the bud, however, America seemed to be back on course, encouraging surveyors of the scene to look ahead to the mother of all futures, the year 2000. "The year 2000, once a bench mark of science fiction, looms only 47 quarterly reports away," noted *US News & World Report* in 1988, the countdown begun as millennium fever picked up steam.[80] The following year, *Life* described the coming event in the monumental terms it deserved, and asked some reasonable questions:

> We await its arrival with the same anticipation we had as children watching the odometer on the family's old Chevy turn to a row of zeros. But when it rolls around less than 11 years from now, will we know how to greet it? Will we call it two thousand, twenty hundred, or perhaps resort to the jingo '80s and just say 20-something? A more serious question looms ahead: Can the next century possibly live up to our expectations for a better tomorrow?[81]

Besides recognizing the historical significance of what would soon take place, *Life*'s editors were decidedly bullish on the next century, confident that the third millennium would at least get off to a good start:

> Much of the future looks promising. We will eat better and live longer. We will work less and stay home more. Technology will befriend us, freeing us of boring tasks and linking us still closer to the world at large. Our newest neighbors may be extraterrestrial, our next platoon a soldier's robotic. As we become increasingly aware of the fragility of the earth, we will have to treat it more kindly.[82]

Contributing to such over-the-top enthusiasm was of course the victory of capitalism, timed rather perfectly with the beginning of the last decade of the millennium. Just two weeks into the 1990s, for example, *Fortune* announced we had entered the "Era of Possibilities," citing the end of communist rule in Czechoslovakia as the final nail in the coffin of the Cold War. "In both the ideological and material realms, the West has triumphed," the business magazine proclaimed a year before the dissolution of the USSR, sending a loud and proud message for "Capitalists of the world, awake!" The previous June,

Francis Fukuyama, a then-obscure State Department planner, had declared in an essay in the magazine the *National Interest* that with the demise of the Marxist/Leninist political model, it was the "end of history," earning him instant fame in the age of the sound bite. It would be economic performance, not military might, that would determine the measure of a nation in this new era, as *Fortune* translated Fukuyama's thesis, proposing that "trade wars may replace Star Wars."[83] Some were even predicting that with the end of the 1980s we were entering a "post-greed" era, with enough signs—Malcolm Forbes's death soon after his $42 million seventieth birthday party, the collapse of Donald Trump's empire (and marriage), and the indictment of Michael Milken, not to mention the recall of Perrier—to suggest they were right. Tom Wolfe, who had so presciently laid out the emerging zeitgeist of the nation at the beginning of the three previous decades, believed in 1991 that "We are leaving the period of money fever that was the Eighties and entering a period of moral fever."[84]

Moral or otherwise, there was no doubt that a handful of seismic international events—the crumbling of the Berlin Wall in 1989, the collapse of the USSR in 1991, and the approaching integration of the European Common Market in 1993—was creating a new world order in which America's long-term role was unclear. Despite *Fortune*'s view that it was high time for capitalists around the world to awake, some were convinced that the next 100 years would not be a repeat of Henry Luce's "American Century." "No one at the end of the 20th century is less prepared for the competition that lies ahead in the 21st century," wrote MIT economist Lester Thurow in his 1992 bestseller *Head to Head: The Coming Economic Battle Among Japan, Europe, and America*, certainly an exaggeration but something that got people thinking that there might indeed be dents in the nation's armor.[85] The country's educational system was of particular concern, especially in technical fields that would no doubt play a huge role in the future. "In a world whose workers require ever more basic education, technological savvy and specialized skill," said Marvin Cetron and Owen Davies in their new book, *Crystal Globe*, "America's schools are the least successful in the Western world." Thurow, not surprisingly, was on the same page, predicting that America was destined to a secondary position in science, engineering, and overall productivity, and that the nation would very possibly be pulling the short straw against Europe and Japan in the twenty-first century.[86]

Thurow wasn't the only one in the early 1990s fretting that the East would soon be going head to head with the West and that the former might come out on top. Although it was now, after an amazing twenty-year run in which it had grabbed fifteen percent of the world's GNP, showing some signs of vulnerability, that Japan remained a huge threat to America's retaining its leadership position in the global economy. "Japan has made technology its arts, commerce its religion, and frugality and patience its culture," wrote economics professor Abu Selimuddin in 1993, asking the reasonable question "Will the 21st century be Japanese?" Selimuddin and others were concerned about the softening of the US economy in the early 1990s, seeing it and other red flags as signs that the nation's best or, at least, most prosperous days were behind it. "Diminishing economic horizons, fewer jobs, stagnating real income, faltering living standards, escalating health care costs, a ballooning national deficit, and accumulating personal and business debts are becoming the critical concerns besetting an America in decline," Selimuddin lamented, looking back longingly to the late 1960s when the United States had accounted for a whopping forty-six percent of the world's GNP and monopolized many industries.[87] Others had different, but equally significant, concerns about America's future at the mid-twenty-first century. "Will 1 percent of the country still be supporting the other 99 percent?" asked Robin Leach, host of TV's "Lifestyles of the Rich and Famous," then asking the more important question (to him at least) "Will caviar reserves have been depleted in 60 years?"[88]

A more competitive economic climate and the scarcity of caviar were mild concerns, however, to those who thought there'd be much bigger fish to fry in the twenty-first century. Some believed that troubles of biblical proportions awaited in the new millennium, a direct counterargument to the majority opinion that the world was becoming more united through democracy and capitalism. "What will we do when the terrorists get nuclear or chemical or biological weapons?" asked Louis Finch of the Rand Corporation in 1990, thinking that "inevitably, they will."[89] The leader of the fin-de-millennium doomsday scenario, however, was Robert Kaplan, whose 1994 article in *Atlantic Monthly*, "The Coming Anarchy," made the *Road Warrior* movies seem like a day at the beach. Random violence, deadly epidemics, common lawlessness, you name it, Kaplan's world of tomorrow was not going to be a pretty place. If Kaplan hadn't been correct about other bad news in the past—including his warning that Saddam Hussein was going to be big trouble—this latest bummer of a prediction would have been quickly dismissed.[90]

While terrorism and anarchy were truly extreme dystopian scenarios, there was little doubt that the twenty-first century would be a much more complex time for all who would inhabit it. Even optimists were concerned about the prospect of a world led by five superpowers—the United States,

China, Russia, Japan, and a European Union—making the bilateral Cold War seem like the good old days. "[We are] returning to a more traditional and complicated time of multipolarity, with a growing number of countries increasingly able to affect the course of events," thought former US Secretary of State Lawrence Eagleburger, a potentially viable situation not unlike that which led to World War I.[91] *Business Week* estimated that there were at least thirty "low-intensity" wars and insurgencies in play in 1994, with a handful of scenarios that likely had geopolitical analysts losing sleep, including a worldwide recession, the breakup of China, widespread ecological damage, conflict among ex-Soviet republics, and, to boot, hundreds or thousands of unaccounted-for nukes.[92] "We are not entering a new century, we are entering a new era," stated Israeli Foreign Minister Shimon Peres in late 1994, words that would indeed describe the next phase of the history of the future as the third millennium unfolded.[93]

The future had been reborn, if you will, in the 1980s, its swagger restored under Ronald Reagan's faith in the power and glory of laissez-faire capitalism. Yesterday's tomorrow was soon just a bad dream, a blip in the nation's divinely ordained mission of progress and the promise of better days ahead. With business again America's first order of business, futurism became heavily corporatized, a marketing tool offering a competitive advantage to those who possessed it. Promoted to the front office, futurism, along with its new trusty sidekick, trends, was now part of the national conversation, the most successful practitioners in the field considered cultural superstars and media darlings. America had become Popcornized, all of us aspiring futurists to better compete in the global economy. With the megatrend of megatrends coming into full view, anticipating tomorrow would become even more important, the budding Information Age about to burst into full bloom.

CHAPTER 6

THE MATRIX,
1995—

"Your mind makes it real."

—Morpheus, in the 1999 movie *The Matrix*

IN JUNE 1996, THE WORLD FUTURE SOCIETY ISSUED A REPORT CALLED "The Cyber Future," listing no fewer than ninety-two ways that information technology would change life by 2025. "Infotech is amplifying our ability to produce the material goods of life, to cure diseases, and to expand the human enterprise into the universe," said Edward Cornish, president of the Society, in explaining how and why the cyber future would make tomorrow a much different place. There was a catch, however. "We are becoming god-like in our capabilities," he thought, but, because the social implications of emerging information technologies were so unclear, "we do not know how to use our growing power wisely." Despite American society becoming richer and better educated, for example, Cornish saw lots more isolation and lethargy ahead for us in a few decades as computers turned today's television couch potatoes into a next generation of technological vegetables.[1]

Cornish's ambivalence about the state of the country and world in some thirty years was typical of the way that many, futurists and nonfuturists alike, were beginning to think as information technology changed much of what we did and how we did it. The future, and the present for that matter, was irrevocably altered in the mid-1990s, when it became clear that the Internet was going to be a major force in our lives. Even in the Dark Ages of the mid-1990s, some were fully aware that we were at the relative beginning of Something Really Big, a conclusion that a four-year-old could now make. Technology had of course always been at the forefront of futurism, but the digitalization of society was, it seemed, swamping almost everything else in its path at startling speed, making the technological revolutions of the past seem downright clunky. Through the dot-com bubble, its bursting, and the mainstreaming of the Internet, many visions of tomorrow shifted from the real world to a virtual one, these visions often a complex mash-up of utopian dreams and dystopian nightmares. More than ever, there was a "catch" to the future, the idea that there were ghosts in our growing number of machines a recurring theme in our prophecies and predictions. With the lines between man and machine and what is real and not real getting increasingly fuzzy, our faith in and fears about the future continue to accelerate, the stakes of tomorrow never higher.

THE ROAD AHEAD

As in the past, the approach of a new century and new millennium brought the idea of the future into high relief, magnifying both our excitement and our anxiety about what was to come. With the mother of all dates coming up fast, it was prime time for virtually anyone with anything to say about the future to pipe in. Experts of all stripes came out of the woodwork, capitalizing on what was probably the biggest interest in tomorrow in at least twenty years, when we hit the three-quarter-century mark and America celebrated its 200th birthday. If the focus in the mid-1970s was trying to catch a glimmer of hope in an overpopulated, economically depressed tomorrow, mid- to late 1990s futurism was mostly about the digitalization of everyday life, especially among visionaries whose feet were already solidly planted in information technology. Bill Gates's 1995 *The Road Ahead*, for example, not surprisingly looked to the digital future (failing to see the rise of universal search and a little company called Google), while Nicholas Negroponte's *Being Digital* of the same year seemed to correctly anticipate a "post-information age" in which the PC would become the cornerstone of life as we knew it (and would ultimately kill television). In his 1997 *What Will Be*, Michael Dertouzos, Internet pioneer and MIT honcho, looked to the Athens flea market of ancient Greece, of all places, as the model for the information marketplace of the future, a virtual community (similar to the one Howard Rheingold had described a few years earlier) in which ideas were exchanged like any other commodity bought, sold, or shared.

Techies weren't the only ones writing books about the future as we crossed over into a new century and millennium, however, with business gurus too adding their own two (or more) cents. Faith Popcorn kept popping off with her 1996 *Clicking* ("an invaluable road map to the newest lifestyle trends," Amazon.com thought), while Strauss and Howe continued their generational view of the past, present, and future in their *The Fourth Turning* of the same year. Jim Taylor and Watts Wacker's *The 500-Year Delta* and J. Walker Smith and Ann Clurman's *Rocking the Ages* of 1997, and my own *The Future Ain't What It Used to Be* of the following year, also offered marketers fodder for future thought, and the Bay Area power trio Peter Schwartz, Peter Leyden, and Joel Hyatt painted a rosy picture of the twenty-first century in their 1999 *The Long Boom*. As expected, there seemed to be no shortage of resources for those wanting to prepare for things to come in the next millennium, and both technology experts and businesspeople were gung-ho on the future.

For filmmakers of the mid- to late 1990s looking ahead to the twenty-first century or beyond, however, it was a much different story. In Terry Gilliam's 1995 *Twelve Monkeys*, for example, just one percent of Earth's population remains in 2035 after a lethal virus wipes out five billion people, forcing the survivors to live underground. Earth's military is engaged in a war against a planet of insects in Paul Verhoeven's 1997 *Starship Troopers*, set in the distant future, while *Gattaca* of the same year presented a sterile world of tomorrow in which one's position in life is determined at birth based on DNA. *The Fifth Element*, also from 1997 (and also, like *Twelve Monkeys*, starring future-world-saver Bruce Willis), takes place in twenty-third-century New York City (where traffic still is congested, unfortunately). Evil, in the form of a dark planet, has arrived as it does every 5,000 years to extinguish humanity, and it is up to an ex-soldier, current taxi driver to rescue the day. With no fewer than 954 Jean-Paul Gaultier costumes used in the film, the future would be a perilous place but at least a fashionable one.

Waking up safe and sound in 2000 did little to ease our millennial jitters, cinematically speaking. No cute aliens could be found in the near-future world of Spielberg's 2001 *Artificial Intelligence: AI*, in which melted polar ice-caps have sunk all coastal cities. In this dystopian fairy tale, realistic robots serve people, but things go awry when one of them expresses human feelings for his mother, a reworking of Pinocchio as Aldous Huxley might have imagined it. There's no crime in Spielberg's 2002 *Minority Report*, based on a Philip K. Dick story, but only because genetically altered humans ("pre-cogs") are able to predict them before they happen. (To create the world of 2054 in the film, Spielberg picked the big brain of Peter Schwartz, who envisioned the very cool personalized commercials, animated cereal box, and continually updating newspaper.)[2]

Rather than plague, interplanetary warfare with bugs, genetics gone bad, or ecological disaster, it was a particularly nasty computer virus that ruined the futuristic day in the 2003 *Terminator 3: Rise of the Machines.* Can the outdated-as-a-Betamax Terminator destroy the much more advanced Terminatrix T-X sent back from 2032, we wonder, making us ask ourselves serious questions about where technology might lead us a few decades out. *I, Robot* of the following year, based on an Asimov story, was another cautionary tale of technology run amok, the threat of robots taking over the world in 2035 (what is it about the year 2035?) a familiar sci-fi device that had new resonance as "smart" robots came into actual being. Movies of the past few years set in the future have been equally dark, a sign that we haven't yet fully recovered from our millennial blues. Great Britain is a fascist state in the 2005 *V for Vendetta,* based on the graphic novel of the same name, the only individual to stand up to the oppressive government considered a terrorist. The UK, or what's left of it, fares little better in the 2006 *Children of Men,* with humankind in 2027 on the brink of extinction due to the infertility of women. Chaos, violence, and anarchy reign in this nightmare of a movie, the only voice of reason an aging hippie living in the woods. (Although it is intended to be hilarious, the 2006 *Idiocracy* is equally frightening.) And in the 2007 *I Am Legend* (the third film version of Richard Matheson's 1954 novel of the same name), a sole survivor populates New York City in 2012 after a biochemical disease kills most of humanity and turns the rest into bloodthirsty zombies. With this string of movies making the Cold War–era Earthlings-versus-aliens genre seem like a day at the beach, was there any hope for our collective future?

Perhaps the answer could be found within the fuzzy logic of the *Matrix* series, these films arguably best capturing our love-hate relationship with technology and our millennium-era anxiety about the future. In the first and by far the best film from, right on time, 1999, a computer hacker discovers that life on Earth may be a virtual reality conceived by evil artificial intelligence machines, that is, the Matrix. Rather than 1999, it is really 200 years into the future, our hero ("The One") learns, and he has been assigned the daunting task of overthrowing the Matrix to free humans from their bondage. Four years later (just enough time to finally figure out the plot for the first one), we have *The Matrix Reloaded* and, just a few months later,

The Matrix Revolutions, in which the rage against the machine continues to unfold in bewildering complexity. In *Reloaded*, thousands of humans are waking up out of their Matrix-induced slumber, attempting to live in the real world. Their numbers continue to grow and the battle moves to Zion, the last remaining real-world city and the front lines of human resistance. Importantly (hang in there), the Matrix's Agent Smith has escaped "deletion" and has morphed into a computer virus, able to infect anyone he touches. Duplicates of Smith and other, new and upgraded agents also have been released, determined to squash the rebellion. In the final installment, the battle between good and evil, human and machine, reaches a fitting if even more convoluted climax, the stakes who or which will survive to see the future.

Although much of the *Matrix* series is pure nonsense (even the actors admitted they didn't quite understand it), its basic premise is simple and compelling. There's a ghost in the machine, we're told, an idea we've heard and seen over and over in darker narratives of the future. Whether it's robots gone haywire or ornery computers robbing our life essence, we should beware of what we wish for as we fall further down the technological rabbit hole. At the turn of the twenty-first century and the third millennium, this idea took on extra significance, reflecting our ambivalence about technological "progress" and everything it brings. The fear that we're already living virtual realities, enslaved to our smarter and smarter machines, is a legitimate one, something that is only going to intensify as the stuff of the future—Internet 2.0 or "Hypernet," which will make the original seem like a Tinkertoy, 24/7 wireless and networked "lifestyles," and yes, microchips in our brains—blur the boundaries between man and machine.

In fact, as farfetched as *The Matrix* is, techies already see something like an uber-computer network emerging, a rather alarming development for any student of science fiction of the last half-century. A computer grid, much like today's mostly invisible electrical power grid, could very well be the next generation of the Internet, in which machines are linked into a single system. "If the nineteenth century was about the steam engine and the twentieth about the combustion engine, I believe that the twenty-first century will be about the grid engine," said Wolfgang Gentzsch of Sun Microsystems in 2002, just one of a host of companies leading the grid charge in the early 2000s. "The grid starts to get really interesting when it links companies, consumers, governments and other institutions to each other," agreed *Newsweek*, "the convergence of wireless technology and smart microchips embedded in inanimate objects and even people [to] change everything." Automated cars, is-it-real-or-is-it-Memorex videoconferencing, digital doubles of one's important possessions for computerized repair, and already FDA-approved biochips sending one's pulse rate to one's cardiologist in real time are just a few miracles the grid promises. The darker side of all this, however, is straight out of George Orwell, Philip K. Dick, or William Gibson on a bad day, the thought of all of us plugged into a single all-knowing, all-powerful system a classic science-fiction conceit. More disturbingly, it was the Global Grid Forum, as frightening a name as could be imagined, the organization that was in 2002 trying to make the whole thing happen, with equally scary-sounding "Globus" software to make the grid self-managing, self-diagnosing, and self-healing. "Machines that can communicate like humans and agents that police the grid all sound chillingly like the sci-future imagined in *The Matrix*," *Newsweek* couldn't help but notice, not at all a deterrent, however, for those wanting to keep pushing technology along its inevitable path through our new century and millennium.[3]

THE BIGGEST TIME BOMB IN HISTORY

Naturally, the coming of the year 2000 was like manna from heaven for those already inclined to think the end was near. Doomsday prophets hadn't had this much fun since the end of the first millennium, when many (at least many of the minority of people aware of the Gregorian calendar) thought it was the end of days. This time around, there were lots more looming cataclysmic events that would sink our ship, with everything from approaching giant meteors to mad cow disease capable of ruining our big New Year's Eve plans.[4] This was all despite the fact that the entire millennium business was mostly silly, of course, just one reason being that the twenty-first century didn't actually start until the year 2001. Besides that, many other cultures around the world used a different calendar, making the Gregorian millennium not very significant. For Muslims, the Gregorian year 2000 equated to 1420, for Hindus 1921, for the Chinese 4697, and for followers of the Hebrew calendar 5760, meaning that for most of the world, the Great Rollover was just another, likely nonapocalyptic, day.[5]

Because many Gregorians were now living in the Information Age, however, it made perfect sense that if the destruction of civilization was imminent, it would arrive in digital form. Very conveniently, computer programming practices of decades past provided the perfect scenario for us to construct a convincing narrative of our demise: Y2K. Mainframe computers loaded with software that omitted the first two digits of dates would think the year 2000 was 1900, many experts in such things believed, the Millennium Bug capable of wreaking major, perhaps total, destruction. "As you spend the waning hours of 1999 waltzing to the strains of Guy Lombardo, our entire information infrastructure will be ticking toward doom," wrote Steven Levy in his 1996 report of what "doomsayers and dread merchants" had been talking about for the past year or so. Not only were businesses at risk, but a host of very scary possibilities—including planes disappearing from radar screens and even the launching of nuclear bombs—could result when "the biggest time bomb in history" silently detonated.[6]

Fearing the worst, organizations were soon hiring "Y2K busters" en masse, their software sifting through Nixon-era computer code (COBOL, no less) in search of two-digit numbers refusing to budge from the twentieth century.[7] As backup, companies were taking out Y2K insurance coverage, the policies to cover the hundreds of millions of dollars in losses from business disruptions and lawsuits should the worst-case scenario occur.[8] The electrical grid posed a particular problem, some worrywarts insisted, with credit card networks, ATMs, elevators, and telephones poised to crash when the double zeros tumbled.[9] "The prospect of this mess has lawyers drooling," said *Forbes* in 1997, with attorneys smelling trillions of dollars in legal and liability costs after the system crashed.[10]

It was no surprise, then, that sales of not just champagne were up as the big day, and possibly Armageddon, approached, but of the same kind of stuff that used to be packed into bomb shelters. Home safes to protect valuables, documents, and cash flew off the shelves, as did the usual use-only-in-emergency paraphernalia of generators, flashlights, batteries, kerosene heaters, water filtration systems, bottled water, canned food, and guns and ammo.[11] By May 1999, more than 200 cities and towns in the United States had already set up Y2K "community preparedness" programs, the fin de siècle version of the civil defense plans of the 1950s and 1960s. "The potential social chaos implications [sic] of this event . . . could precipitate a major setback for human development," fretted John L. Petersen, president of the Arlington Institute, a D.C.-based think tank, that month, about as serious a warning as could be imagined. "Y2K is a test humanity must pass," he continued in dead earnest, with failure leading to nothing less than "the painful future that we deserve."[12]

Not everyone was gnashing their teeth and proclaiming doom and gloom when it came to Y2K, however. Comedian Steve Martin seemed much less concerned than most about what *Newsweek* had referred to as "The Day the World Shuts Down," mocking our collective hysteria in a 1999 essay for the *New Yorker* titled "The Y3K Bug." "Many scientists are beginning to express

concern over the Tridecta Blighter Function, whose circuitry was not programmed to accommodate the year 3000," Martin wrote in the year "2992."
With people now living 600 years, he explained, the stroke of midnight
on December 31, 2999, would usher in some not-very-pretty things, one of
them exploding heads. What to do? "Stay home and let your head blow up,"
Martin recommended, the only downside being that "you're out of commission until a new one grows."[13] A few marketers also were using Y2K as comic
fodder. As the millennium approached, Nike ran a commercial featuring a
man jogging, presumably on January 1, as chaos from Y2K reigned. Neither
flickering lights, cash flying out of ATMs, people running wildly through the
streets, nor a runaway missile streaking through the sky would keep the dedicated, Nike-clad jogger from his appointed rounds, the clever commercial
told viewers. Even funnier was Coors's decision to nominate itself the "official beer of Y2K," much cooler than Miller's meaningless claim as the "official beer of the millennium," the latter just one of hundreds of lame attempts
to somehow capitalize on the event.[14] Although not specifically about Y2K,
both *Mystery Science Theater 3000* and Conan O'Brien's "In the Year 2000"
segment (something he hilariously continues to this day) put our collective
freak-out in much-needed perspective, each, ironically, voices of reason during what we can see in hindsight were some pretty unreasonable times.

Thankfully, Armageddon did not arrive immediately after Dick Clark's
Rockin' New Year's Eve countdown, a big sigh of relief for those fearing the
worst. "Now the biggest problem seems to be disposing of all that tuna fish
we stocked up," wrote Steven Levy, the *Newsweek* reporter who'd been covering the Y2K beat for the past few years, ten days into the new millennium,
justifiably a little embarrassed. Technology geeks had been saying the major
problems had been fixed in most countries, but nobody expected things to
go as smoothly as they did, causing some to suspect that the whole thing
was a scam orchestrated by technology companies wanting to cash in on
a once-in-a-century opportunity. In the United States alone, $100 billion
was spent on debugging computer systems, making the more skeptical think
that Corporate America and the government had fallen for the shell game
of shell games.[15] Whether or not some had exploited the situation, the Y2K
talking heads we had come to know over the past few years looked awfully
silly. "Y2K Chicken Littles have egg on their faces," wrote the *Long Island
Business News* three weeks after a global recession resulting from widespread
computer failures didn't materialize, which some of them had predicted.[16]
As well, Russians did not use the confusion of Y2K to launch a preemp-
tive nuclear strike against the United States, as Internet "gloomies" had cau-

tioned, now wagging their online tails in Internet chat rooms as "pollies" (Pollyannas) rubbed salt in their paranoid wounds.[17]

Of course, there were some Y2K glitches, not worldwide economic chaos or nuclear war, but irritating just the same. A man returning a movie to a video store in upstate New York incurred a $91,250 late charge, and the first baby born in the new year in Denmark was registered as 100 years old. As well, a German salesman was briefly $6 million richer because of a bank error in his favor, and a few prisoners in Italy temporarily were looking at an additional century in the clink.[18] Perhaps to save face, a few Y2Kers insisted we weren't yet completely out of the woods, remembering that experts had said all along that the actual turnover would be just a small part of the problem. Lots of minor but annoying glitches would plague the next few weeks or the entire year, hardcore (or just in-denial) Chicken Littles insisted, demanding we stay on full alert. Nervous Nellies also began looking to the next hoop that computers would have to jump through, February 29, the leap-year-only date that computers had not planned for.[19] "Feb2K," as this scenario became known, was now the catastrophic event that would cause nuclear missiles to be lobbed halfway around the world, something to keep gloomies happy for at least a little while longer.[20]

MILLENNIUM MODE

Y2K heebie-jeebies aside, much turn-of-the-twenty-first-century futurism paled in comparison to that which occurred 100 years earlier, when the promise of the machine made anything and everything seem possible. Thinking long term had generally become more reflective and ambivalent, less predictive and optimistic, recast by the trials and tribulations of the twentieth century (a short list being two world wars, a Great Depression, a counterculture, and about thirty years of additional average lifespan to ponder such things). In its 1950 look at what life might be like in 2000, for example, *Popular Mechanics*, like most experts at the time, had made some bold predictions (scoring with online shopping, microwave ovens, and fax machines, striking out with edible sawdust). Stepping up to the futurism plate again in 2000 to describe the world of 2050, however, editors for the same publication admitted they had "gone out of our way to err on the side of caution." This time around, it was things like pilotless planes, robot surgeons, and virtual reality entertainment—things now already well on the way to becoming realities. The magazine even hedged its bets when it came to one of the classics of futurism, a cure for cancer, seeing only "new treatments and drugs that modify the eating, drinking, and smoking behaviors" that lead to the disease. The reluctance for *Popular Mechanics* to go out on a limb with some truly visionary predictions was much more than being "once burned, twice shy," rooted in our current preference for short-term thinking and, more sadly, a general reining-in of possibilities.[21]

Much of Trudy Schlacter and Roberta Wolf's 1999 book *Millennium Mode* dedicated to the future of fashion also was filled with the kind of wishy-washy predictions now in common circulation, for example, a missed opportunity for leading designers to take a flyer. While some good Old School prophesying could be found in the book ("Just get in the shower and press the clothing sprocket, dip yourself in the clothes and they're hot-wired to computers to keep you warm or cool, change colors, whatever," the designer Stephen Strouse refreshingly imagined), our ecru vision of fashion was now about there being "very few colors" (Isaac Mizrahi) or "a balance between high and low technologies" (Tommy Hilfiger). Donna Karan had apparently abandoned her mid-1970s, rather interesting idea of people one day wearing pieces of fabric lined with ropes, now mushily believing that fashion would become "more holistic, combining our spiritual needs with our earthy ones." Overanalyzed, risk-averse, and politically correct, the future, once as fascinating as literally anything that could be imagined, had become not much more than banal commentary on our own times.[22]

A rash of predictions for the twenty-first century not surprisingly appeared in the media in 1999, many of them sounding awfully familiar. "The twenty-first century will see babies born completely outside the human body as the normal and common way to create children," said Arthur Caplan, the bioethics guru, hardly a new idea. Equally déjà vu was NIMH director Steven E. Hyman's prediction that "mental illness will be curable—and in some cases preventable," a retread that felt more 1930s than 1990s. Technology experts too seemed to be going back to the future, their forecasts straight out of an episode of the *Jetsons* or even *Buck Rogers*. "Virtual reality conferencing will eliminate the need for constant business travel," posited Aliza Sherman, president of Cybergrrl, an idea sporting grandpa's whiskers, matched by food historian Betty Fussell's reheated baked potato that "the electronic superhighway will replace the supermarket," a prediction of the postwar push-button school of futurism.[23]

Being in millennium mode was, as well, the perfect opportunity to trot out the lollapalooza of predictions—world peace. Walter Cronkite's prophecy that "humankind will establish a viable and authoritative world government that will forever abolish war as a means of settling international conflicts" was standard utopia-speak, ignorant of all historical evidence suggesting that the more things change, the more they stay the same.[24] Actor Chuck Norris, of all people, not only thought that war would be a thing of the past ("having gotten too dangerous, [it] will no longer be tolerated," he told *Popular Mechanics* in 1999) but crime and hunger as well, each karate-chopped by good old science and technology. With B-list celebrities' views of the twenty-first century eagerly sought after by journalists digging deep into their Rolodexes, futurism in its most popular form had devolved into standard fodder for the insatiable media universe, not much different than the Hollywood gossip of the week.[25]

Much more interesting was *Glamour*'s (!) sneak peek into twenty-first-century sex, in which the same old same old wasn't simply paraded out in a new party dress. "As the next century begins, the same kinds of great minds that put a man on the moon are concocting better, wilder, smarter and hotter ways to get busy," wrote Erin Bried for the magazine just as 2000 kicked off, consulting not just with the usual suspects but with the love god himself, Barry White. For Ray Kurzweil, an artificial intelligence expert, our future sex lives would imitate circa-1970s art. "By 2019, most people will have a boothlike contraption in their homes for virtual sex," he predicted, the reach-out-and-touch-someone machine much like Woody Allen's orgasmatron in *Sleeper* but capable of digitally enhancing one's lover to make him or her even more desirable. Kurzweil also foresaw, by 2030, robots created just for sex, these sexbots preferred by many to been-there, done-him-and-or-her humanoids. As well, Kurzweil envisioned "mindgasms" in our hot-and-heavy future, with having sex on the brain a much more literal affair by 2040. After swallowing or injecting nanobots, the microscopic computers would position themselves next to nerve fibers in the brain, creating a virtual sensory environment programmed specifically for the dirty deed. Deborah Blum, author of *Sex on the Brain*, saw things rather similarly, expecting "an orgasm pill on the market before 2050," some very good news for pharmaceutical companies should such a thing come to fruition.[26] Comedian Jackie Mason also saw our sexual future through a pharmaceutical lens. "There will be [a] pill to give your wife that will make her think she had a great night while you were watching the football game," Mason prophesied, adding that "you might even catch [her] taking a different pill that makes her think the tennis instructor gave her a steamy night."[27]

Whether or not such jokes were actually funny, millennium mode guaranteed there would be an abundance of satirical takes on the future, if only to relieve the anxiety associated with the turning of such a big page. What better way to poke fun at our own foibles and fears than rocketing them into the twenty-first century, where their comedy or tragedy would be even more apparent? Riffing perhaps on Woody Allen's turning upside-down of red meat, chocolate, and other indulgences, for example, Harvey Fierstein suggested we think twice about our attachment to our precious material possessions. "The collectible gems we valued and squirreled away so that our great-grandchildren could cash in will be worthless," the gravelly voiced entertainer joked, while "the crap we threw out will be priceless."[28] *The Onion*, the popular weekly satirical newspaper and website, not surprisingly weighed in on the future in 2000, publishing that year the front page of an issue dated November 17, 2034, which included such headlines as:

Florida Capsizes Under Weight of Elderly

Budweiser Red Sox Beat Home Depot Cubs 4–3 in World Series Opener

Bill Gates Denies Public's Request for Loosening of Tracking Bracelets

Final Tree Dies in Captivity[29]

With at least one professional sports team already named after (and sponsored by) a beverage (the New York Red Bulls), the *Onion's* faux future may be more prophetic than they had humorously intended.

FUTURE CHANNEL

Although it was obvious that the new century and millennium allowed all kinds of people, qualified and otherwise, to prophesy about tomorrow, voices of future's past could also be heard in the din. By 1993, the Tofflers, once the masters of the game, had all but disappeared from the futurism scene, their most recent book, *War and Anti-War*, a major bomb. In 1995, however, the couple's career was revived as one of their biggest fans, Newt Gingrich, became Speaker of the House and championed their ideas. (Other conservatives at the time were less enthralled; William Bennett said he "never understood" them, while Pat Buchanan called their work "some kind of nonsense.") Gingrich's protechnology politics, including his idea that the government should give all at-risk kids a laptop computer, however, were directly shaped by the Tofflers' *The Third Wave*.[30] In 1996, *Time* claimed that the Tofflers were again at the top of the futurism heap, beating out such heavyweights as Faith Popcorn, John Naisbitt, and Peter Drucker, and tech stars Nicholas Negroponte, Paul Saffo, and Douglas Rushkopf. Hotter than ever because of their affiliation with Gingrich's "cyber-brain trust," the Tofflers did what anyone with at least fifteen minutes of fame would do—go to Hollywood. "There's a History Channel but no Future Channel," said Alvin Toffler, who planned to remedy that situation with a multimedia effort called FutureNet. Cooked up by the Creative Artists Agency, FutureNet would include a weekly *60 Minutes*–type program, a weeknight news show called *NextNewsNow*, and a website, all devoted not to events that had already happened but to those which might.[31]

It was ironic, however, that the more the future was hyped, the thinner it became in terms of real substance, something that didn't go unnoticed by some critics. The complexities of recent times have, it seems, made most futurists want to hedge their bets, base predictions on certain conditions, or simply extrapolate from existing trends, all strategies to avoid being accused of reckless dreaming. Reviewing a flurry of books about the future published within a few months of each other in 1997, Edward Rothstein of the *New York Times* noted that instead of "the promise that there will be vast improvements say, in the power of a car engine, or in the ability to build tall buildings"—the stuff of futurism past—he saw more of "an open-ended promise" and "form without content." More information seemed to be hindering prediction rather than helping it as many (vainly) tried to turn it into something that was linear and logical.[32] "As the stock market lurches between the tugs of bulls and bears, financial analysts armed with statistics and the latest marketing theories throw up their hands in despair when asked to guess what will happen from one day to the next," piped in journalist Malcolm W. Browne in 1998, evidence that now some people were fully expecting to be able to control or manage the future and were surprised and disappointed when they of course could not.[33]

Another example of the shallower nature of our current era of recent futurism is the ambiguity surrounding the Mixmastering of America's population. The demographic upheavals that are certain to come over the next generation or two—the graying of the industrialized world, the rise of China and India, and the growing multiculturalism of the United States—are obviously major forces that will reshape virtually every aspect of tomorrow. As well, computer models have made predicting the nation's demographic makeup easier than ever, with no doubt whatsoever that America's racial deck will be shuffled over the next few decades, resulting in a majority of what were minorities. Most futurists openly admit they cannot or will not predict the social impact of this, however, perhaps out of the fear they will be proved wrong. "The political implications of this new racial landscape have not yet been considered," wrote Michael Lind for the *New York Times* in 1998, rather surprising given the enormity of the issue. For better or worse, yesterday's futurists would likely have imagined either a worst-case scenario for the once-dominant white majority or a happy melting pot of a "beige" society, in other words, but today's visionaries are reluctant to commit to any particular outcome.[34]

It's difficult, then, to resist making the case that our current paradigm of futurism is in some sense "weaker" than those of the past, which typically had more compelling and creative (if more often wrong) visions of what would be. With the notable exception of digital technology, where the world of tomorrow is as wide and wonderful as ever, the future has become a more complicated, responsible, and, resultantly, less interesting affair. Bruce Handy, in a 2000 article for *Vanity Fair*, brilliantly described the decline of futurism, believing that it had by then "become less about the future and more about the past." In place of the twenty-first-century equivalents of jetpacks, picture phones, and grouchy robots, Handy argued, those trafficking in tomorrowlands have simply recycled previous futures, resulting in the scads of "retro-futurism" scattered across American society. "Fresh visions have been in short supply of late, at least compared with the 1930s, 40s, 50s, and 60s," Handy wrote, "years when the future claimed the attention of an avid general public."[35] This thirty-five-year-or-so stretch was, according to Handy:

> . . . an era of dream cars and Kitchens of Tomorrow, of working monorails and cornerless architecture, of science-fiction movies that weren't self-referential, of industrial designers and set designers and architects and other futurists who weren't afraid to make fools of themselves.[36]

Today, however, futurism was, Handy felt, "timid [and] prudent," a sentiment shared by even some of those in the field. "The architects of destiny are all too few and far between," agreed Graham T. T. Molitor, a VP for the World Future Society, also in 2000, just one reason for the wholesale regurgitation of mid-century futurism. Recent examples of futurism in pop culture, including the TV show *Futurama* and the films *Gattaca*, *The Fifth Element*, and even *The Matrix*, drew heavily on science fiction clichés, stuck in a mashed-up twentieth-century time warp. As more evidence, futuresque consumer products like the iMac and VW Beetle were, more than anything else, comfortable, the rough edges of tomorrow rounded off to create cuddlier brands.[37]

The decline of futurism could also be detected by anyone familiar with the history of the field. In the early 1970s, Vice President Gerald Ford was the keynote speaker at one of the World Future Society's annual conferences, indicative of how much futurism was respected at the time. Three decades later, most of the few remaining Future Studies departments at universities were closing up shop, meaning that young people would have little chance of getting exposed to the field. Having "got its start when optimism was easy," as *Newsweek* put it in 2002, there seemed to be less need for futurism when, ironically in a post-9/11 world, being optimistic was not so easy. "Futurology as a kind of faith is gone," the magazine continued, "the glory days are over."[38] With change happening so fast—the Internet, decoding of the human genome, and cloning of a sheep, to name just a few of the greatest hits of the 1990s—who needed the future, one might reasonably ask.[39]

Not Hope Cristol, that's for sure. "Futurism is dead," she boldly proclaimed in *Wired* the next year, really boldly since the magazine she was writing for was, as much as any organization or individual, breathing new life into the field. Despite having an ideal name for the job, Cristol had dropped out of the futurism biz, disillusioned by the state of the art and its loss in social status. No major newspaper had reported that year's World Future Society conference, Cristol noted, and the organization had lost twenty percent of its members over the past decade. As well, a WFS member hadn't been invited to the White House since the Reagan administration, another sign that the field had lost its cachet. Cristol pined for the days when readers had anxiously anticipated the latest prophecies from futurism stars like Asimov, Fuller, and Arthur C. Clarke, intrigued by what might be coming next. Besides now being a ship of fools, she felt, futurism was doomed "because the loosely informed, jack-of-all-trades, trend-watching pontificator (read: professional futurist) is obsolete." Niche consultants and the infusion of risk analysts (armed with actuarial tables, no less) had killed the golden goose, Cristol argued, with the kind of big thinking once common if not required for the job a thing of the past. Even a successful practitioner in the field, Mike Marien, agreed at least in part with Cristol, explaining that with specialization "there isn't a market for someone who can speak about very large, holistic matters with any authority." Cristol's beef with futurism went further than its slide from public view and loss of true visionaries, seeing the discipline as nothing less than a "con." "Futurists don't have a crystal ball," she sneered, "any hausfrau with gumption and a dialup connection can do it."

Since the 1960s, Cristol wound down, futurists had gotten way more predictions wrong than right, evidence enough to make anyone a skeptic when it came to the entire business.[40]

What killed the future, assuming it really was dead? For Handy, it began with the nation's upward mobility—the realization of the American Dream—for many in the 1950s, combined with our loss of trust in authority in the late 1960s. And as our postwar awe of both technology and master planning faded, so did our blind faith in the future, replaced by much darker things to come. Rather than the future shock of the 1970s, however, we now suffer from what Handy called "future ennui," a general numbness to life-altering change. Besides some occasional glimpses of authentic futurism creeping through the cultural cracks—the architecture of Frank Gehry and Rem Koolhaas and Nike's coolest sneakers, for Handy—the idea of tomorrow is, at least for now, out of stock. "What we miss are the hope, the awe, even the scariness of those visions," Handy concluded, in short, "a future that matters."[41]

Much in part to jumpstart a future that mattered, *Wired* did something that was long overdue—make futurists put some money where their big mouths were. Noting that talk is cheap, especially when it comes to making predictions, the magazine set up the Long Bets Foundation (LBF), a project intended to "raise the quality of our collective foresight by incorporating money and accountability into the process of debate." Cooked up by Kevin Kelly, *Wired*'s editor at large, and Well founder Stewart Brand, the LBF pitted experts against each other around a specific prediction, keeping tabs on who turned out to be right, however long that took. The bigger idea, as the magazine made clear, was a very rare examination of the process of futurism, hopefully leading to a "better understanding of how predictions in aggregate work out in reality—what kinds of truths are easiest (or hardest) to forecast, and what kinds of people are right (or wrong) most reliably." The inaugural edition of the LBF (with all winners' proceeds going to designated charities) featured some interesting battles illustrating the state of early twenty-first-century futurism. Craig Mundie, Chief Technology Officer of Microsoft, bet Eric Schmidt, CEO of Google, $1,000 that commercial airline passengers would routinely fly in pilotless planes by 2030, while Peter Schwartz, cofounder of the Global Business Network, made a $1,000 open bet (any takers?) that at least one human born in the year 2000 will still be alive in 2150. Besides asking readers if they "wanna bet," the LBF allowed visitors to its website (www.longbets.org) to make their own bets, a terrific attempt to reverse some of our "future ennui."[42]

In fact, betting on the future actually had a long history within the scientific community, Kevin Kelly made clear, the earliest one on record between the archrival astronomers Johannes Kepler and Christian Longomontanus, in 1600. More recently, cosmologist Stephen Hawking regularly bet other brainiacs on future discoveries (the stakes for a 1975 wager involving a star called Cygnus X-1 were a subscription to *Penthouse*), and for decades Bell Lab employees kept more or less official track of their nerdy intraoffice gambling. Other groups of geeks at Stanford University and Cold Spring Harbor Labs were actively making bets on yet-to-be-determined facts in physics and biology, also helping keep futurism alive by turning it into an interactive and more dynamic exercise. "Betting on the future is more than just entertainment," Kelly told readers, an opportunity to "weed out brainless bragging, insincere speculation, and a tendency—particularly among losers—to forget."[43]

While certainly a valiant effort, *Wired*'s futurism-meets-Texas-Hold-'Em initiative has done little to make the field again a vital part of either intellectual or popular discourse. To celebrate its thirtieth anniversary, for example, *Wilson Quarterly*'s winter 2006 issue was devoted to the idea of the future, with a variety of our current crop of best and brightest contributing essays on where it's been and where it might be going. After neatly tracing the history of futurism in the United States, think-tankers David Rejeski and Robert L. Olson argued that "at the beginning of a new millennium, the future's opportunities and dangers are calling, but we are largely deaf to them." "We pay less attention to the long run today than we did in the 1970s," Rejeski and Olson continued, a thought echoed by Mike Marien, now the editor of the newsletter *Future Survey*, who estimated that there were only half as many books and articles being written on the subject in the United States than there had been thirty years previously. Interestingly, outside the United States the future was doing and continues to do gangbusters business, with many countries around the world embarking on ambitious studies to plan for the long term.[44] Was and is America finally losing its "future-mindedness," something that David Brooks considered an essential component of our national character?

Martin Walker, another think-tanker, would probably say yes, similarly troubled by Americans' recent failure to put futurism into practice, as evidenced by our personal and national debt. "America as an economic community is no longer saving the seed corn," he wrote, noting that the nation's annual net savings have shrunk to miniscule proportions, especially when compared to Europeans and Asians. With the national debt having ballooned to more than a trillion dollars, it appears that even the federal government has officially endorsed the idea that planning for the future is unnecessary. Walker feared that one of Tocqueville's many acute observations about the American character might, after almost two centuries, be coming home to roost. "The prospect really does frighten me that they one day may become so engrossed in cowardly love of immediate pleasures that their interest in their own future and in that of their descendants may vanish," the Frenchman wrote in 1835 in his *Democracy in America*, a warning we should heed, given his own remarkable predictive powers.[45]

AN INCONVENIENT TRUTH

One can only imagine what Tocqueville would have said about jeopardizing our future for immediate pleasures given our current environmental crisis. But while critics might be right in their claim that what can be called "pure" futurism has gone the way of the eight-track, the recent response to the crisis suggests that the idea of tomorrow is hardly dead in the (rising) water. After all, did Isaac Asimov ever win an Oscar? Was Buckminster Fuller ever asked to speak before Congress on his perspective about the future? Had there ever been such a public debate about whether the world was going to end unless something was done pronto? No to all, meaning that Al Gore's campaign to alert the world about global warming is arguably the biggest thing in futurism since Nostradamus made waves with his set of media-friendly predictions. The ex-VP has brought the concept of the future into the mainstream consciousness as all-stars like Herman Kahn never did, using the issue of climate change as a touchstone to think about how our actions today may affect tomorrow.

The debate over what the website for *An Inconvenient Truth* called "the biggest moral challenge facing our global civilization" and what Senator Jim Inhofe labeled "the greatest hoax ever perpetuated on the American people" began in earnest about a decade earlier. "We don't have any evidence that this [global warming] is a serious problem," said Richard S. Lindzen of MIT in 1996, going against the grain of the scientific community, which was gradually agreeing that human activity was seriously altering the atmosphere. The previous fall, a United Nations–sponsored group of scientists came to the conclusion that greenhouse gases such as carbon dioxide were likely contributing to rising temperatures around the world. The panel's worse news was that unless something was done fast to reduce the emission of these gases, the planet would continue to heat up, with probably disastrous consequences, the first time a group of leading scientists had formally made such a claim. Lindzen and some others disagreed, however, believing the computer models used by the group were flawed or, in his own words, "like trusting a ouija board."[46]

In a *Reader's Digest* article published the following year, called "Is the World Really Coming to an End?," Ronald Bailey, an adjunct scholar at the Cato Institute, also pooh-poohed the idea that we were facing an imminent global ecological crisis. After dismissing other popular apocalyptic scenarios of the past few decades—mass starvation and cancer-causing chemicals in Rachel Carson's *Silent Spring*; too many people in Paul Erlich's *The Population Bomb*; the sterility of men in Theo Colborn, Dianne Dumanoski, and John Peter Myers's *Our Stolen Future*; the extinction of species in Norman Myers's *The Sinking Ark*, and, as the coup de grâce, a widely publicized skin-cancer epidemic from the disappearing ozone layer—Bailey shrugged off the global warming scare. "If climate models turn out to be correct, it may be prudent to limit carbon-dioxide emissions in the future," Bailey wrote, seeing no reason to change our behavior yet. "We have a decade or so to collect data and refine our models before we might have to act," agreed Jerry North, professor of meteorology at Texas A&M, typical of the wait-and-see attitude of some scientists during the late 1990s and early 2000s.[47]

In 1998, however, the (also scary-sounding) Intergovernmental Panel on Change, a group of scientists from around the world, forecast that the surface temperature of the planet could increase by anywhere from 1.8 to 6.3 degrees Fahrenheit by 2100, possibly causing rising sea levels, warmer temperatures, extreme weather "events," and the spread of tropical diseases.[48] Spring seemed to come early the following year, a continuing pattern over the past few decades, with two European researchers in the journal *Nature* attributing this to "changes in air temperature." Other researchers in the United States concluded that the 1990s was the warmest decade of the entire second millennium, a conclusion supported by NASA's finding that Greenland's largest ice sheet was melting fast. The US State Department then chimed in, reporting record-high ocean temperatures, which were damaging coral reefs and causing other environmental problems.[49] Because of changes to the Gulf Stream, global warming could, some scientists were now beginning to think, lead not to a hotter planet, as logic would have it, but a colder one, an ice age by the middle of the twenty-first century their worst-case scenario.[50]

Whether it was an endless summer or a very long winter, global warming was, more and more scientists were concluding, a clear and present danger for our collective future. "Evidence for global warming piled up at a furious pace in 2000," reported *Discover*, citing paleontologist Malcolm C. McKenna's shocking photograph of a largely missing polar ice pack and record-fast trips being made through the Arctic Sea as just a couple of disturbing events that year. Old newspaper reports, as well as records kept by Shinto monks, Canadian fur traders, and riverboat captains, too suggested later freezes and earlier thaws than in the past.[51] Mt. Kilimanjaro also seemed to have lost a huge chunk of its ice pack, records from 1912 revealed, with the famous peak to be entirely snowless by 2022 if the meltdown continued at the same rate.[52]

Even with the first six months of 2002 being the warmest on record in the Northern Hemisphere, it was rather surprising when the EPA changed its tune by agreeing that global warming was real and that humans were responsible. Old Testament–style mayhem—droughts, floods, and pestilence—were in the cards over the next century, the EPA report to the United Nations continued, stopping short of recommending that all countries conform to the standards laid out in the 1997 Kyoto Protocol.[53] By 2004, Australia and the United States were the only major industrial nations refusing to limit greenhouse gases, their administrations apparently prioritizing economics over what virtually every scientist was saying was the coming of the apocalypse. That year, however, the Pentagon, Governor Arnold Schwarzenegger, and *Business Week* all added their voices of concern about global warming, suggesting that the issue was well on the way to becoming politically neutral. Climate change causing colossal ocean currents was also the subject of a popular disaster movie, *The Day After Tomorrow*, this too spreading the idea that our future survival relied on decisions made today.[54]

It was Al Gore's *An Inconvenient Truth* that turned the issue into a central one, however, making reports of the death of futurism premature. Gore had been talking about global warming since the late 1970s as a congressman, first using what became known as the "slideshow" in the 1980s. It wasn't until 2005, however, frustrated by the lack of any real action, that he aligned himself with the "green group," as the environmental lobby was nicknamed. This alliance would prove fruitful after one of his talks that year in Beverly Hills, which Hollywood insiders Laurie David and Lawrence Bender attended. In less than a year, *An Inconvenient Truth* (the title borrowed from, yes, Tocqueville's *Democracy in America*) was playing in theaters, instantly launching the cause into a much different orbit and turning the man into someone who has to be considered one of the leading visionaries of our time.[55]

The success of *An Inconvenient Truth* and its contribution to thinking decades into the future cannot be overestimated. The film and companion book, each released in 2006, were hugely popular by any measure, the former grossing about $50 million worldwide by March 2007 and the latter a number-one *New York Times* bestseller. "Al Gore may have done for global warming what *Silent Spring* did for pesticides," wrote James Hansen of NASA in reviewing the book, with sales reaching 850,000 copies by May 2007. Movie critic Roger Ebert wrote, "You owe it to yourself to see this film," something he'd never done in thirty-nine years of reviews, and the documentary went on to win an Academy Award and receive standing ovations at Sundance. Many high schools and universities still use *An Inconvenient Truth* in science class, and the film has been referenced (usually parodied, as a sincere form of flattery) in everything from *South Park* to *Futurama*. In part because today's media universe is infinitely larger, nothing even H. G. Wells or Jules Verne ever created penetrated the zeitgeist like Gore's nerdy slideshow, clear proof that, despite evidence to the contrary, people today are indeed at least thinking about the future. This is quite remarkable, given that the future posed in *An Inconvenient Truth* is as dystopian as any previously imagined, including between-the-wars robots-gone-wild scenarios, postwar interplanetary warfare, or 1970s world-going-to-hell-in-a-handbasket predictions. "If the vast majority of the world's scientists are right," claimed the website for the film and the book, www.climatecrisis.net, "we have just ten years to avert a major catastrophe that could send our entire planet into a tail-spin of epic destruction involving extreme weather, floods, droughts, epidemics and killer heat waves beyond anything we have ever experienced." Proclaiming such devastation has rarely been, with the exception of messianic prophecies, so popular. For the overnight sensation thirty years in the making, however, this was just the beginning. "Live Earth" concerts, a second book focusing on solutions, a kids' TV show, and a reality show were soon in the works, all part of Gore's effort to sway public opinion as a weapon to conquer the many technical and political challenges in bringing the level of greenhouse gases way down. Time, as the film and book made extremely clear, is of the essence. Hansen and Gore agree that it's critical that production of the gases stop increasing by 2017 and be reduced to a fraction of their current levels by 2050 or, as the R.E.M. song goes, it's the end of the world as we know it. With Corporate America increasingly "going green," however, no doubt aware that more than three-quarters of Americans believe that global warming requires immediate action, Tocqueville's "an inconvenient truth" may become more convenient in the decades ahead.[56]

While *An Inconvenient Truth* was the book making the headlines (especially when Gore won the Nobel Prize for it), it was part of or stirred up an entire genre of books published in 2006 and 2007 about global warming.

Tim Flannery's *The Weather Makers*, an international bestseller, explained the science of climate change to make its call for urgent action, while Eugene Linden's *The Winds of Change* showed how the destruction of past civilizations can teach us valuable lessons to save our own. Bill McKibben updated his prescient, titular *The End of Nature*, originally published in 1989, and a handful of other books, including Fred Pearce's *With Speed and Violence*, Joseph Romm's *Hell and High Water*, David Steinman's *Safe Trip to Eden*, and Bruce Stutz's *Chasing Spring*, added to the conversation. With another documentary film narrated by Alanis Morissette and Keanu Reeves, *The Great Warming*, climate change could be said to have tipped, this film positioning the "Great Warming" alongside other crises of humankind like the Great Plague and Great Depression.[57] Critics of those claiming that humans are causing global warming still abound (including Lindzen, who in 2006 accused Gore of exploiting people's fears), but there is no doubt that the issue has become a, perhaps the, cause célèbre of contemporary futurism.

Ironically, Gore has been among the most hopeful of those pronouncing a climate crisis, believing that awareness of the ticking time bomb would lead to a historic shift in how we created and used energy. New kinds of distribution networks for electricity and liquid fuels were on the horizon, Gore foresaw, with renewable sources of energy to end our dependence on the coal- and oil-powered Industrial Revolution. As well, a smart grid or "electranet" (which Gore may or may not take credit for inventing) would make the system far more efficient, and a technology revolution in automobile engines would lead to a 500-mile-per-gallon car. "I believe that this future will come to pass, one way or another," Gore wrote in 2006, the movement he sparked "a rare opportunity for our generation to unite behind a historic mission."[58] In early 2008, Gore, along with the Alliance for Climate Protection, launched their historic mission with a three-year, $300 million marketing campaign to recruit an army of 10 million advocates to fight for laws and policies leading to a reduction in greenhouse gases. Comparing their mission to the invasion of Normandy and the civil rights movement, Gore and his colleagues clearly intended to make their future come to pass sooner rather than later.[59]

RADICAL EVOLUTION

The historic mission to save the world isn't the only way the future is very much part of the present. Many scientists would argue that, if anything, the future is more alive and kicking than ever, living and breathing in such things as gene therapy, "smart" everything, and a seemingly infinite variety of emerging nanotechnologies. Other shape-shifting developments of the past ten years are rocking our world of tomorrow, pointing the way to scenarios very much like those imagined by some scientists of the past. Incredible breakthroughs in biotech are turning the future inside out and upside down; cloning, cryogenics, and anti- and reverse aging are just a few ways the DNA revolution will change the rules of life as we know them. Other ideas actively being bandied about, including the colonization of Mars, seeing dinosaurs again walk the earth via cloning, creating synthetic humans starting with just a brain, and even altering gravity—a scientific no-no if there is one—also are reminiscent of the golden days of futurism, when almost anything and everything was possible. The growing evidence that there seem to be hundreds, thousands, or millions of Earth-like planets outside our own solar system is perhaps the ultimate idea circulating within contemporary futurism and, as well, a throwback to Corn and Horrigan's brand of yesterday's tomorrows.[60]

Despite the incredible change, this era of futurism has been marked by the tendency to see tomorrow not in absolute terms but in relative ones, the mostly black-and-white school of making predictions now many shades of gray. In his review of late 1990s books about the future, Rothstein noted that the authors all "mix skepticism with their fantasy," a rather new development in the field.[61] This more tempered approach to prediction was most prevalent in science as ethical considerations increasingly came into play, particularly when it came to the Human Gene Project. "This is more important than putting a man on the moon or splitting the atom," said Dr. Francis S. Collins, director of the National Human Genome Research Institute, in 1998, adding that "biomedical research will be divided into what we did before we had the human genome and what we did after."[62]

Obvious to all was that the decoding of the gene sequence could very well lead to the realization of one of the classic tropes of futurism—the radical extension of the human lifespan, or the Methuselah scenario. Daniel Kevles, a professor of bioethics at Princeton, made this clear in 1999, writing that "Having extended the life spans of fruit flies, nematodes, and mice, they [biologists] now believe it is only a question of when they will be able to accomplish the feat within humans." While such amazing statements would have elicited pure, unadulterated joy among most in the past, today the prospect of living for as long as 200 years raises as many dystopian concerns as utopian dreams. Besides an out-of-control population, a total meltdown of the health insurance industry, and the fact that long-lived mice are consistently smaller and fatter than their normal kin (bringing to mind a truly nightmarish world made up of billions of George Costanzas), the Methuselah scenario cannot help but recall Aldous Huxley's vision of a two-tiered society in his *Brave New World*. In the book, Delta drones were forced to serve sexagenarian Alpha elites who were engineered to have the physical abilities of a teenager, a vivid image of how class would very likely play a key role in determining whose life was extended and whose was not, should the procedure become a reality.[63] Regardless of the ethics and economics, the possibility of living much longer lives is barreling ahead, as geneticists work their futuristic magic. In his 2001 book *Life Script*, Nicholas Wade, a science writer for the *New York Times*, predicted that with individualized medicine (drugs matched to our specific genotype), organ regeneration, and gene therapy, our normal lifespan could one day be 320 years, perhaps making futurists of the past wish they had been more careful about what they had wished for.[64]

Thankfully, when it came to our future appearance, not all scientists envisioned a smaller, fatter species roaming the earth for a few hundred years. In fact, advancements in bioscience promise to make us all gorgeous, some futurists have thought. By 2034, *People* predicted three decades earlier, baldness might be cured by transplanting stem cells from one's own hair follicles into the scalp, and topical growth regulators used to produce pigment to keep the gray away. Collagen harvested from one's face, grown in quantity, and then injected into wrinkled areas could make our mugs as smooth as a baby's bottom, with DNA-altering pills or creams also nipping crow's feet in the bud. DNA may also be used to grow back missing teeth, *People* reported, perhaps eliminating cavities for good. Our extreme makeover would continue with human growth hormone used to sculpt the body and fight off muscle deterioration, augmented by high-frequency ultrasound waves capable of breaking up fat. Stimulating the stomach with electrical impulses to create a sensation of fullness, as well as hormone-blocking drugs making us feel less hungry, also would have us svelte in the decades to come, the magazine told readers, another step in the direction of designer bodies. Finally, breasts would continue to be enlarged in thirty years (some things never change), but tissue engineering, in which one's own fat cells were used rather than implants, would make the results much more natural looking and feeling. Who said the future would be an Orwellian nightmare?[65]

More beautiful bodies might be just the icing on the cake if some of the hoped-for advancements in bioscience were realized, other futurists believed. That same year, *Wired* saw a host of breakthroughs on the horizon that would perhaps have us living significantly longer, healthier lives. With new chip-based DNA, researchers might have the ability to destroy "bad" genes likely to lead to cancer, with inhalable nanoparticle "cluster bombs" also possibly used in the future to combat the number-two killer in the United States. Number one, heart disease, may also one day be less lethal, with new artificial hearts better than the real thing and regeneration techniques using stem cells expected to keep tickers ticking longer. Other possibilities—a second-generation HIV vaccine to fight AIDS, the development of compounds to inhibit plaque deposits causing Alzheimer's, and, again, various ways to slow down the aging process—are on researchers' drawing boards, the wholesale re-engineering of the human body no longer just the stuff of futurists' dreams.[66]

Joel Garreau, perhaps more than anyone else surveying the scientific scene, has recently recognized the implications of the quantum leaps being made in the field, labeling the emerging universe of biotechnology "radical evolution." In his 2005 book of that name, Garreau laid out different scenarios for how radical evolution may play out, one of them being "Hell," in which an array of nanobots—microscopic, continually replicating and evolving machines "superengineered" to break down the substances of all living things—did just that. (Thankfully, Garreau also included in his book a "Prevail" scenario, in which future technologies will be problematic but ultimately beneficial, and even a "Heaven" scenario, whereby universal connectivity will lead to world peace.)[67] Whether heaven, hell, or somewhere in between, Garreau understood that the idea of the future was shifting from being about transforming the external, physical universe to reconfiguring ourselves. "For the first time," he wrote in 2006, "our technologies are aimed not so much outward at modifying our environment [but rather] inward—at modifying our minds, memories, metabolisms, personalities and progeny." Over the next decade or so, Garreau believed, we would alter what it means to be human, as genetic enhancements and bioengineering continued to progress at alarming speed. Projects already in progress—the ability to go a week without food or sleep, unlimited endurance, regrowing missing limbs, memory pills, to name just a few—are leading to a fundamental alteration in the development of our species, he correctly argued, reasonably concerned that we may not still be fully "human" in the coming future.[68]

Going even further, the top futurist of the day, Ray Kurzweil, believes we're on the cusp of an era so radical that we can't really grasp its implications. Although the days of rock star futurists are over, Kurzweil retains a sort of mythic status, credited with having an extraordinary and original vision reminiscent of that of Asimov and Kahn or even Verne and Wells. Since the 1960s, Ray Kurzweil has been traipsing through the new frontier of artificial intelligence, inventing such things as the flatbed scanner, electric piano, and large-vocabulary speech recognition software along the way. Kurzweil made a cool $1 million in speaking fees in 2006 and, perhaps even more impressive, was occasionally invited to dinner at Bill Gates's house to schmooze over how to design the future. Unlike most futurists, who wouldn't dare to make such a claim, Kurzweil maintained he could see what's coming next with considerable accuracy, the Holy Grail something he called the "Law of Accelerating Returns." The law is actually less than revolutionary, grounded in the premise that the social effects of technology are expanding at an exponential rate. Because of this Moore's-Law-on-steroids idea, Kurzweil argued, we're entering a period of change like none other, leading to a seminal moment he calls the point of "Singularity."[69]

What kind of change are we talking about? Big-time change, the kind that futurists more than half a century ago predicted when we could look forward to a big, bright, beautiful tomorrow. In just twenty or twenty-five years, Kurzweil said in 2007, poverty and disease would be just bad memories, and that was just the beginning. No longer would we be dependent on fossil fuels, proof that Al Gore's "inconvenient truth" of the early twenty-first century was pure hogwash. "Merging with technology is the next stage in our evolution," Kurzweil foresaw, manifested in things like cell-sized, brain-enhancing nanobots coursing through our veins and the ability to upload an individual's consciousness onto a computer. What we've missed, Kurzweil made clear in making these kind of predictions, is that the doubling of technological change every year over a decade equates to a multiple of 1,000, not twenty, as many assume. Change is exponential, in other words, not linear, hence his Law of Accelerating Returns. A perfect example of the validity of his theory is the Human Genome Project, which was scheduled to be completed in fifteen years, he told *Fortune*. After seven years, only one percent of it had been completed, causing skeptics to carp that the thing would never get done. Doubling one percent over the next seven years added up to 100 percent, however, this exponential rate of progress bringing the project in right on time. Humanity itself is now close to that one percent point of technological progress, Kurzweil believed, meaning that amazing stories are to be told in the next few decades. By 2027, computers will be smarter than humans, he predicted, and, in another twenty or so years, the point of "Singularity" reached, a critical time because people will not be able to understand technology as it will be so much more intelligent. Kurzweil had already fully explained the concept in his 2005 bestseller *The Singularity Is Near*, and yes, with a title like that, a movie was soon in the works.[70]

Just as remarkable about Kurzweil, however, is his full intent to be around when most or all of this will happen. Kurzweil not only talked the talk but walked the walk when it came to biotechnology, using his body as what *Fortune* called an "ongoing science project." Besides getting weekly blood tests and intravenous treatments, Kurzweil was popping 230 vitamins, antioxidants, and other supplements a day, all part of his objective to "reprogram" his body chemistry and, in short, stop aging. The top futurist of our times fully believed he had, in his own words, "slowed down aging to a crawl," the fifty-nine-year-old claiming he was just forty, biologically speaking, as he explained in his 2004 book with Terry Grossman, *Fantastic Voyage: Live Long Enough to Live Forever.*[71] Although some justifiably questioned the wisdom of Kurzweil's quest to make it through the twenty-first century ("Two centuries in a cubicle? The inauguration of President Ryan Seacrest? Slightly increased odds of a *Patch Adams* sequel?," joked Scott Feschuk in 2008), his formula for perpetual life will no doubt be his greatest prophecy of all, should he be proven right.[72]

BEING DIGITAL

Besides the expanding universe of science, various emerging technologies—wireless and sensors, especially—are directional beacons pointing the way to the smaller, smarter, and infinitely searchable world to come. It is information technology that will most drastically redirect the trajectory of tomorrow, there is plenty of reason to believe, pushing us further and further toward a truly intimate relationship between man and machine. In his *Being Digital*, for example, Negroponte foresaw how we would one day read, listen, and watch, envisioning "a magical, paper-thin, flexible, waterproof, wireless, lightweight, bright display" in our future (and now just around the convergent technology bend). Negroponte also anticipated the transformation of the media universe from the pushing-out model of broadcasting to one based on pulling in, or "broadcatching" (a term actually coined by Stewart Brand in 1987).[73] By 1999, online culture clearly dominated the idea of the future, perhaps like no other single entity had ever done before. "The Internet has become a powerful symbol of society's expectations about the future—a future of fast moving, disruptive technology that is shifting the terrain not only in business, but also in politics and culture," observed Steve Lohr in the *New York Times* eleven days before the end of the century, something that is only more true today.[74]

Perhaps no dimension of information technology will be as fast moving and disruptive as the anthropomorphizing of machines (or, if you prefer, the mechanization of humans). The ability for machines, specifically computers, to think and feel has endured as an idea for the future as the boundaries between humans and nonhumans get increasingly blurry. Computers will themselves "claim to be conscious" around 2030, Kurzweil wrote in his 1999 book *The Age of Spiritual Machines*, with no "clear distinction between humans and computers by the end of the twenty-first century." "We would like to build models that are so lifelike that they cease to become models of life and become examples of life themselves," echoed Christopher Langton, a researcher in the field of artificial life, his vision not a computer itself but a cyberorganism that would exist within one.[75] All of this sounded strangely familiar, of course, as we had heard something much like it thirty years before in *2001: A Space Odyssey*, in which the computer HAL displayed some pretty anthropomorphic behavior itself. HAL's "birthday" on January 12, 1997, and the dawn of the year 2001 were each occasions for critics to look back on the film to see how much of it had come to pass and how much had not.[76] Although the hardware specs of computers had left HAL in the dust, they had (and have) not yet developed its (his?) sentient capabilities, nor its admirable communications skills. "Thirty years of computer science have given us machines that can beat us at chess, but cannot do the simple things that a 6-year-old can, like walk, talk, recognize faces, learn languages, dream and laugh," Dennis Overbye wrote in the *New York Times* five days before the year 2001.[77]

In the past couple of years, it has become yet more apparent that our future will be a "cyber" one, and in multiple ways. "The Web has just begun, and there's lots more to come," technology guru Paul Saffo understated in 2006, believing that the Internet is already morphing from two-dimensional to 2.5, paving the way toward a three-dimensional online universe over the next ten years. Socializing online via avatars will become mainstream, Saffo predicted, many of us living parallel lives with alternative identities in the digital world. It will be the seamless integration of the real and virtual worlds that will soon upset the technological apple cart, however, Saffo and many other futurists think, with it becoming increasingly difficult to distinguish when we're on- and offline as the Internet continues to encroach on everyday life.[78]

If one can imagine, however, Saffo argues that an even bigger thing than the next generation of the Internet is waiting in the wings—a full-scale robot revolution. It does indeed appear that the robot—arguably the principal icon of the future this past century—is finally moving out of the ivory towers and sci-fi pulps and into our everyday lives, posing new questions about the always contentious relationship between man and machine. By the late 1990s, robots had largely evolved into e-bots or "knowbots," digital helpers ready to obey our every wish and command, much like their tin-can ancestors were imagined. "Knowbots are finally becoming affordable for the home and home office," *Kiplinger's Personal Finance* reported in "2035," using the familiar news-story-from-the-future device in 1997. Intelligent agents programmed to perform tasks ranging from shopping to investing would be part of everyday life, the magazine envisioned, available in either robotic or humanoid form on one's computer screen. Using artificial intelligence software that "learned" users' preferences, knowbots would be our "agent in the electronic world," something of course already being widely used.[79]

Saffo's vision a decade later built on this idea, positing that if the 1980s were about the PC (made possible by cheap microprocessors) and the 1990s about the Web (made possible by bigger bandwidth via cheap lasers), the early decades of the twenty-first century would be about robots (made possible by cheap sensors), something that would have made yesterday's tomorrowists very happy. "The next big consumer revolution that everyone will ooh and aah over will be consumer robots," he prophesied, the director of the Institute for the Future sounding like he could perhaps be director of the Institute of the Past.[80] Artificial intelligence researcher David Levy is predicting a literally intimate relationship between robots and humans, expecting people and androids to get married by the mid-twenty-first century. "People who grow up with all sorts of electronic gizmos will find android robots to be fairly normal as friends, partners, lovers," the author of *Love and Sex with Robots* said in 2008, being "totally convinced it's inevitable."[81] Not everyone is convinced that such a development would be a good thing, however, with Luddites in particular skeptical about our ever-deepening love affair with technology. Journalist and author Chuck Klosterman is not at all impressed with the continued march of technology, for example, seeing "almost no value in the future . . . I suspect that virtually every technological advance since the advent of the gramophone has been—on balance—detrimental to the human race," he said in 2007, his only exception being, quite understandably, air-conditioning.[82]

As in previous big turnings of the clock, futurism exploded at the end of the last century and millennium, the beginning of new ones a prime opportunity to channel our worst fears and greatest hopes. Never before had there been such a wild flurry of utopias and dystopias in play, a feeding frenzy of futurism that served as an apt symbol of the Information Age. Two dominant themes have defined our current concept of the future: the rise of a parallel universe that is increasingly encroaching on the "real" one, and the identification of the basic building blocks of life. Part and parcel of today's view of tomorrow is the questioning of the dynamics of change—the DNA of futurism—specifically whether it is linear or exponential. Much, perhaps even the fate of humans, rests on the answer to that question, such issues no doubt to be explored by a future historian of the future.

Conclusion

THE RECENT HISTORY OF THE FUTURE IS A FASCINATING ONE, ITS twists and turns every bit as revealing as those within any history of the past. Between the two world wars, futurism came into its own as a recognizable field, imbued with the scientific, mechanistic, and often fantastic views of tomorrow. During World War II, however, the idea of the future was scaled back, the thought of a new, improved American Dream enough to make everybody happy. Supercharged by atomic energy, the future of the postwar years took another big leap forward, the consumer paradise that was the American Way of Life imagined as limitless, infinite and, perhaps best of all, exportable. Futurism—the study of the future—too took off like a rocket, the military-industrial complex assigned the weighty task of charting the American tomorrow.

The future suffered a major meltdown in the late 1960s and 1970s, however, when the then-revolutionary idea that perpetual growth was not an American birthright came as a truly shocking revelation. Conversely, though, futurism reached its apex of popularity then, too, the Sturm und Drang of the times reason enough to think long and hard about what might come next. Fortunately, it was not the end of the world, as so many had predicted, the progressive orientation of the 1980s propelling the possibilities of tomorrow to new heights. This time, the future and futurism were in perfect alignment, each in ascendance as the country's confidence, perhaps arrogance, was restored. Finally, the past decade of change has been an interesting time for the future, the dawn of a new technological age making us rethink the nature of reality and even life itself. Depending on your view, futurism is now either experiencing another golden age, due to its ubiquity, or is in steep decline, its magic long gone because so much of "tomorrow" seems to be already here today.

A literally timeless subject, and as certain as death or taxes, however, it's easy to be bullish on futurism. Despite being impossible to predict, there's no doubt many of us will continue to spend an inordinate amount of time and energy thinking about what may lie ahead in order to try to anticipate and control events around us. Perhaps because our own time is limited, and each of our personal futures is known, predetermined, and nonnegotiable, in this life at least, we cannot help but be heavily invested in what tomorrow might bring. The past may be flourishing—a vast resource for our postmodern culture to recycle as "retro" and an anchor in our troubled waters—and the mandate to "live in the moment" also a powerful draw, but I'd continue to place my cards on the future as the most compelling dimension of time. The future is, in many ways, an unbeatable hand, its capacity for infinite possibilities seductive if not irresistible. Anything can happen, as they say: the chance to win the lottery, meet the person of your dreams, maybe even go to heaven is on our minds much—perhaps too much—of the time. For most of us, hope will always spring eternal, it being basic human nature to believe that what can be will be better than what is and what has been. Hoping for the best and fearing the worst, often at the same time, seems to be in our DNA, this biological imperative perhaps the basis for the existential jambalaya that is the future and the practice of futurism.

Unfortunately, futurism since World War I has been largely a failure, its practitioners missing major events and important social movements with impressive regularity. In trying to see the trees, futurists have often missed most of the forest, even the field's elite suffering from a Mr. Magoo–like case of myopia and astigmatism. Beginning with the ascendancy of left-brain thinking in the 1920s, futurism took an inevitable but wrong turn that it has yet to correct, the droppings of quantitative analysis heavily relied upon to point the way to tomorrow. Too many in the field have considered futurism a science, which, history has shown over and over, it simply isn't, as reliability and validity are never terms that can accurately describe the art of prediction. In fact, the only thing we know about the future is that it is unknowable, making most "scientific" attempts to do so ultimately a losing battle. While the future has perhaps improved over the past three-quarters of a century, futurism has, I believe, declined, a victim of too many cooks in the kitchen of tomorrow with numbers instead of imagination.

Within both the academic and applied field of Future Studies, in fact, the dry-as-a-bone school of futurism born between the wars and advanced during the postwar years can still be found. In a valiant but futile effort to canonize the field, logic has ruled despite the overwhelming evidence that logic has little role in futurism. Too often, professional futurists have said things will get better when times are good and things will get worse when times are bad, a swimming with the institutional tide that has let us down. Even the emperors of the field have frequently worn no clothes, failing to use their positions of influence to move forward relevant, usable, and interesting futures. In his nearly epic two-volume *Foundations of Future Studies* published in 1997, for example, Wendell Bell expends great effort to show how the field has been and continues to be an important one, offering "a body of sound and coherent thought and empirical results." Bell and his brainy brethren are determined to demonstrate how Future Studies is a "worthy academic field deserving of respect and support" although, as everyone knows, truly worthy enterprises are awarded respect and support without having to prove or ask for it. Even the subtitle of Bell's book—"Human Science for a New Era"—sounds decidedly old era, a slogan better suited for an exhibit at a 1930s world's fair.[1] With this kind of arcane, pedantic scholarship, it's not surprising that futurism is hardly taught at all at the university level anymore, which is too bad, as nothing is more interesting than the future, especially among young people whose tomorrows are wide open.

Similarly, contemporary futurism is too often obtuse and oblique, written in a language that is foreign to not just general readers but most practitioners in the field. In his 1995 *Visions of the Future*, for example, Robert Heilbroner wasn't kidding about his book's subtitle—"The Distant Past, Yesterday, Today, Tomorrow"—his scope stretching from 150,000 years ago to many millennia into the future. Although just a wee 142 pages, Heilbroner's book has big ideas, too big perhaps for those wishing to learn some actual visions of the future. "Today's vision of the future is certainly not that of the Distant Past, for if there ever was a time in which the shape of things to come was seen as dominated by impersonal forces, it is ours," goes one of his observations, typical of his brand of intellectual discourse, which leaves most readers with more questions than answers.[2]

Much more compelling have been recent writings that have looked at futurism with the skepticism the field warrants. In his 1998 *The Fortune Sellers: The Big Business of Buying and Selling Predictions*, William Sherden was refreshingly critical of almost all kinds of forecasting, summed up by four little words: "It makes one wonder." Regardless of how it was to be used, prediction "contain[s] plenty enough mythology and baloney without the inclusion of such fallacious—albeit lucrative—practices as astrology, divination, and fortune-telling," Sherden thought, reducing the field to "the second oldest profession." "Even with all the advances in science and technology that are available to them, the experts are not getting any better at prediction,"

Sherden continued, setting modern-day futurists roughly equivalent to the Greeks' reading of animal entrails in terms of accuracy.[3] Unlike many futurists, Sherden wasn't being sensational just to sell books. Seymour Martin Lipset, a professor of public policy, has found that between 1945 and 1980, American social scientists blew at least two-thirds of their forecasts, strong evidence that the rigorous methods of "experts" were flawed if not fraudulent.[4] Almost all futurists have regularly gotten it wrong, but the wonks and pundits, armed with their charts, tables, and data, got it wrong while insisting they were right, this largely because their scenarios typically carried an agenda. David Brin, author of the 1998 *The Transparent Society* and a bunch of novels set in an alternative universe (encouragingly named Uplift), recognized that dogma mixes with futurism like oil does with water. "When prediction serves a polemic, it nearly always fails," he said in 2007, convinced that "peering ahead is mostly art."[5] Even worse than their determination to present it as a science and as "evidence" to support a particular doctrine, left-brainers have made the future boring, something simply unforgivable.

Looking back over the recent history of the future, it's rather easy to see that the best, most successful tomorrowists have been those who've ignored attempts to formalize the field and marched to the tune of their own drummer, unafraid to think outside of the prevailing left-brain box. People like Isaac Asimov, Buckminster Fuller, Arthur C. Clarke, Philip K. Dick, most recently, Ray Kurzweil, and, yes, Al Gore have, by taking risks, succeeded in envisioning significantly different tomorrows than today, in my view what more futurists should be doing. *Wired* is also proving that futurism can be not just engaging but dynamic and interactive, its Long Bets Foundation in particular pointed toward the direction the field should be going. In our society, where everyone is and has to be a futurist, such nonelitist opportunities to think about tomorrow offer our best chance to ensure the future remains a vital part of our conversation. In sum, we need to lose most of the analytics, relocate the field to the realm of the imagination, and reposition futurism more toward an art form. With creativity now very much in the air, considered perhaps our most valuable form of cultural currency, it's an ideal time to rethink futurism as a creative enterprise, to redefine its "genre" from nonfiction to fiction, where it started out centuries ago. The future may be more uncertain than ever, but for futurism there is no time like the present.

Notes

INTRODUCTION

1. Anne Fremantle, "Vision in the Novels," *Commonweal*, February 25, 1955, 545.

2. David Remnick, "Future Perfect," *New Yorker*, October 20–27, 1997, 215.

3. David A. Wilson, *The History of the Future* (Toronto: McArthur & Company, 2000), 12.

4. William A. Henry III, "Ready or Not, Here It Comes," *Time*, Fall 1992, 34.

5. Thomas Griffith, "Obsessed by the Future," *Time*, September 3, 1979, 46.

6. Stefan Kanfer, "Is There Any Future in Futurism?," *Time*, May 17, 1976, 51.

7. David Rejeski and Robert L. Olson, "Has Futurism Failed?," *Wilson Quarterly*, Winter 2006, 14.

8. Lewis Lapham, "The Rage Against the Future," *Harper's*, November 1979, 21; James Poniewozik, "Why We're So Obsessed with 'Next,'" *Time*, September 8, 2003, 94.

9. Nassim Nicholas Taleb, *The Black Swan: The Impact of the Highly Improbable* (New York: Random House, 2007).

10. David Orrell, *The Future of Everything: The Science of Prediction* (New York: Thunder's Mouth, 2006).

11. George F. Mechlin, "Seven Technologies for the Future," *USA Today*, January 1983, 62.

12. David Bouchier, "In the Fast Lane with Nostradamus," *New York Times*, 1995, LI12.

13. Isaac Asimov, "Life in 1990," *Science Digest*, August 1965, 63.

14. Lev Grossman, "Forward Thinking," *Time*, October 11, 2004, 58–59.

15. A. S. W. Rosenbach, "Old Almanacs and Prognostications," *Saturday Evening Post*, June 8, 1935, 10–11+.

16. Oona Strathern, *A Brief History of the Future* (New York: Carroll & Graf, 2007), x.

17. F. Pratt, "What's the World Coming To?," *Saturday Review of Literature*, April 2, 1938, 3–4.

18. Ibid.

19. Harry Harrison, "Introducing the Future: The Dawn of Science-Fiction Criticism," in Alan Sandison and Robert Dingley, eds., *Histories of the Future: Studies in Fact, Fantasy, and Science Fiction* (New York: Palgrave, 2000), 6.

20. David Brooks, "Land of the Future," *Newsweek International*, September 16, 2002, 90.

21. Hugh Stevenson Tigner, "Tomorrow Will Not Bring Utopia," *Christian Century*, July 8, 1942, 857. For the definitive study on Einstein, see Walter Isaacson's *Einstein: His Life and Universe.*

22. Tigner, "Tomorrow Will Not Bring Utopia."

23. Kanfer, "Is There Any Future in Futurism?"

24. "Reading the Future," *Wilson's Quarterly*, Winter 2006, 13.

25. Peter Andrews, "The Prediction Game," *Saturday Review*, January 15, 1972, 16.

26. Wilson, *The History of the Future*, 15–16.

27. Roderick Seidenberg, "The Sense of the Future," *Nation*, August 20, 1955, 154.

28. Wilson, *The History of the Future*, 4.

29. Merrill Sheils, "The Cracked Crystal Ball," *Newsweek*, November 19, 1979, 133.

30. Daniel Rosenberg and Susan Harding, "Introduction: Histories of the Future," in Daniel Rosenberg and Susan Harding, eds., *Histories of the Future* (Durham, NC: Duke University Press, 2005), 6.

31. Sandison and Dingley, *Histories of the Future*, xii.

32. Pratt, "What's the World Coming To?"

33. Wilson, *The History of the Future*, 27.

34. L. Dennis, "H. G. Wells's Internationalism," *Saturday Review of Literature*, September 9, 1933, 89–91.

35. Charles M. A. Stine, "Molders of Better Destiny," *Science*, October 2, 1942, 305.

36. Sandison and Dingley, *Histories of the Future*, xiii.

37. Kanfer, "Is There Any Future in Futurism?"

38. Ibid.

CHAPTER 1

1. Julian Huxley, "In Our Stars," *Forum*, April 1933, 245. For more interesting (and often unusual) perspectives from "the other Huxley," see his *Evolutionary Humanism.*

2. Olin Downes, "Present and Future of the Vitaphone—The New Ways of Musical Recording," *New York Times*, September 19, 1926, X6. The Vitaphone was such a

rage in the late 1920s that Warner Brothers formed a partnership with Western Electric to produce sound-on-disk talkies. See Roy Liebman's *Vitaphone Films: A Catalogue of the Features and Shorts.*

3. Olin Downes, "Theremin Opens a Musical Vista," *New York Times*, January 29, 1928, 128.

4. Andre Maurois, "The Formidable Future," *Living Age*, April 15, 1927, 732–734.

5. Ibid.

6. Silas Bent, "The Future Newspaper," *Century*, January 1929, 346.

7. Ibid.

8. Ibid.

9. "Forecasts Big Future for World Television," *New York Times*, February 14, 1930, 6. For a good overview of the development of television, see Gary Edgerton's *The Columbia History of American Television.*

10. Joseph J. Corn and Brian Horrigan, *Yesterday's Tomorrows: Past Visions of the American Future* (Baltimore, MD: Johns Hopkins University Press, 1984), 24.

11. "Directing of Trade by Television Seen," *New York Times*, February 21, 1930, 27.

12. Floyd W. Parsons, "A Look Ahead," *Saturday Evening Post*, April 4, 1931, 150.

13. "Predicts Marvels in Radio's Future," *New York Times*, June 16, 1936, 23. See Kenneth Bilby's *The General: David Sarnoff and the Rise of the Communications Industry* for an insightful analysis of the amazing life and career of "the General."

14. William Burnett Benton, "New Continents Ahead," *Ladies' Home Journal*, October 1938, 4+.

15. "Science in Business Forecast by Filene," *New York Times*, January 11, 1928, 49. See George E. Berkley's *The Filenes* for a history of this Boston family that "revolutionized the retail industry."

16. William B. Stout, "There's a Great Day Coming," *Collier's*, July 27, 1929, 39.

17. Roy Helton, "Sold Out to the Future," *Harper's*, July 1932, 129–142.

18. Henry Ford, "The Promise of the Future Makes the Present Seem Drab," *New York Times*, September 13, 1931, XX3.

19. Henry Ford, "What of the Next 25 Years," *Rotarian*, June 1936, 7, 9. See Steven Watts's *The People's Tycoon: Henry Ford and the American Century* for a comprehensive look at the business legend.

20. Alfred P. Sloan, "The Forward View," *Atlantic Monthly*, September 1934, 257–264. See Sloan's 1963 retrospective, *My Years with General Motors,* for just that; and David Farber's *Sloan Rules: Alfred P. Sloan and the Triumph of General Motors* for a thorough study of "the ultimate organization man."

21. "Looking Backward on the Depression," *Literary Digest*, November 14, 1931, 44–45.

22. Ibid.

23. Ibid.

24. Corn and Horrigan, *Yesterday's Tomorrows*, 12.

25. "What We Shall Be Like in 1950," *Literary Digest*, January 10, 1931, 43–44.

26. Parsons, "A Look Ahead."

27. Norman Bel Geddes, "Ten Years from Now," *Ladies' Home Journal*, January 1931, 3. See Bel Geddes's 1960 autobiography, *Miracle in the Evening*, for more from the brilliant stage and industrial designer.

28. Huxley, "In Our Stars," 242–244.

29. "Fox Foresees End of Vast Fortunes," *New York Times*, May 25, 1934, 19.

30. William Fredrick Bigelow, "Day after Tomorrow," *Good Housekeeping*, February 1935, 4.

31. Corn and Horrigan, *Yesterday's Tomorrows*, 64–77. Alan Colquhoun's *Modern Architecture* is an excellent introduction to the field, while Peter Gossel's *Modern Architecture A–Z* is prime modernist eye candy.

32. Walter Pitkin, "New Houses," *Forum*, December 1931, 343–349.

33. Huxley, "In Our Stars," 245.

34. Corn and Horrigan, *Yesterday's Tomorrows*, 64–77. See Rosemary Thornton's *The Houses That Sears Built* for "everything you ever wanted to know about Sears catalog homes."

35. "Predicts Changes in House Designs," *New York Times*, October 19, 1930, 182.

36. "Directing of Trade by Television Seen."

37. Bel Geddes, "Ten Years from Now."

38. Corn and Horrigan, *Yesterday's Tomorrows*, 50–51.

39. R. L. Duffus, "Charting the New York of the Future," *New York Times*, December 16, 1928, XX3. In his *The Power Broker*, Robert Caro convincingly argues that only the glaciers reshaped New York City's geography more than Robert Moses.

40. Stout, "There's a Great Day Coming," 9.

41. Corn and Horrigan, *Yesterday's Tomorrows*, 15–17. See Roger Shepherd's *Skyscraper: The Search for an American Style 1891–1941* and Roberta Moudry's *The American Skyscraper: Cultural Histories* for more on the history of the tall buildings.

42. Corn and Horrigan, *Yesterday's Tomorrows*, 116–117.

43. Parsons, "A Look Ahead," 145. See Lottie H. Eisner's *Fritz Lang* for a biography of the German filmmaker and his work.

44. Henry Farman, "Future of Aviation," *New York Times*, October 9, 1921, 84. Christopher Chant and John Batchelor's *A Century of Triumph: The History of Aviation* is a fine overview of the first century of flight.

45. Corn and Horrigan, *Yesterday's Tomorrows*, 97. There are a number of good histories of the "blimp," including Dick Hg's *The Golden Age of the Great Passenger Ships*, John Toland's *The Great Dirigibles*, and Dale Topping's *When Giants Roamed the Sky*.

46. T. R. Ybarra, "The Zeppelin's Builder Forecasts Its Future," *New York Times*, July 31, 1927, XX3.

47. "Predict Future Fashions," *New York Times*, September 11, 1928, 12.

48. Josephine Daskam Bacon, "In Nineteen Seventy-Nine," *Century*, January 1929, 269–274.

49. Ibid.

50. Waldemar Kaempffert, "Unsolved Problems of Atlantic Flights," *New York Times*, April 22, 1928, 131.

51. Corn and Horrigan, *Yesterday's Tomorrows*, 97–99.

52. "Edison Forecasts 'Eye' for Fog Flying," *New York Times*, October 3, 1930, 29. Randall E. Stross's *The Wizard of Menlo Park: How Thomas Alva Edison Invented the Modern World* is an entertaining account of not just Edison's technological achievements but his (successful) attempts to turn himself into a celebrity.

53. "Air Service Seen in Stratosphere," *New York Times*, December 26, 1935, 3.

54. "Giroplane Experts Call Future Rosy," *New York Times*, October 29, 1938, 19.

55. Russell Porter, "Science Promises an Amazing Future," *New York Times*, January 20, 1924, XX3.

56. Ibid.

57. Maurois, "The Formidable Future."

58. Ibid.

59. "The Miracles of 2029," *Literary Digest*, February 16, 1929, 19–20.

60. Ibid.

61. Ibid.

62. Hope Satterthwaite, "Human Aspects of the City of the Future," *New York Times*, June 30, 1929, XX3.

63. Irwin Edman, "In Our Stars," *Forum*, November 1932, 270.

64. "What Our Descendants Will Look Like," *Literary Digest*, December 28, 1929, 41.

65. "Forecasts Harnessing of Energy of Atoms," *New York Times*, February 13, 1927, E17. With its roughly 450 entries, Stephen E. Atkins's *Historical Encyclopedia of Atomic Energy* includes pretty much everything one needs to know on the subject.

66. Winston Churchill, "Fifty Years Hence," *Popular Mechanics*, March 1932, 390–397. See William Manchester's two-part biography of Winnie, *The Last Lion*, in which he recognizes 1932 as a key turning point for the man.

67. "Travel to Mars in 2035 Forecast," *New York Times*, April 22, 1935, 19.

68. Arthur Train, Jr., "Catching Up with the Inventors," *Harper's Monthly*, March 1938, 365–373.

69. "Carrel Forecasts a 'Brain Pool' Era," *New York Times*, April 14, 1939, 25.

70. General Eugene Debeney, "The War of Tomorrow," *New York Times*, September 25, 1921, 80; Farman, "Future of Aviation." Chris Bishop's *The Encyclopedia of Tanks and Armored Vehicles: From World War I to the Present Day* shows the development of these fighting machines.

71. Debeney, "The War of Tomorrow."

72. John MacCormac, "War with Rockets Pictured by Oberth," *New York Times*, January 31, 1931, 8.

73. Sir Arthur Salter, "World Without War," *Living Age*, May 1932, 200–203; "Science Knocks at Your Door," *Popular Mechanics*, December 1944, 18–25+.

74. Lawrence Dennis, "H. G. Wells's Internationalism," *Saturday Review of Literature*, September 9, 1933, 89–91. See Anthony West's *H. G. Wells: Aspects of a Life* and David C. Smith's *H. G. Wells: Desperately Mortal* for two different takes on this futurist of futurists.

75. H. G. Wells, "Wells Sees Man Better Off in '88," *New York Times*, January 16, 1938, 41; Corn and Horrigan, *Yesterday's Tomorrows*, 15–17.

76. Wells, "Wells Sees Man Better Off in '88."

77. Ibid.

78. "Official Guide Book of the Fair," Chicago 1933–1934, T501.A4 C42 1933, Wolfsonian. See Robert W. Rydell's *World of Fairs: The Century-of-Progress Expositions* for a useful examination of Depression-era fairs and David Gelernter's *1939: The Lost World of the Fair* for a compelling view of "The World of Tomorrow."

79. *World's Fair Bulletin*, Theme Edition, November 1936, Vol. 1, No. 2, New York 1939–1940, XB1991, 122.1 a–b, Wolfsonian.

80. *Pilgrimage to Tomorrow*, Gemloid Corp., NYC, 1938, New York 1939–1940, T785.P5 P5 C.1, Wolfsonian.

81. Corn and Horrigan, *Yesterday's Tomorrows*, 45.

82. Ibid., 74–75.

83. "Things to See at Highways and Horizons," New York 1939–1940 86.19.63 (Advertisement), Wolfsonian.

84. *Futurama*, New York 1939–1940, TE175.G43 1939, Wolfsonian.

85. Ibid.

86. "The GM Exhibit Building," INT3, New York 1939 87.1653.19.1 (Advertisement), Wolfsonian.

87. "The Ford Exposition New York World's Fair 1940," New York 1939–1940 86.19.167 (Advertisement), Wolfsonian.

88. Sherman Yellen, "Treasures of a Past Glowing with Hope," *New York Times*, July 30, 2000, AR33.

89. "Millikan Depicts Future Marvels," *New York Times*, April 21, 1939, 18. See *The Autobiography of Robert A. Millikan* to read the scientist's story in his own words.

CHAPTER 2

1. Captain Eddie Rickenbacker, "I Live for Tomorrow," *American*, September 1945, 17+. For more on the World War I flying ace, see W. David Lewis's *Eddie Rick-*

enbacker: An American Hero in the Twentieth Century and H. Paul Jeffers's *Ace of Aces: The Life of Captain Eddie Rickenbacker.*

2. Rickenbacker, "I Live for Tomorrow."

3. Ibid.

4. "Great Day Coming," *Time*, June 15, 1942, 76+.

5. Corn and Horrigan, *Yesterday's Tomorrows*, 12.

6. Ibid., 80.

7. "Inventions of Tomorrow," *Senior Scholastic*, March 11, 1940, 5–6.

8. William Fielding Ogburn, "The Future of Your Son," *Ladies' Home Journal*, April 1943, 32.

9. "Bids Women Turn to Small Business," *New York Times*, August 12, 1944, 8.

10. Charles M. A. Stine, "Molders of a Better Destiny," *Science*, October 2, 1942, 309.

11. John Tjaarada, "Your Home, Your Clothes, Your Car—Tomorrow," *American*, May 1943, 44–45+.

12. "Previews," *Better Homes & Gardens*, October 1943, 22–23.

13. "Things to Come," *Better Homes & Gardens*, March 1944, 30.

14. "Quick Looks at Things to Come," *Better Homes & Gardens*, May 1943, 22.

15. "Things to Come."

16. "The Future after Victory," *American Home*, February 1943, 13–15.

17. "Science Within Industry Seen Reshaping Our Life," *New York Times*, July 25, 1943, E11.

18. Waldemar Kaempffert, "Green Light for the Age of Miracles," *Saturday Review of Literature*, April 22, 1944, 14–15.

19. J. D. Ratcliff, "Your Postwar Home," *Woman's Home Companion*, June 1943, 34.

20. Ibid.

21. "Drastic Changes in Living Forecast," *New York Times*, December 12, 1944, 20.

22. 1944 University of Minnesota *Gopher.*

23. 1942 Drake University *Quax.*

24. 1943 Fresno State University *Campus.*

25. 1943 Hardin-Simmons University *Bronco.*

26. 1944 University of Iowa *Hawkeye.* See V. R. Cardozier's *Colleges and Universities in World War II* for more about the intersection between the war and higher education.

27. 1943 West Lafayette (Indiana) High School *Scarlet and Gray.*

28. 1945 St. Cloud (Minnesota) Technical High School *Techoes.*

29. "'Plenitude' Seen for Common Man," *New York Times*, June 8, 1942, 18.

30. "Kaiser Optimistic on Shipping Future," *New York Times*, September 12, 1943, 19. See Albert Heiner's *Henry J. Kaiser: Western Colossus* and Mark S. Foster's *Henry J. Kaiser: Builder in the Modern American West* for more on this captain of industry.

31. "H. G. Wells Urges World Rule by Commissions to Free All Mankind for a 'Dazzling' Future," *New York Times*, January 16, 1943, 6.

32. "Rutledge Describes Post-War World," *New York Times*, February 27, 1943, 11.

33. "Mgr. Sheen Sees Future as Dark," *New York Times*, March 6, 1944, 22.

34. W. M. Kiplinger, "What the Practical Men See Ahead," *Reader's Digest*, September 1943, 36–37.

35. David Sarnoff, "Industrial Science Looks Ahead," *Science*, November 19, 1943, 440.

36. "The Walkie-Talkie Future," *New York Times*, January 21, 1945, 70.

37. Lawrence R. Samuel, *Pledging Allegiance: American Identity and the Bond Drive of World War II* (Washington, D.C.: Smithsonian Institution Press, 1997), 52.

38. Ibid.

39. "Your Home World of Tomorrow," *Better Homes & Gardens*, December 1942, 80–81.

40. Franklin M. Reck, "Tomorrow We'll Go Places," *Better Homes & Gardens*, June 1943, 33.

41. "Previews."

42. Walter Dorwin Teague, "Planning the World of Tomorrow," *Popular Mechanics,* December 1940, 808–811+. Teague's two books of the late 1940s (*Design This Day* and *Land of Plenty*) reveal the vivid imagination of this leading designer.

43. Bruce Bliven, "The Shape of Everyday Things to Come," *Reader's Digest*, March 1941, 121–124.

44. John Chamberlain, "Looking Ahead," *Yale Review*, September 1941, 10.

45. "The Future after Victory."

46. "What Will Our Dream House Look Like?," *American Home*, March 1943, 52–58.

47. "The Future after Victory." For a fascinating account of another company's attempt to construct the prefab house of the future, see Thomas T. Fetters's *The Lustron Home: The History of a Postwar Prefabricated Housing Experiment.*

48. "What Will Our Dream House Look Like?"

49. Ratcliff, "Your Postwar Home," 106.

50. Dixon Wecter, "How Much News in the News Letter?," *Atlantic Monthly*, March 1945, 47.

51. M. G. Morrow, "Grandchildren of the Great War," *Science Digest*, September 1945, 80–81.

52. "Transport Futurama," *Senior Scholastic*, March 22–27, 1944, 44.

53. "Super-Speed Roads of Tomorrow," *Popular Mechanics*, August 1940, 188–191+.

54. Bert Pierce, "Atom-Driven Auto Put Far in Future," *New York Times*, December 23, 1945, 21.

55. Edward R. Grace, "Your Car after the War," *Saturday Evening Post*, November 14, 1942, 12–13+.

56. Ibid. See Stephen Bayley's *Harley Earl and the Dream Machine* for more on the vision of one of Detroit's legendary automobile designers.

57. Corn and Horrigan, *Yesterday's Tomorrows*, 99.

58. "Transport Futurama."

59. Grace, "Your Car after the War."

60. Igor Sikorsky, "The Helicopters are Coming," *Reader's Digest*, October 1942, 128. For more on Sikorsky and other early chopper enthusiasts, see Jay P. Spenser's *Whirlybirds: A History of the U.S. Helicopter Pioneers*.

61. Ogburn, "The Future of Your Son."

62. Roderick M. Grant, "Shape of Things to Come," *Popular Mechanics*, August 1944, 18, 22.

63. Gill Robb Wilson, "The World Is Your Trade Area," *Nation's Business*, November 1942, 28–29+.

64. Reck, "Tomorrow We'll Go Places."

65. "Sees Sky Filled by 500,000 Planes," *New York Times*, October 10, 1943, 17.

66. William A. M. Burden, "The Air Traffic of the Future," *New York Times*, February 20, 1944, SM20.

67. J. R. D. Tata, "The Air Age Dawns," *Rotarian*, January 1945, 20–21.

68. David O. Woodbury, "Your Life Tomorrow," *Collier's*, May 8, 1943, 40.

69. Ibid., 24.

70. Ibid., 48.

71. Raymond Loewy as told to B. Smith Reese, "Looking Backward to the Future," *Collier's*, November 13, 1943, 13+. See Philippe Tretiack's *Raymond Loewy and Streamlined Design* for how the man "created mythical objects which came to be associated with the very image of America itself."

72. Ogburn, "The Future of Your Son."

73. Kaempffert, "Green Light for the Age of Miracles."

74. Roderick M. Grant, "Science Knocks at your Door," *Popular Mechanics*, December 1944, 18–25+.

75. Ibid.

76. Dr. Irving Langmuir, "Across the Nation in an Hour?," *Science Digest*, February 1944, 2.

77. Russell Malone, "The Shape, If Such It Can Be Called, of Things to Come," *New Yorker*, April 3, 1943, 16–17.

78. Waldemar Kaempffert, "Tomorrow Has Arrived," *American*, March 1941, 45+.

79. Waldemar Kaempffert, "Science Charts New Ways of Life," *Science Digest*, June 1943, 30.

80. Kaempffert, "Green Light for the Age of Miracles."

81. Waldemar Kaempffert, "Science in the News," *Science Digest*, April 1945, 83.

82. F. Barrows Colton, "Your New World of Tomorrow," *National Geographic*, October 1945, 385–410.

83. J. D. Ratcliff, "Your Home Tomorrow," *Woman's Home Companion*, July 1943, 54. The "Uranium Age" was officially blessed by President Eisenhower via his famous "Atoms for Peace" speech delivered before the United Nations on December 8, 1953. See Ira Chernus's *Eisenhower's Atoms for Peace*.

84. "Tiny Engine Seen for Future Autos," *New York Times*, August 8, 1945, 9.

CHAPTER 3

1. "The Wonderful, Wonderful Future," *Consumer Reports*, February 1957, 90.

2. "Look 25 Years Ahead—Great Changes Coming," *Changing Times*, June 1957, 30.

3. Corn and Horrigan, *Yesterday's Tomorrows*, 12–13.

4. Ibid., 104, 78–81.

5. "The Wonderful, Wonderful Future," 91.

6. Corn and Horrigan, *Yesterday's Tomorrows*, 81–82. See Donald W. Ballard's *Disneyland Hotel: The Early Years, 1954–1988* for an informative and fun look at the House of the Future and other Disneyalia.

7. David Sarnoff, "The Fabulous Future," *Fortune*, January 1955, 82–83.

8. "Look 25 Years Ahead—Great Changes Coming," 33.

9. Brig. Gen. David Sarnoff, "What I See Ahead," *Reader's Digest*, April 1957, 85–89.

10. Maurice B. Mitchell, "Space-Age Communications," *Saturday Review of Literature*, April 19, 1958, 14, 17.

11. "The Big Show," *Newsweek*, December 14, 1959, 120.

12. Walter H. Waggoner, "Brookings Survey Sees Rosy Century," *New York Times*, July 29, 1949, 10.

13. "Economic Growth Forecast for U.S.," *New York Times*, April 24, 1955, 82.

14. "McNair Sees Department Store of Future Run Like Supermarket," *New York Times*, April 6, 1950, 49.

15. "Look 25 Years Ahead—Great Changes Coming," 27.

16. "The Wonderful, Wonderful Future," 94.

17. "What's Coming," *Newsweek*, December 14, 1959, 90.

18. "Psychologist Calls for Subtle Selling," *New York Times*, May 12, 1955, 42.

19. "The Wonderful, Wonderful Future," 93.

20. Lawrence Galton, "Brookline's Prophet of Things to Come," *Coronet*, March 1951, 127–130.

21. "Polar and Solar," *New Yorker*, January 2, 1954, 15.

22. Leo Cherne, "A Look at Your Life—Ten Years from Today," *Coronet*, October 1955, 29–33.

23. "Showcase for Shoppers of Future," *Life*, December 28, 1959, 170.

24. Charles W. Morton, "Accent on Living," *Atlantic*, January 1955, 88–89.

25. Philip Burnham, "The Odd Shape of Things to Come," *Commonweal*, January 22, 1960, 462.

26. Ernest K. Lindley, "The American Role," *Newsweek*, December 14, 1959, 84.

27. Dorothy Thompson, "The March Wind Doth Blow," *Ladies' Home Journal*, March 1961, 24.

28. Kingsley Amis, "The Psyche of the Future," *Mademoiselle*, January 1962, 40–41+. Zachary Leader's massive *The Life of Kingsley Amis* offers a complete portrait of the British writer.

29. Bill Davidson, "Zolar's Pay-Off in the Stars," *McCall's*, January 1961, 86–87. As recently as 2004, Zolar was still looking to the stars to navigate the unknown, his *Encyclopedia and Dictionary of Dreams* "fully revised and updated for the 21st century."

30. "Boastradamus," *Newsweek*, July 15, 1963, 56.

31. "A Glare into the Future," *New Yorker*, July 11, 1964, 24.

32. Corn and Horrigan, *Yesterday's Tomorrows*, 52.

33. Louis M. Hacker, "A Historian Previews the Sixties," *Saturday Review*, January 30, 1960, 29.

34. Robert F. Wagner, "Forecast of New York in 2012 A.D.," *New York Times*, October 7, 1962, SM24. Jon C. Teaford's *The Rough Road to Renaissance: Urban Revitalization in America, 1940–1985* deftly captures the postwar crisis of the American city.

35. Corn and Horrigan, *Yesterday's Tomorrows*, 53.

36. Bertrand Russell, "The Next Eighty Years," *Saturday Review*, August 9, 1952, 9.

37. "Look 25 Years Ahead—Great Changes Coming," 34.

38. William H. Schelck, "What's Coming in Housing for Families with Children?," *Parents*, October 1957, 72. See Kenneth T. Jackson's classic *Crabgrass Frontier: The Suburbanization of the United States* for a full examination of the bourgeois utopia.

39. "What the U.S. Will Be Like 10 Years from Now," *U.S. News & World Report*, November 9, 1959, 82–83.

40. Ralph Bass, "How We'll Live 50 Years from Now," *Coronet*, December 1959, 82.

41. "2002 A.D.," *Time*, November 17, 1952, 32.

42. Harold Lord Varney, "U.S.A.—2,000 A.D.," *American Mercury*, December 1957, 37–44.

43. Corn and Horrigan, *Yesterday's Tomorrows*, 12–13, 17–18, 23–29.

44. "Look 25 Years Ahead—Great Changes Coming," 30.

45. Earl Ubell, "Hopes and Hazards of the Atomic Age," *Parents*, October 1957, 54.

46. "The 1960's: A Forecast of the Technology," *Fortune*, January 1959, 78; Bass, "How We'll Live 50 Years from Now," 86. See Charles Murray and Catherine Bly Cox's *Apollo: Race to the Moon* for a superb account of NASA's lunar program as well as Gene Kranz's *Failure Is Not an Option* for an insider's perspective.

47. H. J. Rand, "Science Looks Ahead to 2000 A.D.," *Science Digest*, March 1958, 67.

48. Leston Fanuef, "Air Travel 1980," *Science Digest*, July 1962, 19.

49. John Rader Platt, "Can We Foresee the Future," *New Republic*, December 8, 1958, 11.

50. Beryl Tucker, "Fabrics in the Future," *Parents*, October 1957, 158+.

51. "Science Looks at Life in 2057 A.D.," *New York Times*, December 8, 1957, SM7.

52. "The 1960's: A Forecast of the Technology," 74.

53. "Sightseeing in the Sixties," *Saturday Review of Literature*, January 9, 1960, 30.

54. Robert O' Brien, "The U.S.A. in 1970: A Forecast of Things to Come," *Reader's Digest*, January 1961, 28–29. Richard C. Hoagland and Michael Bara's *Dark Mission: The Secret History of NASA* argues that there is much more to the agency's story than we've been told.

55. Isaac Asimov, "Fact Catches Up with Fiction," *New York Times*, November 19, 1961, SM34.

56. Ibid.

57. Wesley S. Griswold, "What'll It Be Like in 2000 A.D.?," *Popular Science*, April 1942, 84.

58. Adlai E. Stevenson, "New Men in New Worlds," *Saturday Review*, July 21, 1962, 17.

59. Corn and Horrigan, *Yesterday's Tomorrows*, 82.

60. "Science Looks at Life in 2057 A.D.," *New York Times*, December 8, 1957, SM7.

61. "I Predict," *Look*, January 16, 1962, 23.

62. J. Bronowski, "'1984' Could Be a Good Year," *New York Times*, July 15, 1962, 141.

63. "Polio Preventive Held Not Far Off," *New York Times*, January 20, 1950, 22. Jeffrey Kluger's *Splendid Solution: Jonas Salk and the Conquest of Polio* tells the full story of one of the biggest triumphs of modern medicine.

64. "World of Future: Electronic Living," *New York Times*, March 25, 1954, 10.

65. "Science and the Heart," *New York Times*, June 13, 1954, E8.

66. Richard Rutter, "Drug Producers Look to Future," *New York Times*, February 15, 1959, F1.

67. "Health and Age," *Newsweek*, December 14, 1959, 111.

68. J. H. Rush, "The Next 10,000 Years," *Saturday Review*, January 25, 1958, 13.

69. Robert O'Brien, "Forty Years from Now," *Reader's Digest*, February 1962, 51.

70. Daniel M. Friedenberg, "New Worlds to Conquer," *New Republic*, February 26, 1962, 24.

71. Corn and Horrigan, *Yesterday's Tomorrows*, 17.

72. Carson Kerr, "At Home, 2004 A.D.," *Popular Mechanics*, October 1954, 154–56+. For the 1964–1965 New York World's Fair, the United States Atomic Energy Commission worked with the Oak Ridge Institute of Nuclear Studies to create "Atomsville USA," a children's exhibit at the fair's Hall of Science.

73. Bert Pierce, "Automobiles: Meeting," *New York Times*, May 31, 1953, X27.

74. "1980's Shape of Things to Come," *Life*, December 12, 1955, 47.

75. "U.S. Doctor Predicts Use Of Radioactive Pills," *New York Times*, August 19, 1955, 5.

76. "Big Changes in Your Life," *Changing Times*, October 1955, 47.

77. L. A. DuBridge, "What about 2000 A.D.?," *Rotarian*, April 1952, 12.

78. "Shapes of the Future: Gas-Turbine Autos, Pocket Phones," *Newsweek,* July 4, 1955, 69; "Through the Looking Phone," *Time*, July 4, 1955, 17.

79. "It'll Be a Big 2000," *Newsweek*, March 18, 1957, 94.

80. "Look 25 Years Ahead—Great Changes Coming," 26, 32.

81. Herman Kahn, *On Thermonuclear War* (Princeton, NJ: Princeton University Press, 1961), v–x.

82. Edmund C. Berkeley, "2150 A.D.—Preview of the Robot Age," *New York Times*, November 19, 1950, SM10.

83. "Tomorrow Jobs—Great Changes, Great Opportunities," *Changing Times*, July 1954, 10–11.

84. "Look 25 Years Ahead—Great Changes Coming," 29.

85. "What's Coming," *Newsweek*, December 14, 1959, 92.

86. Harrison Smith, "How Much Richer Will You Be Ten Years from Now," *Cosmopolitan,* December 1960, 73.

87. "Look 25 Years Ahead—Great Changes Coming," 27.

88. "More about Your Future," *Changing Times*, September 1957, 45.

89. Ibid.

90. Beryl Tucker, Virginia Shaw, and Edith Barnos, "Fashions in Their Future," *Parents*, October 1957, 155.

91. Bass, "How We'll Live 50 Years from Now," 85.

92. Norman Cousins, "Hail Automation, Hail Peace," *Saturday Review*, January 18, 1964, 20; Robert M. MacIver, "On Blueprinting Man's Future," *Science*, April 17, 1964, 278–279.

93. Barbara Ward, "Creating Man's Future: Goals for a World of Plenty," *Saturday Review*, August 29, 1964, 191.

94. R. Buckminster Fuller, "The Prospect for Mankind," *Saturday Review*, Sep-

tember 19, 1964, 180. Lloyd Steven Sieden's *Buckminster Fuller's Universe* is a useful guide to the brilliant and eccentric futurist and philosopher.

95. Lt. Col. Robert B. Rigg, "Fantastic Weapons of Future Armies," *Science Digest*, February 1957, 43.

96. Howard A. Rusk, M.D., "The Fair and Medicine," *New York Times*, July 12, 1964, 4–5.

97. Barbara Tufty, *Science News Letter*, April 11, 1964, 234.

98. "The World of Already," *Time*, June 5, 1964, 40–52.

99. Sheldon J. Reaven, "New Frontiers: Science and Technology at the Fair," in *Remembering the Future: The New York World's Fair from 1939 to 1964* (New York: Rizzoli, 1989), 96.

100. "The World of Already."

101. Ira Wolfert, "Coming: The Most Marvelous Fair Ever!," *Reader's Digest*, January 1964, 91–95.

102. "Material Relating to Automobiles," F128T793.A8 (1–3), New York Historical Society (N-YHS).

103. Rosemarie Haas Bletter, "The 'Laissez-Faire,' Good Taste, and Money Trees: Architecture at the Fair," in *Remembering the Future*, 121.

104. "Material Relating to Automobiles."

105. Tania Long, "Time Capsule II To Get '64 Jazz," *New York Times*, November 29, 1964, 66:3; Barney Lefferts, "Open in 6939," *New York Times*, April 19, 1964, SMA34.

106. "Material Relating to Appliances," F128T793.A7, N-YHS; "Time Capsule II To Get '64 Jazz."

CHAPTER 4

1. William H. Honan, "They Live in the Year 2000," *New York Times*, April 9, 1967, 243.

2. Corn and Horrigan, *Yesterday's Tomorrows*, 19–21.

3. Daniel Cohen, "Psychic Star of the Year," *Nation*, December 13, 1965, 470–473.

4. Tom Buckley, "The Signs Are Right for Astrology," *New York Times*, December 15, 1968, SM30. The cultural malaise of the 1970s served only to fuel less scientific attempts to predict the future ("troubled and confused periods in history may be hell on the stock market or national prestige, but . . . they have turned out to be boom days for anyone claiming a little psychic insight into the future," wrote Peter Andrews in 1972). At New York's Grand Central Terminal, for example, commuters were forking over as much as $7 to get "computer-generated" horoscope readings and fortune tellings at something called the Astro-Flash Booth, and sales of Ouija boards had by now reportedly tripled in recent years, according to the *Wall Street Journal* (Peter Andrews, "The Prediction Game," *Saturday Review*, January 15, 1972).

5. Justine Glass, *They Foresaw the Future: The Story of Fulfilled Prophecy* (New York: G. P. Putnam's Sons, 1969), 7–8. Benson Bobrick's *The Fated Sky* is a wonderful history of the reading of the stars.

6. "The Futurists: Looking Toward A.D. 2000," *Time*, February 25, 1966, 28–29; Max Ways, "The Road to 1977," *Fortune*, January 1967, 94.

7. Philip H. Abelson, "Forecasting Future Developments," *Science*, September 1, 1967, 995.

8. Edward E. Booher, "The Decades Ahead from a Publisher's View," *Science*, November 17, 1967, 882.

9. "Notes and Comments," *New Yorker*, February 24, 1975, 29–30.

10. Ways, "The Road to 1977."

11. "Updating the Crystal Ball," *Newsweek*, November 26, 1973, 101–102.

12. Constance Holden, "Futurism: Gaining a Toehold in Public Policy," *Science*, July 11, 1975, 122. Although they're hard to find and very brief, James Digby's *Operations Research and Systems Analysis at RAND, 1948–1967* and Louis Miller's *Operations Research and Systems Analysis at RAND, 1968–1988* are valuable guides to the company and its work.

13. Ways, "The Road to 1977."

14. "Bringing the Future into Focus," *Nation's Business*, December 1967, 82–86.

15. Pierre Wack, "Scenarios: Uncharted Water Ahead," *Harvard Business Review*, September/October 1985, 73–89; Pierre Wack, "Scenarios: Shooting the Rapids," *Harvard Business Review*, November/December 1985, 139–150.

16. "The Futurists: Looking Toward A.D. 2000," 28–29.

17. Edward T. Chase, "The Super-Futurist," *New Republic*, June 21, 1969, 25–26+.

18. "Forecasters Turn to Group Guesswork," *Business Week*, March 14, 1970, 130–132.

19. "A Job with a Future," *Newsweek*, June 16, 1975, 83.

20. Edward Cornish, *The Study of the Future: An Introduction to the Art and Science of Understanding and Shaping Tomorrow's World* (Washington, D.C.: World Future Society, 1977), iii–viii.

21. "Futurism: Gaining a Toehold in Public Policy," 120–124.

22. Stefan Kanfer, "Is There Any Future in Futurism?," *Time*, May 17, 1976, 52.

23. "What Life Will Be Like 20 Years in the Future," *US News & World Report*, January 14, 1974, 72.

24. Peggy Powers Luedke, "Catastrophe Model: Can It 'See' Crises?," *Science Digest*, February 1977, 68–70.

25. Sally Helgesen, "Visions of Futures Past," *Harper's*, March 1977, 80–86.

26. Frank Trippett, "A Remembrance of Things Future," *Time*, January 15, 1979, 76.

27. Lewis H. Lapham, "The Rage Against the Future," *Harper's*, November 1979, 20, 14.

28. James Traub, "Futurology: The Rise of the Predicting Profession," *Saturday Review*, December 1979, 24, 30–32.

29. Isaac Asimov, "A Planning Challenge Unmet: Seeing the Unforeseeable," *Science Digest*, May 1979, 13.

30. "Futurology: The Rise of the Predicting Profession," 26.

31. Merrill Sheils, "The Cracked Crystal Ball," *Newsweek*, November 19, 1979, 133.

32. Traub, "Futurology: The Rise of the Predicting Profession," 24–26.

33. Alvin Toffler, "The Future as a Way of Life," *Horizon*, Summer 1965, 109–113.

34. Ibid., 114–115.

35. John R. Platt, "The Step to Man," *Science*, August 6, 1965, 607–613.

36. Bernard D. Nossiter, "Reporter on Poverty Turns to Bad Prophecy," *Life*, August 20, 1965, 11.

37. Edward T. Chase, "The Shape of Things to Come," *New Republic*, September 20, 1965, 28.

38. "From the '60s to the '70s: Dissent and Discovery," *Time*, December 19, 1969, 20–26.

39. Gerald Clarke, "Putting the Prophets in Their Place," *Time*, February 15, 1971, 38.

40. "From the '60s to the '70s: Dissent and Discovery."

41. "Apocalyptic Visions for our Fragile Little Planet," *Life*, September 4, 1970, 63.

42. Charles A. Reich, "The Greening of America," *New Yorker*, September 26, 1970, 42–43.

43. Jerome Zukowsky, "Antidotes for Future Shock," *Fortune*, November 1970, 195; Arnold A. Rogow, "Future Shock," *Saturday Review*, December 12, 1970, 39.

44. Robert Claiborne, "Future Schlock," *Nation*, January 25, 1971, 117–120.

45. J. Irwin Miller, "Changing Priorities: Hard Choices, New Price Tags," *Saturday Review*, January 23, 1971, 36.

46. Peter Schrag, "What's Happened to the Brain Business?," *Saturday Review*, August 7, 1971, 12–13+.

47. William Bowen, "A Choice of Futures—Black or Gray," *Fortune*, September 1971, 131.

48. "If Human Race Is to Survive into the Next Century," *US News & World Report*, March 3, 1975, 44.

49. John Thompson, "The Future: Who Wants It?," *Harper's*, August 1971, 89.

50. Jeffrey St. John, "Fear and Fantasy in Future Folly," *New York Times*, December 5, 1972, 47.

51. Loudon Wainwright, "Won't Anybody Hear the Awful Truth?," *Life*, January 28, 1972, 28.

52. Arthur G. Hansen, "The Limits to Growth," *Saturday Evening Post*, Winter 1973, 92.

53. "Pessimistic View of Future Issued," *New York Times*, September 24, 1973, 17; "Updating the Crystal Ball."

54. Melville J. Ulmer, "From Hope to Despondency," *New Republic*, March 30, 1974, 22–24; Walter Clemons, "Things to Come—All Bad," *Newsweek*, April 1, 1974, 78+; Melvin Maddocks, "Quo Vadis," *Time*, April 1, 1974, 82.

55. "What Kind of Future for America," *US News & World Report*, July 7, 1975, 46.

56. Sol M. Linowitz, "Reflections on the American Promise," *Saturday Review*, September 18, 1976, 14.

57. Bernadine Morris, "Fashion Forecast for 2076, Not Next Fall," *New York Times*, June 26, 1976, 32.

58. Kanfer, "Is There Any Future in Futurism?"

59. Isaac Asimov, "Life in 1990," *Science Digest*, August 1965, 70.

60. Richard M. Scammon, "This Is What a Baby Can Look Forward To," *Life*, December 1, 1967, 28–29.

61. "The Frantic Future," *Nation's Business*, August 1968, 34–35.

62. "Pills May Decide Sex," *New York Times*, September 15, 1968, 57.

63. "The Population Bomb, Reconsidered," *New York Times*, November 30, 1978, A22.

64. John Kleiner, "Retro Rocket: When Today Was Tomorrow," *New York Times*, May 25, 1997, TV51.

65. Ulmer, "From Hope to Despondency."

66. Suzanne E. Young, "The Famine Fad," *Science Digest*, July 1975, 85–87.

67. Thompson, "The Future: Who Wants It?," 91.

68. "What Life Will Be Like 20 Years in the Future," 75.

69. Warren R. Young, "What's to Come," *Life*, December 12, 1965, 43+.

70. Theodore Taylor, "Strategies for the Future: Choiceful Future Program," *Saturday Review/World*, December 14, 1974, 59.

71. J. J. Starrow, Jr., "Publisher's Foreword," *Nation*, September 20, 1965, 15–17.

72. "The Frantic Future."

73. Ibid.

74. "Prophet of Optimism," *Time*, May 31, 1971, 51.

75. "Won't Anybody Hear the Awful Truth?," *Life*, January 28, 1972, 28.

76. Robert Reinhold, "Problems of the 21st Century Confound a Parley of Thinkers," *New York Times*, April 10, 1972, 11.

77. "What Life Will Be Like 20 Years in the Future," 72.

78. "Study Forecasts Major Shortages," *New York Times*, February 12, 1975, 77.

79. Walter Carlson, "Advertising: TV '75—Dream or Debacle?," *New York Times*, November 17, 1965, 74.

80. Walter Cronkite, "The World You'll Live In," *Popular Science*, April 1967, 99.

The show's predecessor, "The 20th Century," began in 1957. Mike Wallace picked up the hosting job after Cronkite departed.

81. John Noble Wilfold, "Expert Foresees Profits on Space," *New York Times*, February 21, 1971, BQ103. Michael J. Neufeld's *Von Braun: Dreamer of Space, Engineer of War* convincingly shows how the man was determined to become the "Columbus of Space." Although sycophantic, Bob Ward's *Dr. Space* is also worth consulting to learn more about the ultimate rocket man.

82. Jack Gould, "The Early Bird Is Ready for Its Public Debut," *New York Times*, April 28, 1965, 49.

83. Young, "What's to Come."

84. "In Your Future: Robot 'Slaves,' Instant Knowledge, Sea Farms . . . ," *US News & World Report*, April 10, 1967, 112–113.

85. "The Perils of Underestimation," *Time*, July 5, 1968, 58; "The Frantic Future," 33.

86. "Executives of the Future," *Nation's Business*, January 1969, 71. See Martin Campbell-Kelly and William Aspray's *Computer: A History of the Information Machine* for a sweeping view of the history of the computer, beginning with Charles Babbage's 1883 mechanical prototype.

87. "Executives of the Future," 71.

88. Ibid., 72–73.

89. "What Life Will Be Like 20 Years in the Future," 75.

90. Isaac Asimov, "Asimov's Tomorrow," *Science Digest*, January 1978, 71.

91. Les Brown, "TV: It's Being 'Reinvented'—A Viewing Revolution Looms," *Saturday Review*, January 1979, 56.

92. Mark O'Donnell, "From Here to Eternity," *Saturday Review*, December 1979, 34.

CHAPTER 5

1. Eric Seaborg, "The 1980s: A Hopeful Outlook," *Futurist*, October 1980, 3–11; Val Ross, "As Far as Eyes Can See," *Maclean's*, August 4, 1980, 16–17. For more Learyisms circa the early 1980s, see his 1982 memoir *Changing My Mind among Others*. For much more about "Captain Trips," see Robert Greenfield's 2006 *Timothy Leary: A Biography*.

2. "Viral Infection and Disease," *New York Times*, November 5, 1985, C8.

3. Lynn Langway, "The Doomsday Boom," *Newsweek*, August 11, 1980, 56.

4. "The Doomsday Boom"; "Planning for the Apocalypse Now," *Time*, August 18, 1980, 69.

5. William Watts, "The Future Can Fend for Itself," *Psychology Today*, September 1981, 36, 47.

6. "What Business Will Get Next from Reagan," *US News & World Report*, March 30, 1981, 53.

7. "Upbeat Notes from Business Leaders," *US News & World Report*, May 11, 1981, 91.

8. "Seed Money for a Boom in the '80s," *US News & World Report*, November 30, 1981, 60.

9. Herman Kahn, "Fear Not, Prosperity Awaits Us," *New York Times*, September 19, 1982, 139.

10. "Rumors of Earth's Death Are Greatly Exaggerated," *US News & World Report*, May 9, 1983, A12.

11. Michael Doan, "Miracles, Menaces—The 21st Century as Futurists See It," *US News & World Report*, July 16, 1984, 105.

12. "What the Next 50 Years Will Bring," *US News & World Report*, May 9, 1983, A1–A2.

13. Christopher Lehmann-Haupt, "One Look into the Future," *New York Times*, December 25, 1980, 47.

14. Thomas Griffith, "Guessing Disguised as News," *Time*, December 8, 1980, 101; Frank Trippett, "Looking for Tomorrow (and Tomorrow)," *Time*, April 26, 1982, 90.

15. Trippett, "Looking for Tomorrow (and Tomorrow)."

16. Gerald Nachman, "Future Shuck," *Newsweek*, March 29, 1982, 9.

17. Douglas Colligan, "Your Gift of Prophecy," *Reader's Digest*, September 1982, 145–149.

18. "Social Forecaster John Naisbitt Says He Has Seen the Future—And It Just May Work," *People*, November 8, 1982, 58–61.

19. Emily Yoffe, "John Naisbitt's Clip Joint," *Harper's*, September 1983, 16–22.

20. Edward Ziegler, "Ten Megatrends Transforming Our Lives," *Reader's Digest*, November 1983, 56–62.

21. "The 21st Century: Squinting into the Crystal Ball," *US News & World Report*, May 9, 1983, A41.

22. Michael Marien, "Touring Futures," *Futurist*, April 1983, 13–14.

23. Ibid., 17.

24. "The 21st Century: Squinting into the Crystal Ball," *US News & World Report*, May 9, 1983, A41–42.

25. "The GOP Till 1988?," *People*, December 29, 1980–January 5, 1981, 91.

26. "Interview: Marvin Cetron," *Omni*, April 1985, 86–88+; "Marvin Cetron Says He's Seen the Future, and It's High-Tech Joy," *People*, January 12, 1987, 84–86; "Retiring Baby Boomers," *Omni*, January 1991, 8.

27. David Gelman, "The Megatrends Man," *Newsweek,* September 23, 1985, 58–61.

28. Myron Magnet, "Who Needs a Trend-Spotter," *Fortune*, December 9, 1985, 56.

29. Lena Williams, "The Future They See Works Like Today," *New York Times*, July 19, 1989, C1.

30. Ibid.

31. Susan Lee, "Why the Future Looks So Familiar," *New York Times*, January 7, 1990, BR20.

32. Robert Gardner and Dennis Shortelle, *The Future and the Past: 100 Years from Now and 100 Years Ago* (New York: Julian Messner, 1989).

33. Alvin Toffler, "Powershift," *Newsweek*, October 15, 1990, 86.

34. Richard Lacayo, "Future Schlock," *Time*, Fall 1992, 90.

35. Paul Farhi, "What Do Trend Forecasters Know That You Don't?," *Working Woman*, April 1991, 72–75.

36. Ibid.

37. Gene Bylinsky, "What's Ahead," *US News & World Report*, February 22, 1993, 57–58.

38. George F. Mechlin, "Seven Technologies for the 1980's," *USA Today*, January 1983, 62–65.

39. "What Tomorrow Holds," *Fortune*, October 13, 1986, 42.

40. "Futurists See Growth in Robot Population," *New York Times*, December 27, 1984, A16.

41. Betty Freidan, "Castle Keep," *Popular Mechanics*, July 1986, 166.

42. Gene Bylinger, "Technology in the Year 2000," *Fortune*, July 18, 1988, 92–98.

43. Michael Rogers, "Marvels of the Future," *Newsweek*, December 25, 1989, 78.

44. "A Preview of Life in 2020," *New York Times*, March 23, 1989, C3.

45. Peter Passell, "Fatless Fat," *New York Times*, May 16, 1987, 30.

46. Philip Elmer-Dewitt, "Dream Machines," *Time*, Fall 1992, 39.

47. Ibid., 39–40.

48. Richard Zoglin, "Beyond Your Wildest Dreams," *Time*, Fall 1992, 70.

49. "The Future of Reading," *Utne Reader*, July/August 1993, 110.

50. "Beyond 1993," *US News & World Report*, October 25, 1993, 80.

51. Zoglin, "Beyond Your Wildest Dreams."

52. "Beyond 1993," 78, 74.

53. "The Future of Reading," 105–111.

54. "Beyond 1993," 72.

55. "Technology Titans Sound Off on the Digital Future," *US News & World Report,* May 3, 1993, 64.

56. Daniel J. Boorstin, "The Fourth Kingdom," *US News & World Report*, October 25, 1993, 81–82.

57. Ibid.

58. "Beyond 1993," 73.

59. John M. Eddinger, "21st-Century Office: A Paperless Wonder?," *Nation's Business*, July 1980, 65–66.

60. Ibid.

61. "The Coming Revolution in the World of Culture," *US News & World Report*, May 9, 1983, A8–9, A11.

62. Charlotte Curtis, "Machines vs. Workers," *New York Times*, February 8, 1983, C8.

63. Kenneth B. Noble, "Commuting by Computer Remains Largely in the Future," *New York Times*, May 11, 1986, E22.

64. "The Coming Revolution in the World of Culture," A8–9.

65. Michael Doan, "Miracles, Menaces—The 21st Century as Futurists See It," *US News & World Report*, July 16, 1984, 103.

66. "The Coming Revolution in the World of Culture," A11.

67. "What of the Future?," *Current*, September 1980, 15.

68. Newt Gingrich, "Window of Opportunity," *Futurist*, June 1985, 9.

69. "What Lies Ahead," *USA Today*, August 1989, 3–4.

70. Judith Waldrop, "You'll Know It's the 21st Century When," *Saturday Evening Post*, April 1991, 71.

71. Elmer-Dewitt, "Dream Machines," 39.

72. "Beyond 1993," 73–74.

73. "How the Next Decade Will Differ," *Business Week*, September 25, 1989, 142–186.

74. John C. Szabo and Nancy Croft Baker, "Hot New Markets of the 1990s," *Nation's Business*, December 1988, 21.

75. "Goals for the Future," *USA Today*, August 1989, 3.

76. "Beyond 1993," 72.

77. "How the Next Decade Will Differ."

78. Ronald Bailey, "Raining in Their Hearts," *National Review*, December 3, 1990, 32.

79. "Forecasters Predict Radical Changes," *USA Today*, May 1992, 12.

80. "The 21st-Century Executive," *US News & World Report*, March 7, 1988, 48.

81. "2000: Visions of Tomorrow," *Life*, February 1989, 74.

82. Ibid., 74–75.

83. "The Era of Possibilities," *Fortune*, January 15, 1990, 43; Peter Nulty, "How the World Will Change," *Fortune*, January 15, 1990, 44.

84. Alan Farnham, "What Comes after Greed?," *Fortune*, January 14, 1991, 43.

85. David Gergen, "Winning the World's Biggest Race," *US News & World Report*, April 6, 1992, 35.

86. Bruce W. Nelan, "How the World Will Look in 50 Years," *Time*, Fall 1992, 38.

87. Abu Selimuddin, "Will the 21st Century Belong to Japan?," *USA Today*, May 1993, 52.

88. "Beyond 1993," 80.

89. Nulty, "How the World Will Change," 54.

90. Robert D. Kaplan, "The Coming Anarchy," *Atlantic Monthly*, February 1994, 44; Andrew E. Serwer, "The End of the World Is Nigh—Or Is It," *Fortune*, May 2, 1994, 123.

91. Charles W. Kegley, Jr., and Gregory A. Raymond, "Preparing Now for a Peaceful 21st Century," *USA Today*, September 1994, 20.

92. John Rossant, "Land Mines on the Road to Utopia," *Business Week*, November 18, 1994, 136–140.

93. "The Triple Revolution," *Business Week*, November 18, 1994, 16.

CHAPTER 6

1. "Information Technology," *USA Today*, June 1996, 4.

2. Chris Taylor, "Looking Ahead in a Dangerous World," *Time*, October 11, 2004, 60–61.

3. Rana Foroohar, "A New Way to Compute," *Newsweek*, September 16, 2002, 34.

4. Daniel Menaker, "End Game," *New Yorker*, February 10, 1997, 86.

5. David Ewing Duncan, "The Year 2000 Is . . . ," *Life*, January 2000, 16–20.

6. Steven Levy, "The 1,000-Year Glitch," *Newsweek*, June 24, 1996, 92.

7. John Simons, "The Millennium Bug Looms," *US News & World Report*, February 17, 1997, 54.

8. Alison Rea, "Does Your Computer Need Millennium Coverage?," *Business Week*, March 10, 1997, 98.

9. Steve Levy and Katie Hafner, "The Day the World Shuts Down," *Newsweek*, June 2, 1997, 53–54.

10. Susan Adams, "The Bug Bar," *Forbes*, July 28, 1997, 45.

11. "Y2K," *USA Today*, December 1999, 4–5.

12. John L. Petersen, "Getting Ready in the 21st Century," *USA Today*, May 1999, 56–58.

13. Steve Martin, "The Y3K Bug," *New Yorker*, July 19, 1999, 40.

14. James Poniewozik, "Auld Lang Sigh," *Time*, November 29, 1999, 56–59.

15. Steven Levy, "The Bug That Didn't Bite," *Newsweek*, January 10, 2000, 41.

16. "Doomsayers Admit They Were Wrong about Y2K," *Long Island Business News*, January 21, 2000, 5B.

17. Mariel Garza, "Y2Kaos," *Reason*, February 2000, 17; Barnaby J. Feder, "Problems? What Problems?," *New York Times*, January 9, 2000, P2.

18. "Bugaboo," *Time*, January 17, 2000.

19. "Why Y2K Won't Die," *Newsweek*, January 10, 2000, 38.

20. Garza, "Y2Kaos."

21. Jim Wilson, "Miracles of the Next 50 Years," *Popular Mechanics*, February 2000, 52–57.

22. John Tierney, "Future Shock: A Surgeon as Tailor," *New York Times*, December 11, 1999, B1.

23. "21 Predictions for the 21st Century," *Ladies' Home Journal*, December 1999, 128–132.

24. Ibid.

25. "Famous Americans Predict the Future," *Popular Mechanics*, January 2000, 15.

26. Erin Bried, "21st-Century Sex," *Glamour*, January 2000, 114–117.

27. "Famous Americans Predict the Future."

28. Ibid.

29. "Front Page, 2034," *Newsweek*, January 1, 2000, 110–111.

30. John B. Judis, "Newt's Not-So-Weird Gurus," *New Republic*, October 9, 1995, 16–25.

31. Michael Krantz, "Cashing in on Tomorrow," *Time*, July 15, 1996, 52.

32. Edward Rothstein, "Technology," *New York Times*, April 28, 1997, D5.

33. Malcolm W. Browne, "Science Squints at a Future Fogged by Chaotic Uncertainty," *New York Times*, September 22, 1998, F4.

34. Michael Lind, "The Beige and the Black," *New York Times*, August 16, 1998, SM38.

35. Bruce Handy, "Tomorrowland Never Dies," *Vanity Fair*, March 2000, 114–117+.

36. Ibid.

37. Ibid.

38. Adam Piore, "So Predictably Unpredictable," *Newsweek*, September 16, 2002, 34.

39. Fred Guteri, "Futurology," *Newsweek International*, September 16, 2002, 42.

40. Hope Cristol, "Futurism Is Dead," *Wired*, December 2003, 102, 107.

41. "Tomorrowland Never Dies."

42. "Wanna Bet?," *Wired*, May 2002, 120–124.

43. Kevin Kelly, "A Brief History of Betting on the Future," *Wired*, May 2002, 125–126.

44. David Rejeski and Robert L. Olson, "Has Futurism Failed?," *Wilson Quarterly*, Winter 2006, 21.

45. Martin Walker, "America's Romance with the Future," *Wilson Quarterly*, Winter 2006, 22–26.

46. William K. Stevens, "A Skeptic Asks, Is It Getting Hotter or Is It Just the Computer Model?," *New York Times*, June 18, 1996, C1.

47. Ronald Bailey, "Is the World Really Coming to an End?," *Reader's Digest*, December 1997, 53–60.

48. "And Almost Certain to Get Worse," *Time*, August 24, 1998, 33.

49. "Spring's Sprung Early," *US News and World Report*, March 15, 1999, 60.

50. "How Hot Will It Get?," *Time*, November 8, 1999, 112+.

51. Deborah Hudson, "Clear and Present Danger," *Discover*, January 2001, 59–60.

52. "The Big Melt," *Discover*, January 2002, 68.

53. Josie Glausiusz, "EPA Confirms Global Warming Really Exists," *Discover*, January 2003, 66.

54. Robert Kunzig, "Turning Point," *Discover*, January 2005, 25–29.

55. James Traub, "Al Gore Has Big Plans," *New York Times* magazine, 42–50, May 20, 2007.

56. Ibid.

57. Donna Seaman, "Core Collection: Climate Change," *Booklist*, December 1, 2006, 19.

58. Al Gore, "The Energy Electranet," *Newsweek*, December 18, 2006, E22.

59. Andrew C. Revkin, "Gore Alliance Starts Ad Campaign on Global Warming," *New York Times*, April 1, 2008, 8.

60. Jim Wilson, "Science Does the Impossible," *Popular Mechanics*, February 2003, 60–63.

61. Rothstein, "Technology."

62. Lisa Belkin, "Splice Einstein and Sammy Glick. Add a Little Magellan," *New York Times*, August 23, 1998, SM26.

63. Ibid.

64. David Brooks, "Looking Back on Tomorrow," *Atlantic Monthly*, April 2002, 20–22.

65. "Future Perfect," *People*, April 12, 2004, 264–265.

66. Josh McHugh, "The Cure," *Wired*, May 2004, 172–173.

67. John Tierney, "Homo Sapiens 2.0," *New York Times*, September 27, 2005, A25.

68. Joel Garreau, "Will We Still Be Fully Human?," *Wilson Quarterly*, Winter 2006, 32–34.

69. Brian O'Keefe, Doris Burke, and Telis Demos, "The Smartest, the Nuttiest Futurist on Earth," *Fortune*, May 14, 2007, 60+.

70. Ibid.

71. Ibid.

72. Scott Feschuk, "A Future Filled with Nanobots and Swiss Chalet," *Maclean's*, March 3, 2008, 75.

73. Christopher Lehmann-Haupt, "Vision of a Rosy Future for Man and Machine," *New York Times*, January 30, 1995, C17.

74. Steve Lohr, "The Economy Transformed, Bit by Bit," *New York Times*, December 20, 1999, C1.

75. Rothstein, "Technology."

76. Patrick J. Lyons, "'I Have the Greatest Enthusiasm for the Mission,'" *New York Times*, January 13, 1997, D4.

77. Dennis Overbye, "On the Eve of 2001, the Future Is Not Quite What It Used to Be," *New York Times*, December 26, 2000, F4.

78. "Predictions: Paul Saffo and the Robot Revolution," *PCMag.com*, July 12, 2006.

79. Kristin Davis, "Fifty Years from Now," *Kiplinger's Personal Finance*, January 1997, 98.

80. "Predictions: Paul Saffo and the Robot Revolution."

81. Charles Q. Choi, "Not Tonight, Dear, I Have to Reboot," *Scientific American*, March 2008, 94–97.

82. Chuck Klosterman, "Futurama!," *Esquire*, September 2007, 122.

CONCLUSION

1. Wendell Bell, *Foundations of Future Studies: Human Science for a New Era* (New Brunswick, NJ: Transaction Publishers, 1997), xix–xx.

2. Robert Heilbroner, *Visions of the Future: The Distant Past, Yesterday, Today, Tomorrow* (New York: Oxford University Press, 1995), 13.

3. William Sherden, *The Fortune Sellers: The Big Business of Buying and Selling Predictions* (New York: John Wiley & Sons, 1998), iii–iv, 1–6.

4. *The History of the Future*, 13.

5. David Kushner, "The *Discover* Interview: David Brin," *Discover*, June 2007, 64–67. Brin knew of which he spoke, having anticipated the popularity of cell phone cameras and YouTube in *The Transparent Society* as well as a number of other mega-developments (including the World Wide Web and global warming) in his 1990 novel *Earth*.

BIBLIOGRAPHY

Asimov, Isaac. *Change! Seventy-One Glimpses of the Future.* New York: Houghton Mifflin, 1981.

Bel Geddes, Norman. *Magic Motorways.* New York: Random House, 1940.

Bell, Wendell. *Foundations of Future Studies: Human Science for a New Era.* New Brunswick, NJ: Transaction Publishers, 1997.

Bellamy, Edward. *Looking Backward from 2000 to 1887.* Charleston, SC: BiblioBazaar, 2007.

Blum, Deborah. *Sex on the Brain.* New York: Viking, 1997.

Brin, David. *Earth.* New York: Spectra, 1990.

———. *The Transparent Society.* New York: Perseus, 1998.

Buckingham, Jane. *What's Next: The Expert's Guide; Predictions from 50 of America's Most Compelling People.* New York: HarperCollins, 2008.

Calder, Nigel. *The World in 1984.* New York: Penguin, 1965.

Carlisle, Norman V., and Frank B. Latham. *Miracles Ahead!* New York: Macmillan, 1944.

Carson, Rachel. *Silent Spring.* New York: Houghton Mifflin, 1962.

Cetron, Marvin, and Owen Davies. *American Renaissance: Our Life at the Turn of the 21st Century.* New York: St. Martin's, 1989.

———. *Crystal Globe: The Haves and Have-Nots of the New World Order.* New York: St. Martin's, 1991.

Cetron, Marvin, and Thomas O'Toole. *Encounters with the Future: A Forecast of Life in the Twenty-First Century.* New York: McGraw-Hill, 1982.

Colborn, Theo, Dianne Dumanoski, and John Peter Myers. *Our Stolen Future: Are We Threatening Our Fertility, Intelligence, and Survival? A Scientific Detective Story.* New York: Dutton Adult, 1996.

Commoner, Barry. *The Closing Circle: Nature, Man, and Technology.* New York: Random House, 1971.

Cooley, Donald G., and Editors of *Mechanix Illustrated. Your World Tomorrow.* New York: Essential Book/Duell, Sloan, and Pearce, 1944.

Corn, Joseph J., and Brian Horrigan. *Yesterday's Tomorrows: Past Visions of the American Future.* Baltimore, MD: Johns Hopkins University Press, 1984.

Cornish, Edward. *The Study of the Future: An Introduction to the Art and Science of Understanding and Shaping Tomorrow's World.* Washington, D.C.: World Future Society, 1977.

Dertouzos, Michael. *What Will Be: How the New World of Information Will Change Our Lives.* New York: HarperCollins, 1997.

Drucker, Peter F. *The New Society: The Anatomy of the Industrial Order.* New York: Harper and Brothers, 1950.

———. *America's Next Twenty Years.* New York: Harper Brothers, 1957.

———. *Landmarks of Tomorrow.* New York: Harper and Brothers, 1959.

———. *The Age of Discontinuity: Guidelines to Our Changing Society.* New York: Harper and Row, 1968.

Erlich, Paul R. *The Population Bomb.* New York: Ballantine Books, 1971.

Ferris, Hugh. *The Metropolis of Tomorrow.* Princeton, NJ: Princeton Architectural Press, 1986.

Flannery, Tim. *The Weather Makers: How Man Is Changing the Climate and What It Means for Life on Earth.* New York: Atlantic Monthly Press, 2006.

Forrester, Jay W. *World Dynamics.* New York: Wright-Allen, 1971.

Gabor, Dennis. *Inventing the Future.* New York: Alfred A. Knopf, 1964.

Gardner, Robert, and Dennis Shortelle. *The Future and the Past: 100 Years from Now and 100 Years Ago.* New York: Julian Messner, 1989.

Garreau, Joel. *Radical Evolution: The Promise and Peril of Enhancing Our Minds, Our Bodies—And What It Means to Be Human.* New York: Doubleday, 2005.

Gates, Bill. *The Road Ahead.* New York: Viking, 1995.

Gingrich, Newt. *Window of Opportunity: A Blueprint for the Future.* New York: Tor Books, 1984.

Glass, Justine. *They Foresaw the Future: The Story of Fulfilled Prophecy.* New York: G. P. Putnam's Sons, 1969.

Gore, Al. *An Inconvenient Truth: The Planetary Emergency of Global Warming and What We Can Do about It.* New York: Bloomsbury Books, 2006.

Harrington, Michael. *The Accidental Century.* New York: Macmillan Company, 1965.

Hawken, Paul. *Seven Tomorrows.* New York: Bantam USA, 1982.

Heilbroner, Robert. *The Making of Society.* New York: Prentice Hall (4th Revised Edition), 1972.

———. *An Inquiry into the Human Prospect.* New York: Norton, 1974.

———. *Visions of the Future: The Distant Past, Yesterday, Today, Tomorrow.* New York: Oxford University Press, 1995.

Huxley, Aldous. *Brave New World.* New York: HarperCollins, 1995.

Kahn, Herman. *On Thermonuclear War.* Princeton, NJ: Princeton University Press, 1961.

———. *The Next 200 Years: A Scenario for America and the World.* New York: Morrow, 1976.

Kahn, Herman, and Anthony J. Weiner. *The Year 2000: A Framework for Speculation on the Next Thirty-Three Years.* New York: Macmillan, 1967.

———. *The Coming Boom: Economic, Social, and Political.* New York: Horizon Book Promotions, 1982.

Kurzweil, Ray. *The Age of Spiritual Machines: When Computers Exceed Human Intelligence.* New York: Viking Adult, 1999.

———. *The Singularity Is Near: When Humans Transcend Biology.* New York: Viking Adult, 2005.

Kurzweil, Ray, and Terry Grossman. *Fantastic Voyage: Live Long Enough to Live Forever.* New York: Rodale, 2004.

Lessing, Doris. *Briefing for a Descent into Hell.* New York: Knopf, 1971.

Levy, David. *Love and Sex with Robots: The Evolution of Human-Robot Relationships.* New York: Harper, 2007.

Levy, Steven. *Artificial Life.* New York: Pantheon, 1992.

Linden, Eugene. *The Winds of Change: Climate, Weather, and the Destruction of Civilizations.* New York: Simon & Schuster, 2006.

McKibben, Bill. *The End of Nature.* New York: Random House, 1989.

Meadows, Donella H., Jorgen Randers, Dennis L. Meadows, and William W. Behrens. *The Limits to Growth: A Report for the Club of Rome's Project on the Predicament of Mankind.* New York: Universe Books, 1974 (2nd ed.).

Montgomery, Ruth. *A Gift of Prophecy: The Phenomenal Jeane Dixon.* New York: William Morrow, 1965.

Myers, Norman. *The Sinking Ark: A New Look at the Problem of Disappearing Species.* New York: Pergamon, 1980.

Naisbitt, John. *Megatrends: Ten New Directions Transforming Our Lives.* New York: Warner Books, 1982.

Naisbitt, John, and Patricia Aburdene. *Reinventing the Corporation: Transforming Your Job and Your Company for the New Information Society.* New York: Warner Books, 1985.

———. *Megatrends 2000: Ten New Directions for the 1990's.* New York: William Morrow, 1990.

Negroponte, Nicholas. *Being Digital.* New York: Knopf, 1995.

Orrell, David. *The Future of Everything: The Science of Prediction.* New York: Thunder's Mouth, 2006.

Orwell, George. *Nineteen Eighty-Four.* New York: Plume, 2003.

Pearce, Fred. *With Speed and Violence: Why Scientists Fear Tipping Points in Climate Change.* Boston, MA: Beacon, 2007.

Perloff, Harvey S. *The Future of the United States Government: Toward the Year 2000.* New York: Prentice Hall, 1971.

Popcorn, Faith. *The Popcorn Report.* New York: Currency, 1991.

Popcorn, Faith, and Lys Marigold. *Clicking: 16 Trends to Future Fit Your Life, Your Work, and Your Business.* New York: HarperBusiness, 1996.

Queeny, Edgar M. *The Spirit of Enterprise.* New York: Charles Scribner and Sons, 1943.

Reich, Charles. *The Greening of America.* New York: Random House, 1970.

Remembering the Future: The New York World's Fair from 1939 to 1964. New York: Rizzoli, 1989.

Ritner, Peter. *The Society of Space.* New York: Macmillan, 1961.

Romm, Joseph. *Hell and High Water: Global Warming—The Solution and the Politics—And What We Should Do.* New York: William Morrow, 2006.

Rosenberg, Daniel, and Susan Harding, eds. *Histories of the Future.* Durham, NC: Duke University Press, 2005.

Ruff, Howard. *How to Prosper During the Coming Bad Years: A Crash Course in Personal Financial Survival.* New York: Times Books, 1979.

Russell, Cheryl. *100 Predictions for the Baby Boom: The Next 50 Years.* New York: Plenum Publishing, 1987.

Samuel, Larry. *The Future Ain't What It Used to Be: The 40 Cultural Trends Transforming Your Job, Your Life, Your World.* New York: Riverhead Books, 1998.

Samuel, Lawrence R. *Pledging Allegiance: American Identity and the Bond Drive of World War II.* Washington, D.C.: Smithsonian Institution Press, 1997.

———. *The End of the Innocence: The 1964–1965 New York World's Fair.* Syracuse, NY: Syracuse University Press, 2007.

Sandison, Alan, and Robert Dingley, eds. *Histories of the Future: Studies in Fact, Fantasy, and Science Fiction.* New York: Palgrave, 2000.

Saxon, Kurt. *The Poor Man's James Bond: Homemade Poisons, Explosives, Improvised Firearms.* New York: Gordon, 1986.

Schlacter, Trudy, and Roberta Wolf. *Millennium Mode: Fashion Forecasts from 40 Top Designers.* New York: Rizzoli, 1999.

Schwartz, Peter, Peter Leyden, and Joel Hyatt. *The Long Boom: A Vision for the Coming Age of Prosperity.* New York: Perseus, 1999.

Sherden, William. *The Fortune Sellers: The Big Business of Buying and Selling Predictions.* New York: John Wiley & Sons, 1998.

Simon, Julian L. *The Ultimate Resource.* Princeton, NJ: Princeton University Press, 1981.

Simon, Julian L., and Herman Kahn. *The Resourceful Earth: A Response to Global 2000*. New York: Blackwell, 1984.

Smith, J. Walker, and Ann Clurman. *Rocking the Ages: The Yankelovich Report of Generational Marketing*. New York: HarperBusiness, 1997.

Steinman, David. *Safe Trip to Eden: Ten Steps to Save Planet Earth from the Global Warming Meltdown*. New York: Thunder's Mouth Press, 2006.

Strathern, Oona. *A Brief History of the Future*. New York: Carroll & Graf, 2007.

Strauss, William, and Neil Howe. *Generations: The History of America's Future, 1584–2069*. New York: William Morrow, 1991.

———. *13th Gen: Abort, Retry, Ignore, Fail?* New York: Vintage, 1993.

———. *The Fourth Turning: An American Prophecy*. New York: Broadway, 1996.

Stutz, Bruce. *Chasing Spring: An American Journey through a Changing Season*. New York: Scribner, 2006.

Taleb, Nassim Nicholas. *The Black Swan: The Impact of the Highly Improbable*. New York: Random House, 2007.

Taylor, Jim, and Watts Wacker. *The 500-Year Delta: What Happens after What Comes Next*. New York: HarperBusiness, 1997.

Thompson, William Irwin. *At the Edge of History: Speculations on the Transformation of History*. New York: Irvington, 1971.

Thurow, Lester. *Head to Head: The Coming Economic Battle among Japan, Europe, and America*. New York: William Morrow, 1992.

Toffler, Alvin. *Future Shock*. New York: Random House, 1970.

———. *The Third Wave*. New York: William Morrow, 1980.

———. *Powershift: Knowledge, Wealth, and Violence at the Edge of the 21st Century*. New York: Bantam, 1990.

Toffler, Alvin, and Heidi Toffler. *War and Anti-War: Making Sense of Today's Global Chaos*. New York: Little, Brown, 1993.

Wade, Nicholas. *Life Script: How the Human Genome Discoveries Will Transform Medicine & Enhance Your Health*. Darby, PA: Diane Publishing, 2001.

Wallechinsky, David, Amy Wallace, and Irving Wallace, eds. *The Book of Predictions*. New York: William Morrow, 1980.

Wells, H. G. *The Outline of History*. New York: Doubleday, 1971.

———. *The Time Machine*. New York: New American Library, 2002.

———. *War of the Worlds*. New York: Penguin Classics, 2005.

———. *The Shape of Things to Come*. New York: Penguin Classics, 2006.

———. *When the Sleeper Wakes*. New York: Penguin Classics, 2006.

Wilson, David A. *The History of the Future*. Toronto: McArthur & Company, 2000.

ꟾNDEX

Bell Labs, 187
Bell, Wendell, 203
Bible, 8
biology, 39–42, 71, 97, 154, 187, 193
biotechnology, 156, 176, 193–195, 197
Blade Runner, 142
Blass, Bill, 128
Boorstin, Daniel J., 159–160
Brand, Stewart, 186, 197
Brave New World (Huxley), 5, 41, 83, 96, 194
Brazil, 74, 142
"broadcatching," 197
Buck Rogers, 122, 180

Caplan, Arthur, 180
Cassandra, 7
"catastrophe theory," 118, 147
Celente, Gerald, 153
Century of Progress International Exposition (Chicago, 1933–1934), 29, 30, 47
Cetron, Marvin, 149–150, 152, 167
chaos theory, 13
chemistry, 54–56, 68, 71
Cherne, Leo, 85–86
Churchill, Winston, 42
cities: and alternatives to urban renewal, 131–132; and commissions on Year 2000, 118; floating, 146; and futurism, between-the-wars, 31–34; and futurism, postwar, 88–90; and GM Futurama II, 106; and science, 96; and Teague prediction, 63. *See also* New York City
Clarke, Arthur C., 185, 204
climate control, 122, 125
cloning, 185, 193
clothing (fashion): aviation-inspired, 35–36; and cleaning by supersonic

sound, 102–103; and futurism, World War II, 54–56, 75; and Geddes prediction, 27; and *Millennium Mode*, 180; for space travel, 93; synthetic, 43; throwaway, 127; in 2076, 128
Clurman, Ann, 173
Codrescu, Andrei, 158
Cold Spring Harbor Labs, 187
communications: "automatic telegraph," 71; and de-urbanization, 90; and futurism, World War II, 73–74; 1945 FCC report on, 61; and technological convergence, 159; "telephotophone," 20; "wireless telephony," 45
computers: and career opportunities, 101; and "the cyber future," 171; and demise of print, 159; and Fuller prediction, 103–104; and futurism, late 1960s, 136–138; and *The Matrix*, 174–176; as meal preparers, 102; and modeling and simulation, 13, 150, 183, 189; nanobots, 181, 196; and reduction in work, 115, 149; and technological convergence, 159; thinking and feeling, 198; and "the third wave," 160–164; and Y2K, 176–179
consumerism (shopping): aviation's effect on, 69; and Cherne prediction, 85–86; and Dichter prediction, 84–85; via electronic credit card, 84; and Kahn prediction, 141–142; by "knowbot," 199; and Leary prediction, 141–142; online, 179; "pent-up" consumer demand, 72; by television, 22–23, 74, 83; and "two-of-a-kind urge," 77–78; and war bonds, 62; and wartime forecast for postwar era, 52–57, 80
Cornish, Edward, 109, 117, 171
Cronkite, Walter, 136, 180